## Praise for *Motor City Boomer*

"Part memoir, part cultural history, *Motor City Boomer* is a rollicking reminder of the importance of the auto in American culture. Larry Lankton's love for his boyhood Michigan home and the cars of his youth—from his family's 1956 Packard to his very own 1964 GTO—shine through on every page. Full of quirky and insightful details, this book is a must-read for anyone who cares about the automobile and the way it has shaped everything about America from restaurants to romances."

—Nancy A. Nichols, author of *Women Behind the Wheel: An Unexpected and Personal History of the Car*

"*Motor City Boomer* is a fascinating trip in which the long and winding history of the automobile in America intersects with a personal journey of self-discovery and nostalgia. Along the way, Lankton convinces us that the car is both a ubiquitous and deeply personal object, transporting us through the history of our country and ourselves."

—Laura Walikainen Rouleau, teaching professor of history, Michigan Technological University

"Part history, part 'auto biography,' *Motor City Boomer* draws on Lankton's own experiences to bring the automotive story of the 1950s and 1960s vividly to life. In so doing, it sheds important new light on what the car meant—and continues to mean—to an entire generation of Americans."

—David Lucsko, professor of history, Auburn University

"*Motor City Boomer* is a remarkable account blending automotive history, material culture, and coming-of-age in 1950s and '60s America. Detailed, factual, and—most significantly—personal, it resonated with me. His recollection of family, friends, community, cars, and especially a 1964 GTO mirrored much of my youth. A must-read for boomer gearheads and those interested in post–World War II history."

—John Heitmann, professor emeritus, University of Dayton

I0792541

"Fasten your seatbelt for a thrilling ride through American car culture at its peak in the 1950s and 1960s. Larry Lankton takes the wheel with a two-tone combination of deeply personal memoir and meticulous automotive scholarship."

—Patrick M. Malone, professor emeritus of American studies and urban studies, Brown University

# Motor City Boomer

Great Lakes Books

*A complete listing of the books in this series can be found online at wsupress.wayne.edu.*

Series Editor
Thomas Klug

# Motor City BOOMER

## THE CAR CULTURE THAT DEFINED A GENERATION

Larry Lankton

WAYNE STATE UNIVERSITY PRESS
DETROIT

ISBN 9780814353448 (paperback)
ISBN 9780814353455 (ebook)

Library of Congress Control Number: 2026933069

Cover images from the collections of The Henry Ford. Cover design by Nathaniel Roy.

Wayne State University Press rests on Waawiyaataanong, also referred to as Detroit, the ancestral and contemporary homeland of the Three Fires Confederacy. These sovereign lands were granted by the Ojibwe, Odawa, Potawatomi, and Wyandot Nations, in 1807, through the Treaty of Detroit. Wayne State University Press affirms Indigenous sovereignty and honors all tribes with a connection to Detroit. With our Native neighbors, the press works to advance educational equity and promote a better future for the earth and all people.

Wayne State University Press
Leonard N. Simons Building
4809 Woodward Avenue
Detroit, Michigan 48201-1309

Visit us online at wsupress.wayne.edu.

The Schaffer Drive Kids:
Rick, Bill, Phil, Terry, and Bruce

*and*

The Vermilion Street Cruisers:
Doug, Dave, Dan, and Marilyn

# CONTENTS

# ACKNOWLEDGMENTS

For starters, I would like to thank two special families. For reasons made clear in the book, I wanted to tell the stories of my favorite race car driver, Ralph Donaldson, and my high school girlfriend, Marilyn Kuhn. At a difficult time in his life, Ralph welcomed me into his home twice for interviews. Later, Ralph's children, Denny Donaldson and Marcy Smith, provided photographs and graciously complimented me on my discussion of their father's life and his final days. Similarly, Marilyn Kuhn Palmer's surviving husband, Denny, her daughter, Michele Hecht, and her sister, Alison Caldwell, made my life easier by approving of what I had to say about a teenaged girl back in the mid-1960s.

All the people mentioned in the book are real. I used their real names. I called and emailed many of them, asking them to provide new facts or to verify the stories I thought I already knew. I sent them draft chapters, which occasionally contained embarrassing information. But my old friends (see the dedication) never flinched. They never said "Please don't print that." Sometimes they claimed not to *remember* a given incident, but they never put up any stop signs.

Thanks go to a small army of undergraduates at Michigan Tech who took my "Automobile in America" class. They "volunteered" to Xerox car advertisements that appeared in the fourth-quarter issues of *Time* and *Life* magazines from 1950 to 1969. A physics major, Stephanie Aho, who happened to be the best student in one of my classes, motored one hundred miles over to Northern Michigan University's library to copy all of Charlotte Montgomery's columns in *Good Housekeeping* magazine.

It was truly a blessing to sit down with Pat Kiessling, in her nineties, and reminisce about the time when we were neighbors on Schaffer

Drive, where she still lives. Her husband Arnold, a doctor, treated my dad when he was sick in 1960.

Jean Ellis shared with me the history of Hanse and Jim, who futilely tried to complete an auto trip from Calumet, Michigan, to Chicago in 1908.

Bob Brugger, a book editor, read and enthusiastically responded to the early chapters of my "car book" manuscript. Bob proved to me that there really was a book here.

Several individuals helped me put together the images in this book. Isabella Lenz played a key role. Bella, a family friend and a great basketball player for Michigan Tech, recently graduated with a degree in scientific and technical communications. She managed my image files. Jim Orr, with the Henry Ford Digital Archives Collection, was amazingly responsive to all my requests. Other image or service providers included John Schneiderhan of the Michigan Tech Library, photographer David Lawrence, Joie Chitwood Jr., Justine Duffy of Coyote Classics, Myriss of Getty Images, Dave DeHem of the Michigan Motor Sports Hall of Fame, and Doug of the Glow Shoppe.

I have my own family to thank too. Special thanks go out to Lynn Lewis. When I started writing about her in the book, three times I correctly identified her as my half sister, because that is what she is. Then I switched to just calling her my sister, because that is what felt right. Lynn is thirteen years older than I, and she left our family home and got married when I was only six. Still, we have remained tight over the ensuing seventy or so years. For me, Lynn is the real family historian, and I consulted her often in putting this book together. Lynn and her daughter, Dana Lewis, provided me with family snapshots and stories.

My wife, Rachel, read chapters and caught mistakes. She was exceedingly tolerant and needed to be. While writing this book I sometimes lived like a hermit at the keyboard and was often grumpy, mentally exhausted, and no fun to be around when I emerged from my office. She put up with it, knowing that someday my brain would clear itself of book-fog and I would live in the present again.

My son and daughter, David Lankton and Laura Kloss, never lived in either of my two hometowns of Jackson, Michigan, and Danville,

Illinois. They never met my father and mother, who passed away before they were born. I hope that for them this book reconstructs some of our family's past, including the people who inhabited it. If I gave something to them, David and Laura gave something to me: they offered old Dad computer help, especially in the handling of digital images.

I need to thank Marie Sweetman, Sandra Korn, Emily Gauronskas, Traci Cothran, and Carrie Teefey at Wayne State University Press, as well as Tom Klug, editor of the Great Lakes Books series, and Sandra Judd, my copyeditor. Thanks, too, to the outside readers who caught some errors and pointed me in some new directions.

A debt of gratitude goes out to Michele Toll, an outspoken young assistant professor of English at Monroe County Community College. After I did a little Michigan history consulting job for her in 2022, we spoke on the phone. She was familiar with my prior publications and asked if I was working on something new. I told her I had most of a book written that was about life and cars, but it was dead in the water. This young professor offered an old professor emeritus no sympathy. Basically, she told me to get my butt in gear and get back to work. Finish it, she said. I went back to working on the manuscript the very next day, and I did finish it. Inspiration can come from surprising places.

Finally, thanks to another teacher and a good friend, Martha Kay, who sadly died while this book was being copyedited. I took her one-semester class in rhetoric at Danville High School in 1964. She took a liking to me and thought I had some talent. Since then, she had been my cheerleader and literary critic. I sent Martha the last chapter of this book, and she liked it. Then I sent her another draft where I doubled up the ending. I said the same thing twice, in different ways. She said readers wouldn't need that. She liked the simpler, shorter, to-the-point ending. Change back to that, she said, and I did. When you get to the book's last words, I hope you think that I got it right, with Martha's help.

# INTRODUCTION

*The Car Culture in the Affluent Age of Baby Boomers*

In the early 1970s, I was a graduate student in the American Civilization program at the University of Pennsylvania. My major fields were material culture studies and the history of technology. The faculty at Penn found me quite ordinary at first, until I took the final exam in the material culture portion of the yearlong proseminar class. Professor Pat Malone asked for an essay on this: "Everybody seems to know what the automobile has done to America, but over the last twenty years, what has America done to the automobile?" To borrow a baseball metaphor, that question was right in my wheelhouse, and my answer boosted my academic stature, led to a fellowship, and gave me more incentive to carry on. Once out of Penn, I worked as a curator at the Henry Ford Museum for a couple of years, surrounded by one of the nation's great car collections. Eventually I took a faculty job at Michigan Technological University, where I introduced new courses that examined the interrelationships among science, technology, and society. What could do that better, I thought, than a course called "The Automobile in America"? I introduced it and taught it for thirty years.

The course explored how the automobile impacted both *life* in America and the *look* of America from the 1890s to the present. At the start of the course, I immodestly introduced my favorite laws of technological change. First, there is no such thing as a perfect technology. Second, the technology created to solve today's problems often creates new problems for tomorrow. Third, whenever any major technology is introduced, there will be winners and losers. Fourth, technological change is often accompanied by unintended consequences. And fifth, it is difficult to assess whether a technological change made things better or worse, but it's often easy to say how a change made things *different.*

These laws of technological change were very applicable to the history of the automobile. The Ford Pinto was not perfect, especially when struck in the rear by another car, when it tended to burst into flames. The car early in the century was seen as a problem solver—by replacing horses it cleaned up the urban environment, ridding it of horse dung, urine, and large, dead animals left next to the curb. Fifty years later, the car was seen as a problem maker, because it polluted the air with tailpipe emissions. The automobile made winners out of the manufacturers, dealers, and mechanics devoted to it, while it made losers out of mass transit systems, like streetcars, which disappeared from cities all over the country. Interstate highways made winners out of travelers going as fast as possible through a city, but made losers out of city residents who lived in the way of the new highways and were displaced. Automakers, with considerable prodding from the US National Highway Traffic Safety Administration, installed supplemental restraint systems, or airbags, in cars to better protect drivers and front seat passengers in collisions. One tragic, unintended consequence of this adoption: air bags deployed at two hundred miles an hour could kill young children in front seats. In 1996, in a low-speed, parking lot fender bender, an airbag decapitated a one-year-old girl. Between 1990 and 2008, about 260 infants and children were killed, rather than protected, by airbags. As for a technology making things better or worse, the modern, comfortable automobile and the Interstate highways, taken together, made it possible for travelers to cover far more miles per day than in earlier times. But was that always a good thing? In their haste to get to a destination, didn't Interstate travelers miss having an up-close and lingering view of the landscape, small towns, and cities?

My memoir makes the point that the car was never just about transportation. From Cadillacs to little Nash Ramblers, cars have connected to personal values and needs, family life, rites of passage, courtship, and entertainment. Your vehicle rolls over a landscape equipped with the support system for travel that Americans built, ranging from stoplights and police cars and ambulances to suburban streets, Interstate highways, gas stations, car washes, bump-and-paint shops, motels, restaurants, and tourist traps. Without the car, there would be no Sea Shell City in the northern part of Michigan's mitten, where you can stop to see a "Man Killing Clam!"

From my perspective, the automobile was the single most important technological artifact of twentieth-century America, because its lifetime spanned the entire century and its influence played out on innumerable levels. Especially in the 1950s and 1960s, automobility transformed American life and the American landscape in profound ways, both positive and negative. The car changed the nation writ large, but just as surely it changed the lives of individuals like me and my family and friends.

The car changed where Americans lived, and how the "ideal" woman nurtured and raised her family. The car was a source of entertainment. People went on Sunday drives. They went to auto races, drive-in theaters, and car shows, and they tuned radio dials to pop music stations that blared out songs about love in cars, racing in cars, and even death in cars. People watched new television shows sponsored by car companies. The car industry, while touting its annual model changeovers on television and in magazine ads, strongly expressed the view that the new America being built in the postwar world was much better than the old America. The car culture changed the face of the nation and the American roadside. Small, one-of-a-kind mom-and-pop establishments along older roads got swept aside. Standardized, repetitive architecture and engineering became the norm, as found in look-alike Interstates, suburbs, corporate gas stations, chain motels, and Golden Arches that ran from sea to shining sea.

The 1950s and 1960s were two very different decades. In the 1950s, Americans tried to turn a blind eye to the threat of communism and the Cold War by buying their way to happiness. They practiced rampant consumerism and conspicuous consumption and immersed themselves in materialism. In this decade Americans in many ways made over their personal lives and their country, creating a new way of life very different from the days of the Great Depression and World War II. Tired of living *without*, Americans who could afford it treated themselves to ranch

Comfort, control, convenience, Cadillac. This 1959 Cadillac Biarritz convertible has all the power assists, all the push buttons, a clock, a radio, and air conditioning. (Collections of The Henry Ford)

houses in the suburbs, two cars in the garage, longer vacations, and all kinds of consumer goods. Americans put a premium on things new and big—and they sought to obtain more comfort, control, and convenience in their lives. This was the dawning of "Push Button America," of "Lazy Living," where myriad tasks—whether driving to the grocery store, doing the dishes, or cutting suburban grass—were to be completed with less effort.

In the 1950s, the cultural values of comfort and convenience became embedded in the American home and the American automobile. Home and car were the twin pillars of "modern living." The "modern home" suddenly included automatic washers and dryers, garbage disposals, dishwashers, air conditioners, other large and small electrical appliances, entertainment centers with televisions and high-fidelity music, plus wall-to-wall carpeting and interior furnishings covered with new, easy-to-care-for upholstery. "Modern cars," at the same time, became equipped with air conditioners, heaters, radios, automatic transmissions, power steering, power brakes, power seats, power windows, turn signals, and automatic headlight dimmers. Cars boasted handsome new interiors done up in new fabrics. New colors and polished chrome entered the twin domains of house and car. In the mid-1950s, for the first time a consumer could buy pink toilet paper, pink towels, pink sheets, and a pink Cadillac. Inside her home, a woman could sit on a cushy sofa. Out on the road, she drove a car with a cushy suspension that wasn't good for handling but did take away the bumps.

In the 1950s, America, a new superpower, flexed its muscles and built a permanent, large arsenal. Car styling expressed this exuberance, hubris, and power. Powerful V-8 engines became more commonplace and grew in cubic-inch displacement. Cars became lower, wider, heavier, and longer—and they sprouted fins in the late 1950s that mimicked new military planes. The American auto industry was its own superpower, flying high in the marketplace of cars. The Big Three reigned. They built exactly the cars they wanted, and those cars, in their size, power, interiors, gaudy fins, and chrome, mirrored the American culture of the time.

The American automobile continued to exhibit exuberance in the 1960s, as best exemplified by the mid-decade muscle cars, the 1964 Pontiac GTO, super stock Dodges, Corvette Stingrays, and Chevy 409s. But the 1960s were not the 1950s, and this decade brought much change to Detroit and its products. In the 1960s, the United States stumbled as a global power and became entrapped in Vietnam. The country became less celebratory and more reflective. Instead of swimming in consumerism and materialism, the culture took on social reform and change. In the era of civil rights, the war on poverty, the Great Society, and the budding environmental and feminist movements, a significant number of Americans tried to make the world at home a safer and better place. Try as it might, the auto industry could not run and hide from all this change. It had to adapt to changing expectations and conditions, to a changing market, and live within new limits. Consumers complained that Detroit's cars were too big, too expensive to buy and maintain, too powerful, too wasteful of fuel—and unsafe. Detroit's hegemony in the marketplace eroded. By 1959, foreign cars accounted for 10 percent of all new car sales in the United States, and in trend-setting California, imports accounted for nearly 20 percent. Detroit, with great reluctance, altered its products by building compacts, such as the Ford Falcon and Chevrolet Corvair, introduced in 1960.

Congress and regulators took aim at the industry. Social and political reformers saw the automobile not as a transportation problem solver but as a problem maker. Critics bemoaned the deaths of fifty thousand Americans killed annually in auto accidents. Detroit had launched a safety movement of its own in the mid-1950s, but the Big Three determined that safety didn't sell, so they dropped the idea of engineering crashworthiness into their cars. Reformers responded by passing the National Traffic and Motor Vehicle and Safety Act of 1966, as well as subsequent legislation that set safety standards and design criteria for new cars. Critics, led by Californians, also faulted the automobile's contribution to air pollution: in 1966, auto emissions accounted for 86 of 146 million tons of atmospheric pollutants discharged in the United States, or nearly 60 percent of the total. The United States Congress started to tackle that problem with the Motor Vehicle Air Pollution Act of 1965, to be followed by others that set reduced emissions standards.

In the 1960s, social reformers and critics faulted not only the car but the culture surrounding it. Suburbs were too white and too vacuous. Cars and highways led to urban sprawl and the decline of inner cities, where they destroyed Black neighborhoods and businesses and historic districts. Interstate highways left too big a footprint in rural areas, and the billboards alongside highways blighted the landscape. New corporate, repetitive architecture—cookie-cutter fast-food restaurants, motels, and gas stations—offered boring sameness from one end of the country to the other.

From the mid-1960s on, Detroit was never the same again. It confronted increasing foreign competition as well as federal safety, air pollution, and, in time, fuel economy standards. Highway engineers no longer had full sway over where they would drive through new ribbons of concrete or asphalt. The car culture, too, would never be the same. Millions of individuals remained auto enthusiasts and unabashed lovers of their cars, but society began reining in the car culture. Critics

While American cars grew larger and more expensive, Volkswagen increased its market share by running ads for its Beetle telling Americans to "Think Small" and "Settle for Less." (Collections of The Henry Ford)

damned the automobile for its deleterious effects on natural and built environments, for its vast consumption of oil, a nonrenewable fuel, and for lingering safety issues. Some critics seemed to want the car to become perfect. But perfection, as noted above, was an impossible goal.

Many Americans follow Johnny Mercer's lyrics found in a mid-1940s song that several major singers recorded from 1958 to 1960. They "Ac-Cent-Tchu-Ate the Positive, E-Lim-i-nate the Negative, and Latch on to the Affirmative." They see the 1950s and early 1960s as the glory days. They were the golden years of the car culture, and the high-water mark of General Motors (GM), Ford, and Chrysler cars (and of custom cars and hot rods). The TV show *Happy Days* reminded us of this era, as did the film *American Graffiti*. Today, cultural resource managers and historic preservationists for the National Park Service, as well as state and local governments and numerous small business owners, work to preserve what is left of commercial strips along decommissioned US Highway 66. They want today's tourists to rekindle their memories of "the mother road" from the 1950s or 1960s. They encourage travelers to get off the Interstates and revisit the past, to drive down the stretches of old Route 66 that are still open for business, to eat in mom-and-pop restaurants and sleep in one-of-a-kind motels, many with multicolored

This 1955 Chevy, with period-correct flames engulfing its hood and fenders, participated in the 2018 Woodward Avenue Dream Cruise. (Mustang Joe, Wikimedia Commons)

neon signs out front, that have become historic sites. In the once-upon-a-time Motor Capital of the World, Detroit and surrounding suburbs harken back to the glory days by staging the Woodward Avenue Dream Cruise every August. The event draws 1.5 million spectators and forty thousand classic cars, a great many from the '50s and '60s. All this to celebrate the car and car culture of old. The car culture I grew up in.

I was a young boy in the 1950s and a teenager in the 1960s. Cars changed, the car culture evolved, and at the same time, I changed, too. Whatever stage of life I was in, I always felt connected to cars. I swear that as a kid from southeast Michigan I was groomed to desperately want a driver's license and a set of wheels. I was seduced by the new cars that showed up each fall in auto showrooms, by every pedal car, bumper car, or go-kart that I ever sat in. By anything with wheels. By Matchbox tiny toy cars and AMT plastic models of Buicks and Oldsmobiles. I watched Saturday night races at Jackson Motor Speedway and listened to the Indy 500 on the radio every Memorial Day. I read *Hot Rod* magazine and the car books of Henry Gregor Felsen and listened to car songs on the radio. My folks and I watched Ed Sullivan and Julia Meade sell Mercury and Lincoln cars on television. I rode in the car with my mom to go buy school clothes and with my dad to go to my Little League games. The car took me almost everywhere I went.

While lecturing one day on the postwar era in my "Automobile in America" class, it struck me that my family and I had lived through the social changes I was talking about. These changes didn't happen to somebody else. They happened to us. Move from the city? Check. Relocate to the suburbs? Check. Buy a second car to fill the two-car garage? Check. Have a stay-at-home mom who uses her car to serve as the family shopper and chauffeur? Check. Cruise Main Street with your best buddies while listening to "Maybellene" and "Mustang Sally" on the car radio? Check.

This is my auto biography. Hop in and ride shotgun with me on a road trip through my life with cars in the 1950s and 1960s. Oh, the places we'll go! I hope you enjoy the ride. I know I did—not all of the time, for sure, but most of the time.

# 1

## THE GREATNESS OF EVERYTHING NEW

I was born in Jackson, Michigan, in 1947, making me one of the 3.8 million baby boomers born that year. The city had a thriving downtown, many attractive neighborhoods, and wonderful parks. Jackson called itself "The Rose City," but at its core it was an industrial city of about 51,000 residents, with another 107,000 inhabitants in its surrounding county. Since the start of the century, the city had boasted some twenty-five car manufacturing plants. Jackson produced Buicks for a few years, and it produced Briscoes. Its most successful homegrown auto was the Jackson (sometimes the Jaxon), produced by the Jackson Automobile Company, which produced about ten thousand vehicles before folding in the early 1920s. In 1954, Jackson manufactured its last new car, the Kaiser Darrin. The Darrin and the new Chevrolet Corvette had two things in common: they were two-seater sports cars with fiberglass bodies. The Corvette went on to live forever. Kaiser Darrin produced only 435 cars in its first and only year.

In the year of the Darrin, 1954, my half sister, Lynn, thirteen years older than I, married Ben, who loved cars as much as anybody I ever knew. They held their wedding reception on the topmost floor of the grandest hotel in downtown Jackson, the Hotel Hayes. Opened in 1926, the hotel was named after Clarence B. Hayes, the founder of the Hayes Wheel Company. That company became Kelsey-Hayes, a major American manufacturer of automobile wheels and brakes. Kelsey-Hayes and other parts producers in Jackson shipped their wares eighty miles due east to Detroit or ninety miles north and east to Flint. Throughout my youth, auto parts companies and major railroad repair facilities remained important employers and generators of wealth in my hometown.

Having Detroit as a neighbor had a profound effect on my life. I wasn't born near the Freedom Trail in Boston, or the Santa Fe or Oregon Trails of the American West. I wasn't born in the deep South along the tragic Trail of Tears. I was born near what the Ford Motor Company in many ad campaigns called "The American Road," a road of mythic proportions where cars transported you to family, friends, and interesting places, and to a better way of life.

I became interested in cars at a very early age, I think, because Detroit was close by and the auto companies were shining examples, at the time, of America's styling, production might, and know-how. The carmakers helped the Allies win World War II, and in the postwar world, their cars served as symbols to the world of America's burgeoning economy. The Big Three helped make the United States a superpower.

While some American kids became experts on dinosaurs and comic book characters, I became an expert on American cars. New models rolled out each fall, and I could identify them all from half a block away. I could tell you what it was—a Mercury, a DeSoto, or an Oldsmobile—and I knew how the newest models differed from last year's. I was a big reader as a kid. I consumed all the jokes found in *Reader's Digest*. I read *Boys' Life*, *Sport*, *Baseball Digest*, and *Mad* magazine. I read *True* and *Argosy*. I also read *Hot Rod* magazine, *Rod and Custom*, *Car Craft*, and *Sports Cars Illustrated*. I didn't subscribe to or buy all of these magazines. Often, I just thumbed through them while standing in front of the magazine rack at the drugstore.

Large-format picture magazines, like *Look* and *Life*, were found nearly everywhere, from doctors' offices, to barber shops, to my friends' living rooms. So were news magazines, like *Time* and *Newsweek*. In the fall, when Detroit released its new models, magazines literally blossomed with colorful, boastful ads for all the car companies. The same was true for television. Car companies sponsored many popular shows during prime time. When I heard the voice of Pat Boone, I knew without looking that a Chevy commercial was being aired. Groucho Marx shilled for DeSoto and Plymouth, and Ed Sullivan convinced more Americans to buy a Mercury or a Lincoln than anybody else.

Each fall, my dad and I participated in a ritual that was great fun for me. He took me to downtown Jackson, and we stopped at all the car dealerships. He parked the car at the curb, and we walked up to the big plate glass windows, each one framing another new piece of automotive art from Detroit. (There were no foreign car dealers in Jackson at the time.) The newest cars were cool, especially when spotted in your hometown for the first time.

Later, when I grew up, I learned that Dad and I and millions of Americans had been manipulated by Detroit's automakers. Year after year, Detroit played tricks on us. With appeals to style, status, prestige, comfort, and speed, automakers got Americans to love a car enough to pony up a cash down payment, take out an installment loan, and buy one. Then, the same automakers worked mightily to get customers to fall *out* of love with their cars, so that as soon as possible they would reenter the market and buy a different one. "New," in postwar America, had a short shelf life, particularly in car showrooms.

Alfred Sloan, a longtime head of General Motors, had better ideas about how to sell cars in the Roaring Twenties and thereafter than Henry Ford. Ford had used "Fordism" (mass-production technology and the assembly line) to become the best-selling automaker in the era of the Model T. Under Sloan, GM became the leader of the American auto industry by the late 1920s and early 1930s, and it still ruled over Ford, Chrysler, and all others in the 1950s. Sloanism was a package of marketing strategies. The most fundamental element of Sloanism was the "annual model changeover" or, as some called it, "planned obsolescence." By whatever name, the changeover was as much a part of autumn in America as the changing of the leaves and the migration of birds. Every fall, last year's models left and new models arrived.

To increase sales, GM's marketing strategy included more than the annual model changeover. The corporation did not market just one car line selling at one price. It marketed a stepladder of cars to cover the low-price, medium-price, and fine-car fields. It made buying a car easier by offering installment loans and good trade-ins for used cars.

To compete with GM, other auto companies had to act like GM. In the 1950s, GM, Ford, Chrysler, and surviving independents like Studebaker, Packard, Hudson, and Nash practiced Sloanism with wild abandon. In no other decade, before or since the '50s, did American cars change so radically in size, style, paint colors, trim, interior design, engines, and power assists. General Motors aggressively expanded its sales to stay ahead of the pack. Ford and Chrysler did what GM did, feeling that otherwise they would wither and die. GM had its stepladder of cars to cover all market segments. Moving up the ladder, from Chevy to Pontiac to Oldsmobile to Buick to Cadillac, each step meant a bigger car, a more powerful engine, more features as standard equipment, and a more expensive car. GM's stepladder established price points in the market that other automakers struggled to match, or they faced a loss of market share. If you didn't have a car that matched the Buick or Oldsmobile in price and amenities, you lost sales to Buick or Oldsmobile. So Ford had its stepladder that positioned Ford, Mercury, Edsel, Thunderbird, Lincoln, and Continental at various points in the marketplace, while Chrysler Corporation countered with its Plymouth, Dodge, DeSoto, Chrysler, and Imperial lines.

The stepladder of cars in the 1950s led to a proliferation of models and styles. Looking at the bottom rung of the ladder, Chevy, Ford, and Plymouth not only competed with each other in the low-cost field, they also competed with other makes within their own corporation. The '57 Ford needed to appear different from the '57 Chevy and the '57 Plymouth, but it also needed to look different from its corporate sibling, Mercury. And, of course, the '57 Ford needed to look different from the '56 Ford, too. The same was true for DeSoto, Chrysler, Pontiac, and Buick. Each used change to try to get some elbow room in the market, to try to set itself off from the others.

In the 1950s, the industry brought the idea of having stepladders within stepladders into full flower. It wasn't enough to have just a single Ford, Chevy, or Dodge model. Each make had to come in multiples. Ford developed a stepladder of Fords, from cheapest to most expensive, and so did all of the others. At least in terms of full-size, six-passenger cars, the automakers offered something for every taste and pocketbook.

In 1956, Dodge sold the Coronet, the Royal Lancer, and the Custom Royal. It also offered some specialty models, such as the "Texan," sold only in Texas, and the "La Femme," pitched at women. In 1959, Buick sold the LeSabre ("The thriftiest Buick"), the Invicta ("The most spirited Buick"), and the Electra ("The most luxurious Buick").

I had a wonderful, challenging time as a kid keeping up with proliferating models, names, and styles. Each car line seemed to have two- and four-door sedans; two- and four-door hardtops (a new style pioneered by GM that had fewer pillars supporting the roof); convertibles; and station wagons. Rampant Sloanism in the 1950s produced rampant variety. In 1955, the Ford Motor Company, once champion of the singular, black Model T, offered its Ford in sixteen body styles and eleven *two-tone* color combinations. Three years later, in 1958, Ford's ill-fated, short-lived Edsel came out of the gate with eighteen different models spread over four series (Ranger, Pacer, Corsair, and Citation), and you could get your Edsel, if you were one of the few who wanted one, in ninety different color combinations.

Success and excess marked the 1950s for Detroit. To my amusement, it was a decade of *more*. The only auto dimension to shrink was height: cars became lower, but longer and wider. If a little of something worked, more of that something presumably worked better. The small fins that sprouted on Cadillacs in the late 1940s grew to become the giant fins of the late '50s. One chrome strip down the fenders and door panels branched into many. Two headlights had sufficed until 1957 and especially 1958, when every car seemed to need four. Six-cylinder engines grew to eight cylinders, and eight-cylinder engines grew in cubic inch displacement and horsepower. In the late 1950s, a film crew making "The Cars in Your Life" interviewed Raymond Loewy, the leading industrial designer who had worked for Studebaker and who had designed cars that looked lean, trim, and spare in comparison with the behemoths surrounding them on the road. Asked about the evolution of Detroit automobiles, Loewy replied:

> The sales department evaluation of what the next product should be is based on an existing product and they try to go . . . one better. So, why

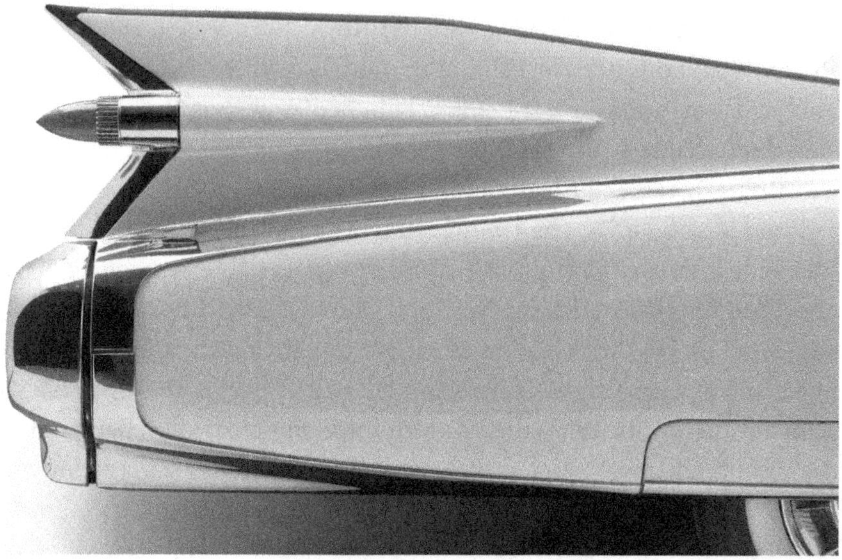

This knife-edged fin on the 1959 Cadillac Biarritz convertible was excessive, to be sure, but as a piece of automotive art it seemed more handsome than any fins found on Chrysler Corporation cars. (Collections of The Henry Ford)

> not make it a little bit bigger, a little bit larger, a little bit more powerful, a little bit roomier, a little bit more gaudy, a little bit more jazzy, and it's a continuous process which leads to monstrosities.

Carmakers constantly trumpeted their products' newness. Print ads and television commercials bombarded consumers with the words "new," "newer," and "newest." Nobody sold newness like the auto industry. In 1950, Packard proudly offered new simplicity, new smoothness, new economy, new quietness, and new safety. Ford said its offering for 1950 was "50 Ways New, the One *Fine* Car in its Field." Ford's improvements ran the gamut from new "super-fitted pistons" to a new V-8, new heater controls, and new push button door handles. Oldsmobile, with its Rocket 88 engine and automatic transmission, promised a "new thrill" to all who purchased a Futuramic Olds.

In 1951, a two-page spread for Packard in *Time* magazine used the word "new" eighteen times. Packard was an old company, largely surviving on tradition, on its reputation for having been a fine car.

Packard nevertheless entered the "new" battle and advertised new restful riding and new soundproofing, steering, body construction, and upholstery. Every little part of a car could be lauded for its newness. In 1953, a Chrysler television commercial made its pitch: "new low silhouette, new one-piece windshield, new pull-type door handle, new rear deck, new rear deck lock, new rear fender design, new rear door design, new wheel covers, new taillight design, new gas filler cap location." In an ad in *Time* magazine, General Motors avoided the word "new," yet still conveyed the same message: "Our finger-on-the-future stylists—originators of the hardtop, the panoramic windshield and, most recently, the 4-door hardtop—have advanced automotive design many a fashion furlong further in our '56 Oldsmobiles, Buicks and Cadillacs."

In 1957, Chrysler Corporation raced ahead a few fashion furlongs itself and promoted "The Forward Look," calling its Plymouths, Dodges, DeSotos, Chryslers, and Imperials "The Newest New Cars in 20 Years." In 1957, Buick finally hopped on the newness bandwagon. Earlier in the '50s, Buick had behaved like one of the "fine" car lines it so wanted to be. Cadillac, Lincoln, and Imperial, instead of touting newness, touted tradition, luxury, and prestige. Instead of trying to sell itself to the public in the manner of Chevrolet, Pontiac, and Oldsmobile, Buick opted to sell itself like Cadillac, an aristocratic car. But in 1957, Buick threw in the towel and entered the fray to be seen as the newest, rather than the best. In an advertisement in *Time*, this General Motors division announced, "Here is Newness for the Sake of Greatness—Newest Buick Yet." The two-page ad used the words "new," "newer," or "newest" thirty-five times.

In 1958, Ford Motor Company expanded its stepladder of cars by introducing the Edsel. Meant to attract sales away from General Motors, Edsel was "the one that's new, and the lowest priced, too." It wasn't a look-alike car, such as the many GM models that shared styling touches. The Edsel was something else. It was "truly new from nameplate to taillights." It presented "new looks" from all angles, "new from the front, new from the side, and new from the rear." The 1958 Ford heralded its own newness. In a lengthy commercial featuring Ford

In 1957, the new "Forward Look" DeSoto looked extremely wide because of its massive horizontal bumper, four headlights, and broad hood ornament. It looked long, with chrome moldings along the sides. And, supposedly, its fins made it look like a jet plane. (Collections of The Henry Ford)

spokesmen Hugh Downs, Dick Powell, Arthur Godfrey, and Tennessee Ernie Ford, Hugh Downs first asked, "What makes a new car new? I mean really new, in all the things that count?" He extolled the '58 Ford because of its "new styling, new power, new performance, new handling, new comfort, new ride. There's nothing newer in the world." All told, the commercial used the words "new," "newer," or "newest" a total of thirty times. Following up on the theme of "nothing newer in the world," print ads and television spots pictured Fords in such far-flung places as Vietnam, Paris, the Swiss Alps, Turkey, London, and Yugoslavia.

Chevrolet refused to concede the newness crown to Ford. In one 1958 commercial, Pat Boone stood beside a Chevy and rather breathlessly uttered, "Now, did you ever see anything as new and fresh looking as that?" A deep, disembodied voice (rather godlike) answered back: "It's so new, it's almost too new to be true." In 1959, Chevy proclaimed it was "All New All Over Again!" "Never before," ran the copy in a *Time* ad, "has an automobile manufacturer made such sweeping changes two years in a row." Dodge kept the drumbeat going, saying that its cars had "The Newest of Everything Great! The Greatness of Everything New!"

Detroit wordsmiths trumpeted the qualities of a car's constituent parts. They avoided generic terms, such as "automatic transmission" or "windshield" or "coil springs." In advertising copy, each manufacturer named its own windshield, body style, or shock absorber. Ad agencies made up many new words and fell in love with mechanical words like "torque" and "turbine," with hyphenated words, and with suffixes like "-amic" and "-matic," which consumers presumably associated with the whole words "dynamic" and "automatic." Ad copy surrounded freshly minted names for car parts in a sea of capital letters and exclamation points, all to scream out newness.

Windshields came with new names that promised wide views of a grandiose America: "New Horizon Super-Scenic" (1955 Chrysler), "Scene-A-Ramic" (1955 Nash Ambassador), and "Vista-Panoramic" (1959 General Motors). Different cars exhibited "Futuramic," "Sweep-Ahead," "Forward Look," "Beauty-Action," or "Metal-in-Motion" styling. In 1955 and 1956, Chevrolet targeted younger buyers, not the middle-aged, when hawking its new "Motoramic" styling. Chevy said that Motoramic styling was "sassy" and "new," and announced that "the hot one's even hotter!" Chevy's "frisky new models" promised "more of the dynamite action that's zoomed its way into America's heart."

The soft suspensions on 1950s cars cushioned riders from harsh road shocks but tended to wallow over bumps and dip going around curves. Americans rode on "Hydra-Coil," "ParaFlex," or "Quadruflex" springs, with help from "Level-Flite Torsion-Aire" suspension, "Unitized Knee-Action Ride," "New-Matic Ride," "Air Pillow Ride," or "Oriflow Ride." New transmissions and drive trains also bore all ilk of monikers. The 1950 DeSoto featured "Tip-Toe Hydraulic Shift." General Motors introduced Powerglide in the Chevrolet, Dynaflow in the Buick, and Hydra-Matic in the Pontiac, Olds, and Cadillac. By 1957, Chevrolet had "Triple-Turbine-Powerglide," which was one turbine more than Buick's "Twin-Turbine Transmission" of 1959. In the early '50s, Mercury had both "Merc-O-Matic" and "Touch-O-Matic Overdrive." Ford introduced "Ford-O-Matic" and later, "Cruise-O-Matic," while Packard had its "Ultramatic," Dodge its "Gyro-Matic" and later "PowerFlite" transmissions, and Plymouth its "Hy-Drive." The "Gyro-Torque Drive" on the '53 Dodge had a "Scat" gear for safer, faster passing.

The 1958 Buick was a huge car, dripping with chrome. Its "Dynastar Grille" featured a mere 184 square, chromed "jewels" sitting under the lip of the hood and behind a massive, chromed bumper. As an eleven-year-old kid, I loved this beast of a Buick. I was a lover of all this chrome and newness. I assembled a '58 Buick model car kit and kept it in my bedroom. For good measure I assembled a '58 Oldsmobile too.

In the postwar world, Americans viewed high-tech aircraft and missiles with a mixture of fascination and fear. For sure, travel in the skies in the 1950s evoked excitement and adventure, as many Americans took their first commercial flights on a Lockheed Constellation or aboard the first jetliner, the Boeing 707, flight-tested in 1954 and put into service by Pan American Airways in 1958. But the skies were clouded by threats too. In 1949 the United States lost its nuclear monopoly when the Soviet Union detonated its first atomic bombs, and a year later the Soviets sent MiG-15 jet fighters to Korea to dogfight with American F-86 Sabre jets. The fear of atomic warfare escalated as Cold War tensions and bomber-building and missile-building programs grew. Nobody in my neighborhood in Jackson built a personal bomb shelter in their basement or backyard, but one hundred thousand or so Americans did. Civil Defense fallout shelters, stocked with food and water, proliferated across the country. Many were in schools, including my Ella Sharp Park grade school. That's where Bill, Phil, Rick, and I learned to duck and cover to survive a nuclear attack.

Despite our fears, Americans, including automakers and me, swooned romantically over new planes and rockets. In a junior high English class, I wrote a research paper on jets after seeing a story about them in *True* magazine. Detroit seemed bent on having their cars break the surly bonds of Earth. They launched their own air forces, using words, imagery, and styling to mimic flight. They applied aeronautical and astronautical words and terms to cars. They adopted swoopy logos, such as Chrysler Corporation's flying wings logo introduced in the mid-1950s, and new hood ornaments modeled after rockets or planes.

Detroit had both historical and current connections to aircraft production. During World War II, as the lynchpin of the Arsenal of Democracy, automakers provided approximately 20 percent of all war materiel produced in the United States. Besides manufacturing 12.5 billion rounds of small-arms ammunition, 245 million artillery shells, and over five million bombs, auto companies accounted for about twenty-seven thousand complete airplanes and an immense number of aircraft engines. Auto companies ran two of the largest war plants in the United States. Ford operated the Willow Run plant in Ypsilanti, Michigan, where it produced 8,642 B-24 Liberator bombers (6,792 fly-aways, and 1,850 knock-downs, shipped to others for final assembly). Dodge, meanwhile, operated a vast aircraft engine facility in Chicago. The Defense Plant Corporation funded the construction and equipping of numerous war plants. The auto industry—including Dodge, Chevy, Buick, Ford, Studebaker, GM-Allison division, and Packard—operated ten of the sixteen most expensive facilities built with government dollars. After the war, the Arsenal of Democracy was disarmed, but the new military-industrial complex took up the slack when it came to military research, development, and production. In the 1950s, several automakers remained active in the defense industry.

After World War II ended, it took Detroit a few years to tool up to produce cars that were clearly different from prewar cars. Almost as soon as these cars appeared, Detroit's "air force" took flight, as the industry forged connections between cars and planes. The legendary Harley Earl and his designers at General Motors led the way in styling the 1948 Caddy. Before the war, the designers went to Selfridge Air Base near Mount Clemens, Michigan, to examine an early Lockheed P-38 Lightning fighter bomber. This novel plane had twin tails that terminated with a vertical fin or stabilizer. Frank Hershey, one of the GM men who studied the P-38 before the war, harkened back to the profile of the aircraft's tails when working on postwar Cadillacs. His recollections ultimately led to the smallish tail fins found on 1948 Cadillacs, tail fins that grew and grew on Cadillacs and other makes through the 1950s.

Another GM marque led the way in taking Detroit into the heavens. In 1949, Oldsmobile offered a new, high-compression V-8 engine called the "Rocket." Soon, Olds not only had its "Rocket engine"—it also had its "Rocket 88" and more expensive "Rocket 98" model cars. The Rocket

Olds engine and space motif carried Olds throughout the 1950s and beyond. Olds tweaked the Rocket theme from year to year and sometimes gave it a new logo. In 1950, the catch phrase was "Oldsmobile Rockets Ahead!" In 1951, Olds told Americans to "Ride the Rocket and Save!" In 1954 the message was "there's more than a touch of tomorrow in the Rockets of today." Olds used themes built around the Rocket engine to make its cars seem ultramodern and special. Under the hood, the engine's valve covers carried the words "Rocket Oldsmobile." Atop the hood, Olds affixed a rocket-like hood ornament. Beneath the ornament, on the lip of the hood, a chromed Oldsmobile medallion represented planet earth, with orbital rings around the equator. On the first Olds badge, the earth was stylized and showed lines of latitude and longitude. A few years later, Olds changed the badge so that Mother Earth clearly showed the outlines of North and South America.

Oldsmobile print ads in the 1950s made heavy use of rocket imagery. The first depiction of the Olds rocket had an elongated ballistic shape with four stabilizer fins. Although it resembled a German V-2, this was clearly a friendly rocket. It was always aimed upward, and never down. Following Oldsmobile's "Ride the Rocket" theme, a happy man sits astride the rocket with a woman right behind him, holding on to his waist. Speed lines and flames at the base of the rocket provide a sense of rapid propulsion. He holds on to his hat, while his tie streams out behind him. Her over-the-shoulder purse streams behind her. Seeing the rocket and its travelers up in space, a bright cartoon moon carries a happily surprised look on its face. Other rocket riders in the ad campaign included a baby in diapers and a woman dressed in full equestrian gear. She was symbolic of the upper class, and the ad made it clear that she and her husband should purchase the top-end Olds, the Rocket 98 Holiday Coupe. Oldsmobile's rocket riders disappeared for a while in magazine ads, but in 1958, after the Soviet Union launched Sputnik, they returned, making space once again seem like a happy place, not a threatening one.

The Big Three were not alone in pushing air and space motifs. In 1950, Nash trumpeted its "Airflyte Construction," patterned after aircraft construction: "In Nash the entire frame and body, floor, roof, rear fenders and pillars are built as a single, rigid, welded unit." Nash claimed to build "The World's First Cars to Apply the Modern Developments of Aviation to the Building of Automobiles." The company told potential buyers that "you sit inside a twist-proof, all-welded fuselage," inside a "Sky-Lounge Interior" with five-position "airliner reclining seats." In 1950, Studebaker announced that "this 'next look' in cars is a 'jet-propelled' look!" Sporting a new aerodynamic design, Studebaker noted that "most people say it's a car so startling, they half expect to see it take off and fly!" In 1952, during the Korean War, Studebaker called its Commander V-8 a "jet-streamed wonder car," and an ad depicted the Studebaker in the foreground with drawings of four Air Force planes in the sky beyond. The ad noted a direct connection between Studebaker and the jets—"National defense now has enlisted Studebaker competence extensively—for jet engines and military vehicles."

In 1952, GM reminded the public that the giant corporation made more than cars (and household appliances); it built tanks, engines for submarines, and jet aircraft flown by the Air Force and the Navy. Packard, meanwhile, extolled its past—it built 55,523 Rolls-Royce aircraft engines during World War II—and in the 1950s it manufactured "new J-47 Turbo-Jet engines . . . for the Air Force's new B-47 Boeing Bomber."

In 1953, Dodge offered a "distinctive Jet Air-Flow hood" and "Pilot View" curved windshield. In 1955, Ford eased into the aircraft motif by calling out its "jet-like rear fender." Chevy, that year, parked a yellow-and-white car on an airfield with a US Air Force jet fighter right behind it, plus a control tower and three other jets in the distance. The ad helped sell Chevy's "new 'Turbo-Fire V-8.'" Pontiac, in 1955–56, promised a quick ride to the stratosphere with its "New Strato-Flight Hydra-Matic Coupled with Pontiac's 227-H.P. Strato-Streak V-8." Buick truly applied the high tech of aircraft to its transmissions: "We took a tip from aeronautics. When we tell you these eager new Buicks use the modern airplane's principle of 'variable pitch' propulsion, we mean that literally." Buick said, "You do what a pilot does when he heads his plane down a runway. You do in oil what he does in air—*you cut down take-off time by using 'variable pitch propellers.'*" Buick went on to explain, sort of, that the stator deep inside the Dynaflow Drive transmission had blades that changed in pitch. Like a plane's variable pitch propellers—which had one pitch for takeoffs and steep climbs and another for gas-saving cruising—the pitch of the Dynaflow Drive changed to give you fast starts or fuel economy. Buick no doubt hoped that potential car buyers appreciated this new technology, even if they didn't understand it.

In 1955 the Chrysler Corporation created the "Forward Look" and launched a series of ads and commercials that linked aircraft to all Chrysler Corporation cars. Chrysler knew no boundaries when it came to presenting itself as a builder of cars that damn near could fly. In a teaser ad done before its November 15, 1955, release date for new cars, Chrysler posed nine men in front of a new model, thus hiding much of its styling. The nine men were high-tech modernists for sure: "These 9 top aircraft designers salute Chrysler Corporation's all-new 1955 styling." Chrysler identified the designers as coming from Republic Aviation, Sikorsky, Lockheed, Societe Ateliers d'Aviation, Northrop, Piper, Bell Aircraft, and two from Glenn L. Martin Co. The designers admired the new models' long, low lines and "felt a sense of motion even when the cars were standing still."

In 1956, Chrysler Corporation pitched its new "Flight-Sweep Styling" across its entire line, from the lowly Plymouth all the way up to the luxurious Imperial. All, said Chrysler, exhibited "Youthful Aerodynamic Styling." For all, "The almost wedge-shape silhouette—like that of a jet plane—conveys *motion* and *power*." In a commercial aired just before the '56 models were released, the announcer sat on a stool with nothing but sky and clouds visible behind him. "Well, as you can plainly see," he says, "we're way up in the clouds tonight. And I'm pretty excited because tonight's the night we start telling you about the great line of all new cars of the Forward Look of 1956." The Chrysler products had "all new style along with jet-plane power." The commercial showed a jet in flight, followed by eight performers who sang and danced in front of a drawing of a jet. The commercial flashed images of US Air Force jets doing barrel rolls and other maneuvers. The message was, "Flight-Sweep styling is just about the nearest thing to the look of flying you can have in car design."

Chrysler, in magazine ads, posed its 1956 Plymouth Belvedere in front of a military jet. Plymouth, read the ad, had "all-new 90–90 Turbo-Torque Power . . . for Top Thrust at Take-off!" In a different Plymouth ad, readers were asked to appreciate the "fabulous new beauty that ranks Plymouth first in the styling frontiers of the jet age. Note Plymouth's steeply swept-back 'fins.'" In a Dodge commercial of the same vintage, three young men in uniform leave their suburban houses and get into Coronet, Royal Lancer, and Custom Royal Dodges with "Jet Fin Styling for '56." They meet, fall into line, and drive into the country. When they cross a large bridge, they travel in a V-formation, and then they pull up at an airfield. All disappear briefly and then reappear in flight suits. Soon, they are piloting three Air Force jets streaking across the sky, while the announcer intones, "See and drive the car with the look, the feel, the power of success, the '56 Dodge, value leader of the Forward Look!"

Another Chrysler Corporation commercial of 1956 spent a Saturday morning with a new PowerStyle Chrysler. The husband puts his golf clubs in the trunk, and his wife drives them away from their expensive house in an exclusive suburb. Their car attracts attention. "Notice how your neighbors look with admiration as you drive, . . . and no wonder. From the rakish flare of its new Flight-Swept rear fenders, right up to its bold but elegant new front styling, the new PowerStyled Chrysler emphasizes the Forward Look of Power in Motion." The wife drops her husband off at the course, and a golfer says with admiration, "Looks like it's still moving, even when it stops!" She continues on to the grocery store. The bag boy taking her groceries out to the car stops in his tracks and exclaims, "Wow! That rear end looks just like a jet plane!"

In 1957, Ford got more into the swing of all things aeronautical by adding a bit more fin to the T-Bird (and other '57 Fords) and by taking the T-Bird and the rest of the line out to Nellis Air Force Base, home of the flying Thunderbirds. A television spot shows Air Force Thunderbirds streaking over the runways in new F-100 Super Sabres powered by Pratt & Whitney J57 engines "manufactured by the Ford Aircraft Engine Division." The commercial shows the T-Bird with jets in the background, then other Fords drive up in front of the Super

Sabres—Fairlanes, Customs, even station wagons. A jet takes off, and then the Fords race down the runway.

Buick joined the air force in 1958 when it introduced "The Air Born B-58," which "looks and feels like flight on wheels." Buick ads pictured a climbing jet with four engines and read, "It is literally born of aviation principles—starting with the fact that it makes greater use of aluminum than ever before." It was "a car born of more aviation principles than any other car in history." When driving it, "you float over bumps like a pilot flying over the weather." This Buick was a massive car, one of the largest and most chrome-laden behemoths of its time, yet one ad called it "buoyant." Another showed it seemingly sailing through the air, with three delta-wing planes climbing with it into the sky, accompanied by the tagline, "It's the new face of fashion—the new feeling of flight." (This was one case where Detroit won the race with plane manufacturers and the military. General Motors had its Buick B-58 in 1958; the Air Force did not operate B-58 bombers within the Strategic Air Command until 1960.)

In the face of criticism that the fins on cars of the late 1950s represented styling run amok, Chrysler Corporation fought back. In 1958, Plymouth ads proclaimed that "directional stabilizer fins" were "for safer travel on the nation's highways." A 1959 Chrysler Corporation ad for all of its car lines, in a text block located next to a drawing of a big fin, opined that "true aerodynamic styling not only sets the pace for design but also makes a real contribution to your car's driving stability on the highway." Chrysler did not retreat from its commitment to exaggerated "aerodynamic" styling and high-tech auto components. In 1959, an ad announced that in the Chrysler car, "Space travel . . . it's pushbutton driving ease with room to spare." Consumers were advised to "start your count-down—at Chrysler's unique control center," which was modern lingo for "driver's seat." This Chrysler even had "Auto-Pilot Selector"—something that later, when the fascination with aircraft finally wore off, would simply be called cruise control.

In 1949, Oldsmobile launched Detroit's metaphorical space race by introducing its Rocket Olds engine, which morphed into Rocket 88 and 98 Oldsmobile cars. Over ten years, the auto industry made innumerable allusions to air and space that were sometimes accurate but more often tenuous, hyperbolic, and even laughable. But in 1958, Chrysler finally made the space deal real. It connected the road below to the heavens above.

I saw this for myself. The Cold War and the race to space intensified after the Soviet Union launched one Sputnik into orbit in October 1957 and quickly followed with another. In our grade school class, we sometimes got to watch rocket launches on television; we watched America try to catch up. Some launches were spectacular failures that came back down to earth faster than they went up. These failures hurt our national pride and diminished our confidence, so Americans tried to turn these failures into a kind of win. The Communists ran their space program in secret. They hid any failures and announced only their successes. Meanwhile, our rockets and their gantries stood tall and in the open at Cape Canaveral. The whole world could see a liftoff, good or bad, and that elevated us above the secret, closed society of the Soviet Union.

In the late 1950s, Chrysler built the most baroque, outlandish cars coming off American assembly lines. But Chrysler also built Redstone and Jupiter rockets. On January 31, 1958, a Jupiter C rocket finally launched our first satellite, Explorer, into orbit. That was something to cheer for!

Kudos to Detroit!

# 2

## COLOR, CHROME, AND LAZY LIVING

After having their dreams and aspirations throttled by the Great Depression and World War II, Americans in the late 1940s and 1950s were primed to get on with the good life. They were generally optimistic and believed the future would be better than the recent past. Marriages and births abounded, and millions of new, young families, with their baby boomer kids, set out on buying sprees to acquire the things that would make them secure and comfortable. Working wages doubled, at least for whites, and producers and advertisers worked hard to sell new families all the things they ever wanted, things that promised happiness and a sense of accomplishment, a sense of having *made it*.

The happy consumers depicted in ads and commercials did not look like my folks. They looked younger. In 1954, I was a young seven, but my dad was fifty-one and my mom forty-three. My half sister, Lynn, was twenty and married Ben at the start of the year and left our household. Despite being older, my folks acted much like younger parents. They went on a buying spree to cement their place in middle-class America. My mom, for a few years, took up waitressing and hosting again, including at the toney Drum Room Restaurant in the Hotel Hayes. Presumably she did this to help the family build up a nest egg. I don't know how much money they spent or how much debt they incurred, but it was substantial.

Between 1954 and 1959, they bought a brand-new three-bedroom ranch house. They bought two new cars. To me, it didn't seem that they transferred many furnishings from Emmett Street in Vandercook

In 1949 a Ford photographer foreshadowed what the post–World War II car culture would look like and how it would contribute to a new good life for Americans. Two young couples cruise around in a new-model Ford Custom Club Coupe. They stop at a Richard's hamburger stand in Southern California. They drink Cokes out of paper cups and eat fries out of little paper bags. (Collections of The Henry Ford)

Lake to the new house on Schaffer Drive. We had an automatic washer and dryer in the utility room, and in the kitchen, a new refrigerator, stove, kitchen table, and chairs. Our countertop glistened with new chrome kitchen gadgets. Mom and Dad filled the living room with new chairs and a couch, and after an expensive trip to the one nearby furniture store, they returned with high-quality, solid maple beds, dressers, and nightstands for their bedroom and my bedroom. They put an air conditioner into my bedroom. We used the third bedroom as a den, which my parents equipped with a second "portable" television on a metal stand, a pull-out sofa, and a parakeet cage. The garage, besides housing cars, became home to two lawn mowers (a riding mower and a walk-behind), a wheelbarrow, a seed or fertilizer spreader, and all kinds of shovels, rakes, and trimmers.

My family spent many evenings watching television in our living room at 1861 Schaffer Drive. Mom usually sat on one end of the couch, placed along the wall opposite the picture window. Dad sat in an easy chair that swiveled, so he could spin from focal point to focal point. I sat at the other end of the couch but often got on the floor to sit cross-legged on the wall-to-wall carpeting. Before a favorite show came on, we made trips to the kitchen and put our beverages and snacks on the low, blonde coffee table that stood in front of the couch on its spindly Hollywood legs. The Zenith television looked like the finest piece of furniture in the room. Its hardwood cabinet had doors we could close to hide the screen, if we wanted to. Those doors never made sense to me. Why put solid shutters in front of America's new window to entertainment?

Television also served as the window to conspicuous consumption. As far as the television business was concerned, everyone was a consumer, even my older parents and a little kid like me. Shows did their darnedest to sell me Ovaltine, Alpha-Bits cereal, Pepsi Cola, and Mounds and Almond Joy candy bars. Poor Mom got bombarded with a plethora of new products to keep her house sparkling clean and her family healthy. The tobacco industry hit Dad with Marlboro, Winston, and Pall Mall

The Lankton family, shown in 1950–51. Lynn, Mom, Dad, and me. (Courtesy of Lynn Lewis)

commercials; the personal products industry hit him with Gillette Blue Blades and Safety Razors, Vitalis, Brylcreem, 'Lectric shave, and Lava soap; the keeper-of-your-castle industry hit him with Dutch Boy paints and Lawn Boy mowers. And beautiful Dinah Shore looked right out of the television at our family and sang, "See the USA in your Chevrolet." Then she blew us all a kiss.

At the start of the 1950s, four million households had televisions. By 1959, 90 percent of all households—forty-four million of them—owned sets. Commercials for soaps, soups, soda pops, and cereals weren't the only ones that delivered visual entertainment. Automakers reduced their expenditures on print ads and bought more airtime for car commercials. The auto and television industries fed off one another, reinforced one another. Cars and stars went together in the 1950s.

The televised faces that sold GM cars in the 1950s were famous ones, like Dinah Shore, Pat Boone, Dave Garroway, and that comedic singer with the big schnoz, Jimmy Durante. GM hoped you'd laugh all the way to the dealership, having been encouraged to do so by Jackie Gleason, Red Buttons, or Uncle Miltie (Milton Berle), the most famous cross-dresser in the country. GM-sponsored shows included the Pontiac Football Scoreboard, Buick's *Tales of Wells Fargo*, and Chevrolet's *Treasury Men in Action*, which introduced new actors James Dean and Charles Bronson.

Chrysler countered with its troupe of entertainers, including Fred Astaire, Jack Benny, and Bob Hope. Danny Thomas, who starred in one of the most popular situation comedies, *Make Room for Daddy*, shilled for Dodge. Plymouth sponsored the most famous musician with a thick accent and a bubble-making machine, Lawrence Welk. Chrysler Corporation had Americans singing along with its commercial jingle, "It's delightful, it's de-lovely, it's DeSoto!" DeSoto made it possible for millions of Americans to wait for a duck to fall out of the sky, once a game show contestant had finally said whatever the "secret word" was that night on *You Bet Your Life*, hosted by Groucho Marx. One message from the cigar-smoking, mustachioed comedian was always the same: "Friends, go in to see your DeSoto, Plymouth dealer tomorrow. And when you do, tell 'em Groucho sent you!" Late in the 1950s, Groucho, who had a mischievous, if not lecherous, look in his eyes for the ladies, had another message: "Beauty doesn't always mean quality. That's true of women and certainly true of cars. Looks can be deceiving. But here's one car that has as much quality as it has beauty: the magnificent '58 DeSoto."

My family was fond of a new folksy singer with a drawl and hillbilly demeanor, Tennessee Ernie Ford. On his show, which we watched every week, he fittingly sold Fords to Americans and thanked our "little pea-pickin' hearts" for buying them. B-movie actor Glenn Ford helped sell Fords too. Ford Motor Company introduced the Edsel in October 1958 by airing a live broadcast, "The Edsel Show," on CBS. Ford's greatest automotive flop of the age was launched by one of the greatest stars of the age, crooner Bing Crosby, with a galaxy of guest stars, including Louis Armstrong, Frank Sinatra, and Rosemary Clooney.

The *Ed Sullivan Show* and Ford's Lincoln-Mercury division had the best synergistic bond between a car company and commercial television. Sullivan's hugely successful variety show occupied prime time on CBS on Sunday nights. My family never missed this show, which showcased the best comedians, singers, and dancers. Diverse performers came and went every week, but a Lincoln or Mercury starred in every show. Like a celebrity, the car sat right onstage. Ed Sullivan extolled its virtues, helped by "the lovely Julia Meade," an actress/spokesperson who dressed as if she were going to dinner at her country club. When the commercial spot concluded, the camera panned to the live audience, where every member was shown applauding the commercial performance.

Ed Sullivan and Julia Meade (whose husband, Tom Foldes, did his own commercials for Ford) taught us to understand that the modern car, the modern home, and modern culture are all interconnected. They wanted their viewing families to live a stylish and comfortable life, both at home and on the road. A Lincoln spot went like this:

> ED SULLIVAN: This is really a push-button age.
>
> JULIA MEADE: Yes, Ed, we're living in a push-button age and now I'd like to show you what amounts to a push-button car, the one fine car designed for modern living—Lincoln.

Lincoln had "push-button luxury that takes all the effort out of all your driving." It had all kinds of power assists, "and even air-conditioning." In other spots, Meade intoned that the Lincoln interior, with its "glamorous fabrics" and its "really full range of colors," is "just as up to date as your modern home." Lincoln was "truly the one fine car designed for modern living and completely powered for modern driving." In yet another spot, Meade said the Lincoln was "designed to reflect modern living as you find it in the modern home."

Other car companies also drew comparisons between house and car. In both 1954 and 1957, Dodge promised potential buyers that "you open the door and enter a world . . . as tasteful, as colorful as your own home." In a 1956 commercial for Dodge, Danny Thomas did not sit behind the wheel to sell Americans on push-button shifting. He told his audience, "Folks, this is the greatest thing that's happened to driving in years: The Dodge push-button control. All you do is push a button and go. . . . It's terrific." Instead of being in a car, Thomas held a push-button shifter unit in his hands while sitting in a kitchen—with a toaster just behind him. In 1957, Ford's chief stylist, George Walker, told *Time* that to please the modern woman, "We've spent millions to make the floor covering like the carpet in her living room." In 1959, GM and Fisher Body touted their "*Living-Room Interiors*, whose contour-molded carpeting, durable chrome metalwork and lock-stitched fabrics make time stand still."

In the decade after World War II, Henry J. Kaiser served as a direct connection between car and home. While making Kaiser and Henry J automobiles (and my hometown's short-lived Darrin sports car), he planned to build ten thousand new suburban homes a year. Powell Crosley produced about seventy-five thousand small and inexpensive automobiles between 1946 and 1952. At the same time, his firm produced refrigerators, washer-dryers, stoves, televisions, and radios. In the October 17, 1949, issue of *Life* magazine, GM ran an ad titled, "Key to better living." A General Motors key illustrated the ad, and the text noted that "not every General Motors product needs a key to make it go. GM still stands as a symbol for value, not only in motor cars, but things for the home—products that keep food fresh, people comfortable, and daily burdens lighter. . . . No matter what the product is—refrigerator, electric range, automatic washer, television or automatic home-heating equipment—it benefits by the same GM fundamentals applied in its automotive products." Instead of picturing Buicks and Cadillacs, this GM ad featured its Frigidaire and Delco divisions and pictured a Frigidaire-equipped kitchen with cold-wall refrigerator and electric range, plus Frigidaire automatic washers and dryers, electric irons, and water heaters. Chrysler Airtemp did its part by manufacturing air-conditioning and heating equipment for the modern American house, and Nash-Kelvinator produced a wide range of home appliances.

When American families like mine went into debt to purchase their two big-ticket items, their houses and cars, they cast their ballots, dollar by dollar, rather than vote by vote, for the way of life they wanted. They embraced comfort, control, and convenience. By 1953, a woman could serve her family a turkey dinner with all the trimmings from her all-electric kitchen, merely by popping Swanson frozen TV dinners into the oven. No prep time, and no cleanup time, because the Swanson aluminum "dinner plate" went straight into the garbage. Americans liked automatic things. In 1954, Westinghouse televisions introduced a "new electronic eye" that automatically adjusted the picture tube's brightness as the room got lighter or darker. In 1955, Cadillac and Oldsmobile introduced the "Autronic-Eye," an "automatic headlight control" that turned off your brights when a car was coming and put them back on when no car was coming. Maybe Americans had never realized what a chore it was to push a dimmer switch on the car floor with their foot, but GM informed us that at night, meeting an average of two oncoming cars per mile, we pushed the dimmer switch (on-off-on-off) two hundred times per hour. The Autronic-Eye eliminated one of driving's "most irksome jobs" and cut back on "night-driving work and tension." In 1959, Chrysler offered its own "Automatic Beam Changer," as well as an electronic "Mirror-Matic." At night, the rear-view mirror automatically dimmed when bright lights approached from behind.

For our home, Mom and Dad did not opt for a dishwasher or garbage disposal, but we did have an electric vacuum cleaner and an automatic clothes washer and dryer. Adhering to old-time ways, Dad put up a clothesline in the backyard, so on warm, bright days my mom could still hang our laundry outside to dry. She thought things smelled better when dried in the sun. Americans turned away from the old-fashioned push, reel-type lawn mowers and moved to gas-powered ones, and so did we. The new 1956 car that Mom and Dad picked out had an automatic transmission, power steering, and power brakes. Many Americans then were buying cars that came with even more: power windows and power seats. These power assists came earliest on higher-priced cars but quickly trickled down to the mid- and low-priced fields. By 1955, even the buyer of a Plymouth—the bottom rung on Chrysler's stepladder of cars—could equip a car with power brakes and steering, a PowerFlite automatic transmission, Easy-Glide power seats, and Easy-Lift power windows. And just as more houses were air-conditioned, more cars came with air-conditioning too—but not ours. By 1955, if the interior of the decked-out Plymouth became too hot, its driver could push one button to close the windows and another button to cause a cool breeze to blow out from his Chrysler Airtemp air conditioner. My family had no such recourse. When visiting hot Indiana and Illinois nearly every summer, all we could do was crank down the windows, open the wing vents, and sit in the hot wind.

The 1950s became the decade of the push button, when consumer goods promised that a small push of a finger could make life better. The push button, to be sure, had earlier origins. The Eastman Company in the late 1880s and early 1890s democratized photography by developing Kodak cameras using roll film. "You press the [shutter] button, we do the rest," the ads said. In 1891, W. S. Mullaly published a "You Press the Button, We Do the Rest" song that touted "new wonders," like push buttons that were "bobbing up each year." Push-button light switches bobbed up in American homes, and in commercial settings, elevators moved up or down with push-button controls. In the 1950s, such controls proliferated, especially in what *Popular Mechanics*, in its December 1950 issue, called "Push-Button Manor." This house happened to be in my own hometown. Arthur Railton started his article about this special house with a question: "Remember those wartime dreams of lazy living in postwar homes with push buttons to do all the work?" Jackson's Emil Mathias made those dreams come true by stringing seven thousand feet of wire in his six-room house and installing "innumerable switches, relays and motors." Push-button switches controlled a homemade elevator from the first floor to the basement. And if you pressed the Mathias doorbell at night, the porch light automatically went on—and then if no one answered, a thermostatic switch turned it off after three minutes.

Most Americans didn't have to invent push-button servants; they just bought them. Black Flag sold aerosol insect killer: "Just press the button," the ad said, and "BUGS DROP DEAD!" While Black Flag peddled push-button death, General Electric peddled "Push Button Cooking" on its automatic electric ranges. The Gibson "Diamond Jubilee" electric range of 1952 sported two ovens, two broilers, four burners, and a control panel filled with a clock, cooking timers, and four vertical rows of eight push buttons each.

Hotpoint washers gave a woman "Touch Command"—"One touch of your finger gives you the correct washing method for every known washable!" The Westinghouse 1000 washer-dryer set of 1959, with miracle wash-and-wear garments in mind, had a new "program computer" that "thinks out and carries out your choice of 8 custom programs. . . . All you do is push one button." General Electric and Westclox offered button-controlled snooze alarms on their clocks.

Watching television on Schaffer Drive entailed a lot of getting up and down. That was my job, since I had the youngest legs. If a variety show ended and we wanted to watch a western on another network, I popped up, walked to the television, and turned its channel knob, clicking through its stops till I reached channel 2, 4, or 7, all out of Detroit. Maybe I also adjusted the volume. If the picture was snowy, I could try to make it sharper by changing the direction of our rooftop antennae. I turned the dial on the rotary box sitting on top of the TV. It whirred and clicked a bit while up above the antennae rotated. *Have Gun Will Travel* now filled the screen, and the sound and picture were good. I sat back down.

I could have avoided this labor if our Zenith had come with remote control, but it didn't. In 1950, Zenith offered a remote control called

"Lazy Bones." This device had numbered buttons that corresponded to TV stations, and on-off buttons too. So, I could've switched channels without getting up. A cable connected this controller to the television, which was a bit of a problem. The cable could get twisted up or people could trip over it. In 1956, Zenith produced a wireless remote, called "Space Command." Life got better when a viewer could "change programs from across the room!" By the mid-1950s, the push-button technology that changed TV channels also raised and lowered heavy garage doors, thanks to the "Genie" radio-controlled, automatic garage door opener.

New push buttons in cars matched those found in homes. Buttons controlled windows, power seats, radios, heaters, and air conditioners. By 1953, over 1.5 million American autos already sported power windows, and 86.5 percent of all Lincolns had them. *Steel* magazine, in its April 27, 1953, issue, announced that "muscles . . . are on the way out," and that power assists and push buttons "make the car easier for the little woman to operate."

In 1954, GM added the "selector bar" to its new Delco radio. Just touch it with one finger and "the magic of electronics takes over, tuning in the nearest station on your dial with pinpoint precision. Touch it again to change stations . . . and so on across the dial. . . . It's all done so smoothly, so accurately, so effortlessly, you need never take your eyes from the road ahead!" Mercury bragged that no other car in the mid-price field offered automatic push-button lubrication, which they called "Multi-Luber." Dodge in 1958 announced that "orderly rows of buttons on a gleaming panel welcome you to the first all-pushbutton car with fingertip control of driving."

In the 1950s, car dashboards and control panels on electric ranges, washing machines, and blenders all had buttons. For Detroit, the ultimate "modern miracle," as Chrysler called it in 1956, was push-button drive. General Motors managed to avoid the short-lived phenomenon of push-button transmissions, but Packard, Chrysler, Dodge, Plymouth, Mercury, and Ford's new Edsel jumped right in. They stripped away the gearshift lever and replaced it with a box of push buttons mounted near the steering column or, in Edsel's case, in the center of the steering wheel. Each button had a letter on it, such as P for Park, D for Drive, or R for Reverse, which prompted Mercury, drawing an analogy to the typewriter, to call its system "Merc-O-Matic Keyboard Control." A 1957 Mercury ad showed a woman's hand with painted nails pushing its keyboard's seven positions. Keyboard control "turns the engine on—controls drive, low, neutral, reverse, and park—releases the brake at a touch!" Edsel's "Teletouch Drive" was "as easy as flicking a light switch," and Chrysler's "push-button Powerflite" allowed a single finger to "tame a tornado of torque."

With their tail fins, new upholstery, carpeting, and push buttons, the American car became a curious amalgam in the 1950s: part jet plane, part living room, part kitchen range or washing machine. While consumers cued up to buy them, and while I found them quite fun and entertaining to look at, social critics lined up to pan them. Some thought that success and high sales had led Detroit to excessive interior and exterior designs in a chromed-ugly era. Louis Mumford called American automobiles "insolent chariots." A *New York Times* writer called them "overblown, overpriced monstrosities built by oafs for thieves to sell to mental defectives." Another critic opined that they were "huge, vulgar, dripping with pot metal." Famed designer Raymond Loewy said they were "juke boxes on wheels." Brock Yates, an auto journalist, historian, and enthusiast, called the 1950s an era "when finned, snaggletoothed dinosaurs with three-toned pastel skins ruled the road."

Detroit stylists did not conjure up their excessive cars in a cultural vacuum. Americans in the 1950s liked big over small, fast over slow, new over old, and colorful over drab. We bought suburban ranch-style houses that were lower and longer, and we flocked to auto showrooms to buy lower and longer cars. Detroit stylists didn't have to sell consumers on chrome or new colors. Those things were ubiquitous in the culture and showed up in department stores, appliance stores, and any place that sold towels, plates, furniture, tiles, or toasters. Producers of household goods and appliances had a message to Americans: adopt a new palette of colors for the things you live with.

New housewares arrived made of polystyrene plastics, such as Monsanto's "Lustrex" and Dow Chemical's "Styron." These plastics came in a rainbow of colors that brightened a home after being formed into bread boxes, pitchers, cake covers, canisters, measuring cups, salt and pepper shakers, butter dishes, plates, and bowls. Manufacturers molded another plastic, "Melamine," into nearly indestructible dinnerware: blue, pink, red, yellow, pewter, coral, burgundy, emerald, and chartreuse plates. Pyrex sold blue, red, green, and yellow mixing bowls. Rubbermaid contributed "bright new ideas" executed in four colors for shelf liners, plate racks, laundry baskets, storage bins, wastebaskets, tissue dispensers, pails, and dish drainers. Alcoa Aluminum built a greater home products market for its favorite material. "Gay and colorful aluminum," an ad said, "anodized, or porcelainized, or brushed to satiny richness, . . . create[s] table arrangements as original as a Gauguin canvas." Colorama sold anodized aluminum tumblers, pitchers, mugs, and dessert bowls in green, gold, copper, red, blue, and silver. West Bend produced Delphinium Blue, Sunset Gold, and Cherry Red coffee percolators. In 1955 the Federal Enameling and Stamping Company, makers of a full range of pots and pans, advertised "Fabulous Federal Cookware" in "Fabulous PINK." My mom had a pink electric can opener. One dessert surged in popularity in the 1950s—Jell-O! Jell-O was a snap to prepare, and it came in shimmering colors too.

Koppers plastic tiles, "in a rainbow of colors," brightened baths, entrance halls, game rooms, and kitchens. Republic Steel sold metal kitchen cabinets finished in pink, yellow, and turquoise, as well as white. Youngstown Kitchens in 1950 offered countertops in "ten new colors." In 1955, Kelvinator (a division of American Motors) brought color into the house: "Now you can blend your appliances with any kitchen color scheme with the new Kelvinator Electric Ranges and matching Refrigerators in 8 new decorator colors." In 1959, Hotpoint appliances came in "four lovely Colortones" plus white, which allowed the consumer to color coordinate range, refrigerator, dishwasher, clothes washer, and dryer.

The International Harvester Company—maker of McCormick farm equipment and Farmall tractors—also made refrigerators and freezers. Refrigerators, given their size, became prime sheet-metal canvases for manufacturers infusing American homes with color. International

Harvester enthusiastically credited itself with the "Most Exciting Idea in Refrigerators Since the Ice Cube!" Its 1951 advertisements told housewives they could "Pick a Color from the Rainbow" and obtain "Door Handles Color-Keyed to your Kitchen!" True, this "femineered" refrigerator was still white, but "sleek door handle plaques" or surrounds, in ten gorgeous colors, could match or contrast with any kitchen color scheme. A few years later, International Harvester introduced the "Decorator Refrigerator," whose front door was designed to be covered in "any pattern—any color fabric you choose." Admiral refrigerators followed suit in 1956 by offering a "Fashion Front." A woman could change the look of the upper freezer door by applying one of five color panels that came in a kit. Each panel was shiny, washable, precut to fit, and had an adhesive backing, "So you can put them on and peel them off in a wink. . . . Each change is as stimulating as a new hat!" That same year, Westinghouse introduced its own "Choose-N-Change" vinyl panels to apply to freezer doors. Five main cabinet colors, plus ten panel colors, gave the consumer 50 different color combinations to choose from.

ScotTissue was "Mad about Color," and in 1956 it sold white, blue, green, yellow, and pink toilet paper. On towel bars near a roll of ScotTissue, a homemaker could hang Cannon towels in "eighteen lighthearted colors." The family not only *dried off* with towels—they *decorated* with towels, which brought a "whole NEW look to your bath with every change." Moving from bathroom to bedroom, Mom and Dad slipped between Cannon sheets of aquamarine, true blue, sunset rose, moonlight yellow, lagoon green, pink lilac, shell pink—or plain old white.

Color was everywhere in the house, and so was chrome. Sometimes they went together, as in the Magic Chef "color-chrome" gas range. The top and sides of the range carried porcelain enamel in willow green or coral rouge. The entire front and the control panel behind the burners glistened in "easy-to-clean gleaming chrome." Chrome-plated steel, plus polished stainless steel and aluminum, gave the American home a modern, smart look. Pots and pans gleamed. Chromed toasters sat on Formica countertops, right next to chromed Sunbeam waffle makers,

Osterizer blenders, and coffee percolators. Chrome plumbing fixtures glistened in kitchen and bathroom sinks. Consumers pulled on chrome handles to get into the refrigerator or oven. Chrome bezels framed clocks and dials and stove burners, and chrome letters spelled out manufacturers' names.

Many American families, including mine, ate their meals sitting at chrome dinette sets. Lloyd Chrome Plated Furniture promised that the "bright, gay beauty" of its products would give "a festive note to the simplest breakfast—or 'company-best' dinner." Chromcraft offered a dinette in the Duncan Phyfe style. These dinettes had chromed table and chair legs, bright seat coverings done in Duran or another plastic, table skirts of stainless or chrome-plated steel, and laminated plastic tabletops that stood up well to alcohol stains and cigarette burns.

A museum curator, if putting together an exhibit on the 1950s, could do no better than to juxtapose a chrome dinette set, a two-tone refrigerator, and a Buick. Even the most casual observer would discern that the same culture had produced them all at the same time. A 1956 Chevrolet magazine ad featured nineteen Chevrolets, every one bedecked in chrome trim and a two-tone paint job; a 1956 Westinghouse ad showed fifty refrigerators, in fifty different color combinations. The movie *Funny Face*, filmed in 1956, featured the song "Think Pink." The lyrics informed that "Pink's for all the family," and that "red is dead, blue is through, green's obscene, brown's taboo." Americans should "drive in pink, come alive in pink." They should "think pink on the long road ahead." American life, in this instance, imitated art. In the mid-1950s, manufacturers turned out pink cookware, pink toilet tissue, pink plates, pink kitchen cabinets, and pink stoves—and General Motors sold pink Cadillacs.

When car production picked up after World War II, the solid, dark prewar colors of black and maroon proved most popular for a while, before color preferences changed. An article, "Bright Car Colors Gain Favor," appeared in the July 1953 issue of *American Business*. According to data collected from the manufacturers, black remained the most popular color for only two makes: high-priced Cadillacs and Lincolns. Black was the second or third most popular color on some other expensive cars: Chrysler, Buick, and Packard. Black wasn't even an option for Plymouth, Nash, or Kaiser-Frazer.

Low- and mid-priced cars led the color revolution in the 1950s. They wore different shades of green, blue, red, and gray, often combined to make two-tones. By 1953, 24 percent of new Chevrolets carried two-tone paint jobs, a figure mirrored by Mercury (28 percent) and substantially exceeded by Pontiac (36 percent). Geography also contributed to the automotive pallet. In the 1950s, Los Angeles became a bellwether of cultural change in America, and it moved car colors in new directions. People in L.A. and Detroit drove the same cars, but of a different color. Ten to 13 percent of all new cars sold in Detroit remained black, while only 1 to 2 percent of the new cars in Los Angeles were black. Car buyers in cloudy, cold Detroit purchased black, dark blue, dark green, and dark gray cars; those in sunny California drove light blue, light green, light gray, and beige automobiles.

During the 1955 model year, DeSoto asked consumers, "Have your favorite colors?" Buyers could "choose from fifty-five combinations of various reds, frosty blues, greens, an artist's range of pastels." The next model year, DeSoto outdid itself, offering "85 color combinations." In 1953, General Motors bragged that "one thing that everyone seems to notice about this year's [GM cars] is the gay beauty of their colors." In 1956, Pontiac announced, "*Here is high fashion at its haughtiest!* The shimmering beauty of jewel-like new two-tone colors." In 1958, Buick enthused about itself: "Wait till you see . . . the colors! Bold, fresh—gay, but not garish."

Chevrolet, GM's main entrant in the low-priced field, competed in the color race against Ford and Plymouth. In 1949 Chevrolets came in eight colors (four of which were metallic): black, maroon, blue, and ivory—plus two grays and two greens. It offered a couple of two-tone combinations, pairing "Satin Green" with "Live Oak Green," and "Grecian Grey" with "Vista Grey." Into the early 1950s, manufacturers typically created their two-tones by painting one shade of a color on the roof and another shade of the same color on the rest of the body. Or, they might paint the roof white, off-white, or gray to obtain the two-tone look. They avoided juxtaposing distinct and different colors.

By 1955, things looked a whole lot different. Chevrolets came in fourteen solid colors, including gold, bronze, copper, red, and coral. Chevy mixed and matched these colors to produce twenty-three two-tone combinations. Some of these conservatively paired two greens or two blues, but others paired black over ivory, ivory over red, bronze over beige, or gray over coral. In 1957, Chevy added yellow and silver to its solid colors.

In November 1957, while admiring a trailer-load of new '58 models passing by, a Detroit secretary gushed, "Chrome is my favorite color!" Indeed, automakers decorated their cars in the late '50s with shiny chrome, polished aluminum, and stainless steel. The chrome added luster, and as cars grew wider, large chrome bumpers added to the sense of massiveness that automakers wished to convey. In this era the Big Three wanted cars in all price levels to look large and spacious. Manufacturers hoped that liberally applied chrome made a Ford look nearly as big and good as a Lincoln, or a Chevy as big and sexy as a Cadillac.

Chrome hood ornaments, often in the shape of planes or rockets, conveyed a car's identity and a sense of speed. Linear chrome moldings applied to the sides of cars conveyed a sense of going forward, even when the car was parked. As cars grew longer and lower, designers called for chrome to serve as "speed lines" running from headlights back to taillights. These lines added visual excitement, especially when paired with swooping fins and the notions of flight they were meant to symbolize.

In the 1950s, I participated in a paint-by-number fad that democratized "art." I proved that anybody could become a painter, using a kit complete with canvas, paints, and brushes that Mom bought me at the hobby shop. Lines printed on the canvas set off bounded spaces, and each space had a number inside, corresponding to a paint color. Follow the numbers, paint inside the lines—and you created your little masterpiece that thousands of other Americans painted at the same time. Chrome moldings on the cars of the 1950s allowed manufacturers to do their own "paint-by-number" thing. The chrome moldings set off spaces on a car body that could be painted in different colors. They served as color boundaries.

Colors could be applied in new patterns. A red-and-white '55 Chevy might have a red top, a white hood and trunk, white carried on the doors and quarter panels down toward the tops of the wheel wells, and then red again at the bottom. A cream color flowed out over the top, hood, and trunk of a 1956 Packard Caribbean hardtop and ran half the way down its sides. Two parallel strips of chrome provided a stop for the cream color, and in the space between them ran a band of blue about five inches high. Beneath the bottom strip of chrome, down to the bottom of the rocker panels, a band of a darker third color, about eight inches high, ran the length of the car. The 1956 three-tone Dodge Royal Lancer used chrome to separate the white top from the red and black on the hood, trunk deck, and sides. The 1955 and 1956 Pontiac car bodies were virtually identical, but by moving chrome moldings around, which allowed them to move paint colors around, GM made them look more different than they really were.

Chrome served another important function. Like chevrons on a military uniform, it served as a sign of rank. In the 1950s, each of the Big Three still had a basic "stepladder" of cars from one division to the next, where each step up promised more amenities and power, more status—and more cost. The successive rungs at GM, from bottom to top, remained Chevy, Pontiac, Oldsmobile, Buick, and Cadillac. At Chrysler, one progressed from Plymouth, to Dodge, to DeSoto, to Chrysler, to Imperial. But in the 1950s, the automakers implemented a stepladder of cars not only *between* divisions but *within* divisions. There were cheap Dodges and more expensive Dodges—the Cornet, Royal Lancer, and Custom Royal Lancer—which were trimmed out differently. Pontiac had its version of "Three Little Indians" and offered the Star Chief, Super Chief, and Chieftain. In the mid-1950s, the model "One-Fifty" Chevy carried a shorter length of chrome on the side than the "Two-Fifty" Chevy, and the shorter chrome strip altered its two-tone paint scheme. The Bel Air was the top Chevrolet until the Impala came along. By 1958, the Chevrolet Impala had chromed faux vents mounted in front of the rear wheel wells and at the rear of the roof panel. The Chevy Bel Air lacked these trim pieces. The Impala had three taillights inside chrome surrounds; the Bel Air, only two.

1956 Fords came in three model groups. The basic "Mainline" models had less chrome than more expensive Fords and came with a 137-horsepower 6-cylinder engine or a 202 h.p. V-8. The "Customline" Fords had enhanced chrome trim on their rooflines and sides and came with 176 and 202 h.p. V-8 engines. Top of the line "Fairlane" Fords came with still more chrome, especially the "Crown Victoria," whose crown was a chrome strip rising up and over the roof from the B-pillar on one side of the car to the B-pillar on the other. Fairlane Fords came with the 225 h.p. "Thunderbird Special V-8," with fender skirts on the rear wheel wells and bold color combinations, like black and yellow. In 1958, Buick created the Limited, a car meant to introduce a "new sense of magnificence." To set the Limited off from other chrome-laden Buicks, General Motors added fifteen slanted bars of chrome to each rear quarter panel and four horizontal chrome bars to each taillight. Like military insignia, the additional chrome bars indicated that this Buick pulled rank on all others.

The smaller, independent car companies produced their own stepladder cars. In 1954, Hudson offered six versions of its four-door sedan: the Jet (listed at $1,858), the Super Jet ($1,954), the Jet Liner ($2,056), the Wasp ($2,256), the Super Wasp ($2,465), and the Hornet ($2,768). Nash offered six versions of its four-door, priced from $1,795 to $2,595. Studebaker, too, had six four-doors, ranging in price from $1,801 to $2,438. Packard had four models. Kaiser and Willys had two.

Detroit's crazy-for-color era peaked about 1955–56; its crazy-for-chrome era peaked a few years later, in 1957–59. Detroit also went crazy for fins. Perhaps the most baroque, over-the-top cars ever assembled were the Chrysler Corporation cars of 1959. Chrysler carried every design, color, and chrome element to the extreme and somehow, with a straight face, said its cars were the finest expression possible of Chrysler "engineering." This bit of hyperbole no doubt had Walter P. Chrysler spinning in his grave. "Showmanship," not "engineering," was the operative word while Detroit produced a circus of cars in the late 1950s.

Detroit didn't come up with outlandish designs on its own. It borrowed fins from the aircraft industry; new textiles—floor carpets and seat covers—from the home; colors from refrigerators, tiles, plastic plates, kitchenware, toilet paper, and towels; push buttons from washing machines, electric ranges, and blenders; and chrome from toasters and kitchenette tables. Love or loathe the consumers and carmakers of the 1950s, they shared a coherent view of what the good life was all about: comfort, convenience, color, and chrome.

# 3

## SOMEWHERE THAT'S GREEN

It was a beautiful summer day at 1861 Shaffer Drive. An overflowing mound of petunias filled the big planter that ran the length of the house's dining room wall. A big green-and-white 1956 Packard occupied its space on the left-hand side of the two-car garage. A small 1958 Hillman, light green and gray, stood on the right side of the recently asphalted driveway, near the petunias. The Hillman spent most of its life banished to the driveway, because riding and walk-behind lawn mowers, a bicycle, and carpentry and yard tools usually occupied its half of the garage.

Dad and Mom worked in the front yard. On weekends, from May to October, it seemed you could always find them in the yard somewhere. Today, they were mowing, raking, and trimming out front. I was messing around, doing nothing in particular. In the garage, I found a ping-pong ball, used as a projectile to be shot from my pneumatic, bazooka-like toy gun. You pushed the ball into the barrel, past a rubber-ring seal, and then you moved the gun's pump action back and forth. Each stroke put more air pressure behind the ball until—wopp!—a burst of air blasted the ball out past the seal and toward the target.

I bounced the ping pong ball off the garage floor. If I tossed it down harder, of course it bounced back higher. This led me to wonder: could you make it bounce higher some other way? Sometime during my eleven years on earth, I learned that hot air rises. The ping-pong ball had air in it. What if you heated the air inside a ping-pong ball—would it bounce higher?

I opened the driver's side door of the Hillman and got in. Mom and Dad both smoked, so I was sure there would be some matches in the glove compartment. I leaned across the seat, got the book of matches out, and peeled one off. I struck the match, held it in my right hand, and with my left I put the ping-pong ball over the flame to heat it up. That's when the experiment went awry. I hadn't counted on the flammability of the ping-pong ball. It burst into flames. Stunned, I did what any smart kid would do—I dropped the flaming ball. It then rolled under the Hillman's front seat, which was padded with horsehair. I leaped out of the Hillman, ran into the front yard, and grabbed the hose that my folks had been using. I raced back to the car, turning the nozzle on as I went. My parents looked up just in time to see me dive back into the front seat, carrying a garden hose at full stream. They rushed to the car themselves. By the time they got to it, I had put the fire out. There remained, of course, some explaining to do.

* * *

In the postwar era, many Americans, especially young families, dreamed of moving into a new suburban house. In the movie *Little Shop of Horrors*, a musical comedy, the character Audrey sings of her deep longing for suburbia. Audrey lives a hapless, threatened life within a grim city. Her boyfriend, Seymour, is a meek flower-shop worker who is caring for a huge, man-eating plant always in need of blood. Audrey, understandably, hopes to escape all this. She wants to flee the city with Seymour to a place where the vegetation is green, but not carnivorous. She wants a matchbox house of their own, with a fenced yard. She wants a charcoal grill on the patio. Seymour will rake and trim the grass, mow, and weed. Inside, she will have a garbage disposal, a washer, a dryer, and an ironing machine. In her kitchen, she will cook like Betty Crocker and look like the television star Donna Reed. She'll put plastic on the furniture to keep it clean, and the inside air will smell like Pine-Sol. After cooking a frozen dinner, she and Seymour will snuggle up and watch *I Love Lucy* on their twelve-inch television. Their place is perfect, like some picture in *Better Homes and Gardens*

Taken in the summer of 1954, this Ford promotional photo captured the company's view of the American dream. Two well-dressed white women stand next to a new-model Ford Thunderbird. They live in an upscale suburb of fine houses and perfect lawns. (Collections of The Henry Ford)

magazine. They'll be far from the city's skid row. They'll be somewhere that's green.

Had it been real, Audrey's house would have shared many characteristics with another 1950s suburban house, erected, of all places, in Moscow, Russia. In 1958, the two saber-rattling superpowers, the United States and the Soviet Union, stepped back from their nuclear arms race and initiated cultural exchanges. In the summer of 1959, the state-supported Soviet National Exhibition opened for a few months in New York City, and a bit later, the American National Exhibition opened in Moscow.

We sent the Russians artifacts thought to represent the American way of life, including twenty-two new American cars, a $250,000 futuristic kitchen, and a suburban house, split in two so that the 2.7 million

Soviets who attended the exhibition could easily pass through it. The single-story, single-family ranch house had six rooms, modern kitchen appliances and entertainment centers, wall-to-wall carpeting, and furnishings from Macy's department store. This house, the Soviets were told, could be bought in the United States for $14,000, meaning the average American worker could afford it. The model home was a replica of a real suburban house designed by architect Stanley H. Klein and located at 398 Townline Road in Commack, Long Island.

America's self-portrayal contained powerful icons—cars, kitchens, and a suburban house filled with consumer items—that captured our country's postwar way of life. Vice President Richard Nixon attended the opening of the American National Exhibition. Nixon, who had built his political career by stoking the fires of anticommunism back home, stood proudly alongside the truculent Soviet premier, Nikita Khrushchev, in the futuristic kitchen and in the model American house. Soon, the notion of an educational cultural exchange gave way to Cold War competition, as these two men entered a "kitchen debate," caught on television, over whose system was best, communism or capitalism. Instead of debating nuclear weapons proliferation or the race into space, Khrushchev and Nixon debated houses, appliances, and televisions. Nixon asked Khrushchev if it was not "far better to be talking about washing machines, than about machines of war, like rockets."

The global struggle between communism and capitalism boiled down to which economic system gave people what they most wanted. In the Soviet Union, as characterized by Nixon, the government stifled competition and change, while "the American system is designed to take advantage of new inventions and new techniques." Americans lived in a land of diversity, where they could exercise their right to choose: "the fact that we have 1,000 builders building 1,000 different houses is the most important thing. We don't have one decision made at the top by one government official. This is the difference." Nixon went on, "Let the people choose the kind of house, the kind of soup, the kind of ideas they want. We have many different manufacturers and many different kinds of washing machines, so that the housewives may have a choice."

American freedom, as expressed by Nixon, was not freedom of

speech, or freedom of religion, or freedom of assembly, or any other hallowed freedom—it was the freedom to buy what you wanted. And in the 1950s, millions of Americans, including the Lanktons, exercised this freedom and bought a suburban house.

Much transformative change occurred in American society during the 1950s. After population increases of less than 10 million in the 1930s, and 19 million in the 1940s, the US population jumped by 30 million in the 1950s, rising from 150 to 180 million. Postwar adults embraced marriage and created babies. These families looked to acquire houses, and federal policy supported their search. The GI Bill passed by Congress in 1944 created federally guaranteed mortgage loans, which encouraged lenders to make money readily available to potential buyers, who did not have to pony up a down payment. Buyers could stretch low monthly mortgage payments over thirty years, and they got a break on their federal income tax. Builders, too, had access to federally guaranteed loans, so they could develop large suburban housing tracts without investing much of their own money. Buyers and builders alike seized opportunity in the 1950s. Single-family housing starts increased, and thirteen million new houses were built. Eleven million of these houses stood in suburbs. In the nation's twenty largest metropolitan areas, the population of core cities grew by only 0.1 percent, while the surrounding suburban population increased by 45 percent. Car sales and house sales in this decade had a symbiotic relationship; each supported the other. With a car, you could buy a house in the 'burbs and still get around; if you lived in a suburban house, you needed a second car so Dad could go to work and Mom could go shopping. In the 1950s, the number of automobiles in the United States increased by 50 percent; the number of Americans living in suburbs increased by 47 percent.

The most famous, or infamous, postwar suburb stood on four thousand acres of plowed-over potato fields on Long Island, New York. Abraham Levitt had become one of the largest home builders in America, even before he broke ground on this new community, dubbed Levittown. Levitt pioneered streamlined methods of clearing building sites, delivering construction materials, and assembling them into completed houses. Two thousand houses stood in Levittown by 1947. This number grew to 10,000 by 1950, and to an astronomical 17,447 houses (with 82,000 residents) by 1953. The initial two-bedroom, Cape Cod houses offered a very standardized appearance, inside and out. They sat on a slab, with no basement, no garage, and no separate dining room. They offered some amenities: a twelve-by-sixteen-foot living room with a fireplace; a backyard, perhaps with a company-planted fruit tree or evergreen; and appliances in the kitchen. The development featured swimming pools, playgrounds, parks, baseball diamonds, and curvilinear streets. Of most importance, Levittown houses sold at a low price. Without any down payment, veterans could buy a house in Levittown for $56 per month, far less than the average apartment rental of $93 per month they would pay in a nearby city. As noted by Kenneth Jackson in *Crabgrass Frontier: The Suburbanization of the United States*, "This early Levitt house was as basic to post–World War II suburban development as the Model T had been to the automobile. In each case, the actual design features were less important than the fact that they were mass-produced and thus priced within the reach of the middle class."

Levittown's success led other large building companies to launch similar developments across the United States, from Boston and Baltimore and Cleveland and Chicago, to Houston, to Phoenix, to Los Angeles and San Francisco. In smaller cities, smaller builders developed suburbs on a more modest scale. In short order, the suburban house became a ubiquitous feature on the landscape. Postwar suburbs attracted millions of buyers, but over the decades they also attracted numerous and diverse critics. Folk singers; feminists; social, environmental, urban, and architectural historians; new urbanists; and social scientists and planners—all have chimed in. The Levittowns of America became places that many commentators loved to hate. Detractors argued that in the 1950s and beyond the biggest threat to the American way of life was not the Soviet Union or the arms race. The biggest threat was not the Red menace but the suburban menace.

In 1962, Malvina Reynolds, a folk singer and songwriter, was driving with her husband from Berkeley, California, to La Honda. While at the wheel, Malvina steered her way through Daly City, but after spying the suburban Westlake development, she pulled over and told husband Bud to take the wheel, because she felt a song coming on. That song was "Little Boxes," and it condemned the houses in places like Westlake *and the people who lived in them*. There was no originality here—and no individuality, only conformity. The clustered houses (or little boxes) all looked alike, even if they were different colors: blue, pink, yellow, or green. They were ticky tacky, or tasteless. The people living inside the houses had gone to university and learned a profession, but in this suburb they all looked the same and acted the same. They played golf, drank martinis, and produced pretty children—who went to school and then university, before ending up just like their parents. They got into a business, had a family, and lived in their own ticky tacky houses.

"Little Boxes" became a well-known critique of postwar suburban life, thanks largely to folk singer Pete Seeger, who released the song as a 45 r.p.m. single and included it on several albums over the decades. "Little Boxes" resonated with other critical portrayals of suburbia in the way it faulted both the place and the people who lived there.

As a place, the suburbs had too much of some things and too little of others. Suburbia had too much vapid architecture, too much sameness. The houses looked like cookie-cutter creations put up by builders wanting to save on construction costs by eschewing novelty or uniqueness. Suburbs swept away farmland and large, old trees, while they increased urban sprawl and decreased human interaction and a sense of community. The houses lacked front porches, the developments often lacked sidewalks—both of which discouraged residents from walking from house to house, meeting face-to-face with neighbors, and saying hello. Instead, residents sat inside, maybe talking on the telephone, or glued to their new televisions, while enjoying their air conditioning and not the evening breezes.

The suburbs also lacked corner stores, places to work, theaters, hospitals, libraries, and mass transit. In short, they lacked what any real town or city had. Author James Howard Kunstler, in his book *The Geography of Nowhere: The Rise and Decline of America's Man-Made Landscape*, tells of his boyhood, part of which was lived in a ranch house in the Long Island suburb of Northwood, twenty miles east of Manhattan.

Starting at age twelve, Kunstler went off to a boys' camp in Lebanon, New Hampshire, which had a traditional New England layout. There, he got his "first glimpse of what real American towns were like." Lebanon, with a population of only eight thousand, had big trees, capacious porches fronted by sidewalks, and a town square lined with commercial, civic, and cultural buildings:

> As I thought about it, I realized that a town like Lebanon was what a place like Northwood could only pretend to be: that Northwood, lacking any center, lacking any shops or public buildings, lacking places of work or of play, lacking anything except the treeless streets of nearly identical houses set on the useless front lawns, was in some essential way a mockery of what Lebanon really was.

Suburbanites were as roundly criticized as the tract developments they inhabited. They were just as interchangeable as their nearly identical houses. They were conformists who lived the same way and had similar aspirations for themselves and their children. Residents of a given suburb came from the same economic class. Families with less, and families with more, lived somewhere else, often in a different suburb for people just like them.

Suburbanites were too alike in age. They tended to be young adults. In a short 1957 film called *In the Suburbs*, which *Redbook* magazine directed at potential advertisers, the new suburbanites bought a house, had children, talked about their kids, pets, and schools—and bought things. They lived in a "happy go-spending world," and as "buy-it-now" young adults they lived by the automobile, driving off to new shopping centers, where they purchased "Easy Living." *Redbook*, of course, meant all this in a complimentary fashion, while critics of suburbia treated the same behavior with scorn.

The suburbs were too lily white. Not a single Black American lived in Levittown in 1960. Whites fled cities to find "somewhere that's green," to find a place of their own that offered more privacy and safety, good value for the money, lower taxes, less congestion and grime, and greater segregation from any urban dwellers they cared not to mingle with.

Whites moved out of inner cities, while Blacks, having fewer financial resources and facing housing discrimination based on race, remained behind in center cities often weakened by the population-sucking suburbs that ringed them.

The litany of suburbia's sins went on and on. Suburbs trapped women into unfulfilling lives. Isolated at home, they spent their days endlessly repeating the same mundane tasks. Families and children suffered, because the nuclear family in the suburb was separated from the traditional extended family. The grandparents weren't around. In these low-density housing developments spread out beyond cities, residents more than ever had to rely on the automobile to get around, which accelerated the use of nonrenewable fuels. And all these new suburbs demanded large-scale and expensive relocations of businesses, governmental services, streets, and utilities—because institutions had to move out to the fringe as the people moved out. Critic Lewis Mumford, in assessing postwar suburban development, put it very succinctly: "The end product is an encapsulated life, spent more and more either in a motor car or within the cabin of darkness before a television set."

Surely, millions of Americans who lived in the suburbs in the 1950s and early 1960s, had they read Mumford and all of the critics, would have been very surprised to discover just how miserable and limited their lives were.

* * *

When I was born in 1947, my parents, Mary and Larry, lived on Stanley Avenue, in a house within the city limits of Jackson, Michigan, about a mile from the heart of downtown. Here, I learned to talk, walk, put a spoonful of food into my mouth, and go potty. Lots of childhood development happened on Stanley Avenue, yet I have little recollection of the place, and if old photographs didn't trigger my memory, I'd recall almost nothing of the house itself or the life I lived there.

The Stanley house was an older frame dwelling, two stories and an attic. It carried little detail, architecturally speaking, save for a modest pediment over the front door. The clapboard siding was painted a light color, white or yellow, which contrasted nicely with nearby dark green shrubs and evergreen trees. It had a small front yard, with a sidewalk along the street, and a back yard, where the grass shared space with a detached garage. I lived there for only three or four years. Later, I couldn't recall the plan of the house, my room, or the names of any neighbors. Thanks to photos, I can vaguely remember dressing as a cowboy with a hat and six-shooters holstered to my sides; playing outside with neighbor boys and dogs; and romping outside with Uncle Darrell, visiting from Detroit, who used to pull me around in a wagon.

I didn't know why my folks moved off Stanley. Maybe they thought the neighborhood was "turning," so they left for whiter surroundings. They never talked like that had been the case, but maybe it was. On the other hand, maybe my parents, married in 1945, were just restless in the late 1940s and early 1950s, so they moved around. They couldn't blame this restlessness on youth, surely, because Dad was in his mid-forties and Mom in her mid-thirties. Who knows just what they were looking for, what they might have been trying to recapture from previous places, previous lives. Dad had been born in Adrian in 1903, had run a cartage company in Detroit during the Depression, but had also lived, quite recently, in very rural Moscow, Michigan, a tiny crossroads settlement twenty miles southwest of Jackson, where he had acreage and kept horses. Mom, born in 1911 on a farm near tiny Kingman, Indiana, had six brothers and sisters, five older and one younger. Mary Atkinson never graduated from high school. About the time she might have been doing that, she headed off bravely to California by herself, where she made a living as a waitress through the Depression. Then she moved to Detroit by 1940, still waitressing, living there with her sister, Millie, and other female friends, like Marge and Bernie.

The postwar couple, Mary and Larry, never sat down to tell me what they were looking for in terms of a house and a neighborhood. They left Stanley for Emmett Avenue in Vandercook Lake, about three and a half miles to the south. The Emmett Avenue house had a nice porch, but other than that it was unattractive and in need of repair. It seemed a step down from our house on Stanley. Built about 1910, the single-story dwelling, covered in asphalt shingles, had small rooms and a very small yard, front and back. Its narrow driveway ran slightly uphill from the street to a detached, single-car garage at the back of the house that had barn-style doors. Off the drive, a chute led into the basement, and inside, beneath the chute, stood a pile of coal that Dad, in winter, shoveled into the furnace.

The small houses lining both sides of Emmett were less than grand. Some were well kept up; others weren't. The narrow, paved street had no curbs. The asphalt bled into sand and gravel on each side, which bled into mown weeds or grass. Since it carried little traffic, neighborhood kids played in the street, chased each other, rode bikes, and on hot days, begged the milk man for some ice out of his truck.

On Emmett, by age five or six I was old enough to form solid memories, and for the first time I learned what a neighborhood was. Plenty of young kids lived on my block. Some were nice; some were bullies. Some of the adults on his block yelled, drank, and could be mean as the dickens. Others were nice and friendly. We lived next door to the Harts, an older couple whose children were grown and gone. The Harts had Emmett's nicest yard, a big garden, and a well-cared-for white house. They often invited my family over for a meal, to play games, or just to visit and snack on cookies or cake. Mrs. Hart made popcorn balls for Halloween, making her house a favorite stop on my trick-or-treat route. On the opposite end of the block lived the Ritsons, Roy and Alice, with their children, Danny (the same age as I) and Pam. Roy loved the outdoors. He always had dark brown arms and a tanned, deeply creased face beneath his butch haircut. Roy lived to hunt and fish. Danny and I, with our dads, spent happy early mornings on small ponds, pulling in bluegill and sunfish. Alice Ritson was my mother's best friend on Emmett. She loved her flowers and garden, liked to bake cookies, and laughed at everything and enjoyed every day she ever lived.

I went to kindergarten and first grade while living in Vandercook Lake. I remember the good and bad that happened there. I remember getting tart apples from the tree across the street. You got more fruit if you threw some fallen apples up at those still clinging to the branches, bringing them down. One day, my throw downed a bee's nest instead of an apple, and I ran the hundred feet home, being stung all along the way.

On Emmet, I received my first jackknife. I whittled with it, and Danny and I played "stretch" with it, out in the yard. I also stabbed myself in the arm with it, while attacking a cardboard box. The blade hit a big metal staple and deflected right into a vein at mid-forearm. I ran screaming into the house. I'd never seen so much blood. Dad was right there, but I wanted nothing to do with him. I wanted my momma—who had to be summoned from the Harts' house—to bandage me up.

On Emmet I received my first lever-action Red Ryder BB gun. Plinking cans was a lot of fun, but the BB gun, in my immature hands, spelled trouble now and then. I stood in the driveway, drew a level bead on a nearby telephone pole, and pulled the trigger. The BB hit the pole, came straight back, and plunked me hard in the forehead. I busted a window across the street with an errant shot and had to fess up to it. After ten or fifteen attempts in the back yard, I finally hit the flower stem with a shot, only to discover that decapitating one of Mom's tulips was nothing to be proud of. It didn't make her happy.

Dr. Spock's book on baby and childcare had been out since 1946, and it became the childrearing bible for the parents of baby boomers. But my father never read it, and soft nurturing and constant protection weren't in vogue at our house on Emmett. Dad used the "sink or swim" approach to teaching me things. In Vandercook Lake, he took me out to where it was over my head, held me for a bit, then let go, leaving me to sink or swim on my own. Learning to ride a bike, it was the same thing. Dad held the back of the bicycle seat and told me to pedal—don't worry, he'd hold me up! Dad ran alongside the bike for a little bit, but after five seconds at most, I realized that Dad had let go, and I was on my own to cope with turning, stopping, or crashing, whichever came first.

I walked from Emmett about five blocks north on Hague Avenue to get to kindergarten, which was in the same building as Vandercook Lake High School. I remember rolling out clay snakes, making them long enough to ring all the way around the outside edge of the classroom's low, circular play tables. I remember taking naps on a pallet on the floor. We had a gift exchange, where everybody put a present under the Christmas tree, and then each student walked up to the Christmas tree and received one. I won a talent contest among my youthful peers one night in the school auditorium, when I recited from memory the full text of the book *Gerald McBoing-Boing*, which Mom had read to me a thousand times. By the end of the book, Gerald, who had trouble talking but could make all kinds of animal sounds, was a star on the radio and got to ride around in a big limousine. I remember the little soda shop across from the high school. When Mom took me there I ate the best grilled cheese sandwiches ever. Walking home from school, I often stopped into Shine's tiny barbershop to say "hi." Halfway home there was a small variety store that sold groceries, candies, and drinks. I liked to go there to get a Baby Ruth or a Clark bar. One day, I waited in line while another little boy got his treat. While I was paying, the little boy ahead of me burst out past the store's screen door and ran into the street. A car coming down Hague Avenue hit and killed him. Next out the door, I was the first person on the scene. I stumbled home, dazed, to tell Mom what had happened.

Some other memorable moments happened while I lived on Emmett. A couple involved the family car, a new 1950 Ford. Somehow, when I was sitting in the car alone, I sent the car rolling down the drive and into the street. That was frightening, even at two miles an hour. On another day, Dad ran over our cat while backing out of the garage. We acquired another feline, and that cat, taken for a car ride, jumped out the door at a gas station and ran off, never to be seen again. From then on, it was all dogs for us.

A good part of living on Emmett was its proximity to Vandercook Lake, a half mile from our house. Once, the lake had been home to an extensive amusement park with rides, but that was gone. Still, it had a nice sandy beach, a park area with tall trees and tables for picnics and birthday parties, and a concession stand. With any luck at all, I could talk Mom into buying me a push-up pop. But the lake, despite providing sun, sand, and smiles, provided some tears and heartbreak. Riding back from the lake one evening, hitching a ride on the back fender of my sister's bicycle, I got my foot caught in the spokes and broke my ankle. On a good day for swimming, Uncle Darrell and I splashed around until I noticed that a woman nearby had been floating face down for too long. Uncle Darrell checked and then called others over to help. The woman had suffered a heart attack, and no amount of trying could revive her lifeless body once it had been laid out on the shore. About seven years later, Mom pulled the car into the gravel parking lot at this same Vandercook Lake and stopped. She picked the car, and the lake, as the place to tell me that Dad, badly sick for months, was going to die soon. But that is getting a bit ahead of the story.

We left Vandercook Lake in 1954, after my parents bought the Schaffer Drive house on June 30. Located in Summit Township, it was a mile or two south of the Jackson city limits. Sister Lynn had married Ben earlier that year, so it was just the three of us now. When we landed on Schaffer the family seemed more stable and set. Dad worked for years as a tool-and-die maker at Mechanical Products, which made circuit breakers. Mechanical Products was located eight or ten miles north of Schaffer Drive, way over on the other side of town. He drove off in the car early every weekday morning to get there, and quite often on Saturdays too. Before getting married, Mom worked full-time for at least fifteen years. When we lived on Emmett, she worked part-time for a few years. On Schaffer Drive, she was a stay-at-home mom.

The house at 1861 Schaffer was the first and only brand-new house I ever lived in. In this part of Summit Township, near the intersection of two old country roads, Horton and Badgley, Jackson County was growing. It seemed that nearly every house within a mile of 1861 Schaffer Drive had been built since 1950. Before then, not many people lived in this neck of the woods. There had been an orchard, a dairy, a gas station, and one tiny store, but only a few houses and a few roads. Development during the 1950s changed all that.

New houses sprang up along both sides of Badgley, and then to create more building sites, developers put in new roads. The land was not flat or regular. It had rolling hills, woods, creeks, ponds, and marshes. Developers didn't have any contiguous acreage for building a large tract of suburban housing, so they put in smaller tracts here and there. They

1861 Schaffer Drive. Three-bed, one-bath, 1,072 square feet of living space, with a two-car garage on a half-acre lot. (Collection of the author)

ran short roads off Badgley and Horton, wherever they could easily put them, and then built houses on their flanks.

About 1950, Schaffer Drive, a short, curving street only one block long, was cut through from Badgley over to Horton Road. The land belonged to Allen and Ica Schaffer and became the Hillbrook Subdivision, where lots were plotted out for new houses. At about the same time, other developers put in Roosevelt Circle. It headed east from Horton, ran in a loop, then came back upon itself. The new Mardee Road was U-shaped. It led south off Badgley, turned east and ran a block, then turned north to reconnect with the main road. Within the decade, developers added other roads: Plateau and Brookside Drives off Badgley, and Hillcrest, further out on Horton Road, right near the Jackson Country Club. The small subdivisions along these roads didn't look anything like the sprawling, cookie-cutter Levittowns of the era, to be sure. No two houses in any cluster were identical and no subdivision ran on, block after block. The subdivisions were small and disconnected, bounded and separated by small streams or marshes. Still, they exhibited great commonality. Their ranch houses were all new and sat on good-sized lots. And the residents were couples—white, middle class, mostly young, and mostly with children.

House number 1861, which my family moved into, was the last one built on Schaffer Drive. The single-story ranch sat on a cinderblock foundation wall that enclosed a crawl space with a dirt floor. The wide, horizontal wooden siding on the house was painted tan; the window and door trim and the roof edging and soffit were dark brown. Light brown asphalt shingles protected the roof, which was topped with a spindly TV antenna. Most windows were narrow, rectangular units mounted high on the walls—jalousie windows that cranked open and shut. The major exception was the living room window at the front of the house, which was a much bigger rectangle, maybe five feet high and six feet long.

The facade's dominant architectural feature was the two-car garage on the east end. The garage had a concrete slab floor and was drywalled on the inside to cover the studs and rafters. A small louvered cupola sat atop the garage roof. A wooden tool bench and some storage shelves occupied one wall of the garage, and two small doors led away from it. One opened off a rear corner to the back yard, right by one of Mom's T-shaped clothesline poles; the other, near the front of the garage, opened into the house's utility room, which served as a buffer between inside and outside.

The utility room had a place for coats and hats to be hung and for dirty or snowy boots to be taken off. It also had a large sink, a washer (the automatic kind, not like the old wringer washer on Emmett), and a dryer, which Mom could fire up if she chose not to hang the wash outside. A gas furnace in the utility room heated the house via forced air passing through ductwork. A water heater and water softener stood in the room. The house was not connected to a municipal water source but had its own well. The electric pump for the well sat in the crawl space directly under the utility room. When the pump needed to be oiled, Dad went to the back of the house, climbed down into the crawl space through a window, and then crawled on hands and knees to the pump. After a few years of that, he got smart and cut a trap door in the utility room floor.

A doorway from the utility room led straight into the kitchen. The kitchen had a stainless-steel sink centered beneath a window on the exterior wall; a run of countertop the full length of that wall; overhead cabinets finished in light maple; a four-burner stove and oven; a white Norge double-door refrigerator with a large freezer; and a rectangular kitchen table with four chairs. The tabletop was dark blue Formica, with a four-inch band of maple around the perimeter. The table stood on shiny chrome-plated legs, as did the four chairs that came with it. On the countertop rested polished canisters for flour and sugar, a Mixmaster mixer, an electric can opener, and a chrome Toastmaster toaster with dark brown, Bakelite handles. The cabinets held colorful, anodized aluminum tumblers—red, blue, green, gold, and silver—that I drank my milk out of. Some cabinets were full of inexpensive, everyday plates and bowls, but others held pretty blue-and-white Woods Ware china from England that depicted "English scenery" on plates, saucers, bowls, gravy boats, and serving platters. My mother inherited this china from her mother, and she held it dear. Whenever this china came out, I knew a special meal would soon follow and guests would be breaking bread with us. A few times, to try to enlarge her collection or to replace a broken piece, Mom and I drove to the grand J. L. Hudson's department store in downtown Detroit to find or order more Woods Ware.

A second door in the kitchen led off to the small dining area at the front of the house, which opened directly into the living room. A long couch, framed by matching end tables and lamps, sat beneath a big, framed mirror against the back wall of the living room; the couch faced the big window at the front of the house. Two upholstered easy chairs and a low coffee table with Hollywood legs took up other space, and at the far end of the room, against the wall, sat the Zenith television set.

A doorway led from the end of the living room into the house's short interior hallway—a hallway of doors. Above your head was a door of sorts, concealing a pull-down ladder to the attic. To your left was a door to a bedroom, except we didn't need it often as a bedroom, so we turned it into a den. Straight ahead was the door to the bathroom, tiled in light and dark green with a white tub, basin, mirrored medicine cabinet, and toilet. Opposite the bathroom was the door to my parents' bedroom at the front of the house. Yet another door opened into my bedroom at the back of the house. Early American maple furniture occupied both bedrooms. Closets, with sliding doors of light wood, offered plenty of space for clothes. All the walls in our house were painted a light color; the ceilings, an off-white. Wall-to-wall carpeting covered the floor in the dining area and living room. Linoleum underlay the utility room, kitchen, and small entryway by the front door. The interior hallway and bedroom floors were maple.

Our house sat on a big half-acre lot. At the back of the lot, a hill ran down from the higher lots up on Badgley. The soil was none too good, nor was the drainage. Typically, moving out to the suburbs in the 1950s is portrayed as moving out to "green space," a land of well-mown, grassy yards. People forget, though, that at the start, subdivisions were not green but brown. The first yard at 1861 Schaffer was dirt, the driveway was dirt, even the street was dirt. For a couple years, the US Post Office recognized Schaffer Drive as a frontier outpost, and its mail trucks refused to go there. Residents couldn't put mailboxes up on posts at the end of their driveways; they had to put them all in a row on Horton Road, where Schaffer intersected it.

It took my parents two or three years to work the yard at 1861 Schaffer into shape. They raked and raked to get the stones out, laid down the seed, then watched a torrential downpour wash it all away. In the back yard, between the foot of the hill and the house, a nice little pond frequently formed. Dad laid drain tile in trenches to take care of that problem. They planted bushes in front of the house and fruit trees atop the hill at the back, and Mom put in a rock garden, where she could see it when looking straight out the kitchen window. Eventually, the problem of growing grass gave way to the problem of mowing grass, and a riding mower moved into the garage and parked alongside the gas-powered, walk-behind rotary. My dad put a little putting green in the backyard, so my friends and I could pitch and putt anytime we wanted. In the front of the house, we had the driveway paved, the township paved the street, and the Post Office let us put a mailbox in front of our own house. The neighborhood had arrived.

Nine ranch houses stood along Schaffer. They were green, tan, white, yellow, and red. Seven of the nine families had children. The dads worked for the phone company, sold auto parts, ran a lumberyard, performed blue-collar work, or did accounting. One dad was a doctor, a general practitioner, setting up his first office. Dr. Kiessling's family occupied the biggest spread on Schaffer Drive. They owned an additional lot or two, and the lots had a stream running through them. The doctor put in the neighborhood's one and only fishpond, plus the only swimming pool for humans.

Pat Kiessling managed her husband's office, and Shirley Crossley worked at a bank, but most Shaffer Drive women were stay-at-home moms. Everybody on the block was white and Christian. Two families were Catholic, which set them apart a bit. The Catholic Horn family had the most kids, while the Kiesslings sent their children to a parochial grade school before sending them to public high school. All the other kids in the neighborhood went to the same public school. Two-parent families occupied all the houses. No parents were missing.

A couple of gas stations, a furniture store, and a tiny convenience store, the "Cheesebox," did business near Schaffer. There were no nearby supermarkets or other retailers. For grocery shopping, moms got in their cars and drove toward downtown Jackson, or over to Vandercook Lake. Vandercook didn't have much, but it did have Polly's grocery, the Weatherwax Drug Store, Krupa's Marine, Mitch's Bar, the Summit Township Library, a small hospital, and several churches and garages. Closer to home, the grade school that served the Schaffer neighborhood was a mile north on Horton Road, and just past the school sat some real treasures, Ella Sharp Park and its municipal golf course. A beautiful rose garden graced the park, as did a small zoo. The park had a nice pavilion for picnics and family reunions, woods, grassy fields, and plenty of baseball and softball diamonds.

Most mornings, I could see the men of Schaffer Drive get in their cars and drive off to work. My dad had one principal job, the one at Mechanical Products, that paid all the bills. To be sure, he worked around the house, sometimes very hard, fixing whatever needed fixing, and he did the heavy yard work. In terms of parental responsibilities, dad handled the sports—fishing, baseball, football. He sometimes drove twenty miles to take me and my buddies to play county Little League games, and if an umpire failed to show up, he volunteered for the job. He once called me out at third when I was sure I had slid in safely. I didn't talk to my dad during the ride home in the car.

Dad also handled tool-wielding skills and taught them to me. This is how you hammered nails or sawed wood. This is how you put gas in the mower or put a bicycle back together after foolishly taking it apart. He helped me with schoolwork, especially on those few occasions when math perplexed me. I can remember being whacked only once in my life by my dad. We disagreed on how to solve a math problem in seventh grade. I allowed as how my dad was being dumb, and he whacked me.

Mom took care of everybody and, it seemed, everything. This included our spiritual needs. In an era when the Sabbath counted for something, churches were open on Sunday, but most businesses weren't. On the days we attended church, my Methodist mom got us there. Dad, baptized a Presbyterian, went to church without complaint if that was what Mom wanted, but otherwise he didn't attend. Grampa Lankton and two of his sons were seriously religious. They observed the Sabbath and did not believe in drinking, smoking, swearing—or divorce. My dad failed his family on all those counts. Dad was well liked at Mechanical Products, where he worked, and he was well liked by all the neighbors on Schaffer Drive. But he was pretty much a black sheep in his own family.

We identified as Christians, but God was not at the center of our Lankton household, not by any means. Mom was far less pious than some of her siblings, who positively embraced Methodism, and she felt no compulsion to herd us off to church every Sunday. I think that as a mom, she thought she should introduce me to the church and Christianity as part of my education. Learn the rituals, sing the hymns, memorize the Lord's Prayer and the Doxology, and enjoy the fellowship. To teach me more about Jesus, she gave me the ten-volume set *The Bible Story*, written by Arthur S. Maxwell and published between 1953 and

1957. She read some of Maxwell's four hundred stories to me, but we didn't come close to exhausting all ten volumes. Religion was a part of our lives, to be sure, but it was "more honored in the breach than in the observance."

Mom bought our food and made the meals. She was a good cook, especially of the belly-filling comfort food she'd learned to make while growing up on an Indiana farm. She made great fried chicken and the best gravy in the world, and she baked lots of things from scratch, including bread, cookies, pies, and cakes. I especially loved being in the house when she was baking bread—it smelled so good throughout every room! She took me shopping for clothes, did the laundry, took me to the dentist and doctor, and served as home nurse. She kept house like a fanatic—partly because that was her character and partly because I suffered bad allergies as a kid. If it walked on four legs (dogs, cats, horses), I was allergic to it. If it grew in dirt (grass, weeds, trees), I was allergic to it. To ease my allergy problems, the folks put an air conditioner in my room in the mid-1950s, while the rest of the house went without. A speck of dust or pollen didn't stand a chance inside my bedroom, because Mom dusted and swept it every single day. I hope I thanked her for all this, but I probably just took it for granted.

Mary Lankton needed her own car to complete her myriad tasks and serve as the family's buyer of goods, runner of errands, and chauffeur. On Schaffer, we became a two-car family. In 1956, a green-and-white Packard Clipper became the prime car. This big, roomy land yacht, powered by a V-8, became our take-a-Sunday-drive car, our summer vacation drive-to-Indiana car, and Mom's drive-to-the-store, to-the-library, to-the-doctor, to-downtown-Jackson commuter car. Mom got the good car to run around town in, while Dad drove to and from work in a succession of lesser cars: a big, black 1949 Dodge Wayfarer sedan, then a gray over dark blue 1953 Hillman, and then a new, light gray over light seafoam green 1958 Hillman Minx four-door (the one I nearly torched with the flaming ping-pong ball).

Driving a Packard set my family apart. Nobody else on Schaffer Drive had one. That was Packard's problem. Once it had been a quality, upper-end car. Now, few wanted one and Packard in the mid-1950s was on its last legs. The Crossleys and Kiesslings drove Fords; the Reynolds, a Pontiac; and the Cosiers, Buicks. Only the Lanktons had a rare Packard. The car did have one slick feature that amused me: torsion-level suspension. If you put a lot of weight in the trunk, a little motor gizmo lifted the back end of the car up, leveling it. Whenever new friends came over to play, I liked to chat them up in the garage, then sit them down on the Packard's rear bumper. Boy, did they jump when suddenly the car whirred and the bumper lifted!

I was just another pampered, spoiled member of the baby boom generation. My main "job" was to go to school and to study and get good grades. In the realm of education, my parents made it clear that I was expected to do well. Other than school, I helped a bit around the house, mostly outside work in the yard. Despite being allergic to all the dusty things kicked up by a rotary mower, I helped cut the grass at home, and I cut the Macy family's grass, a couple doors down on Schaffer, for a couple bucks at a time. I sold Christmas cards and surplus tomatoes to neighbors to raise some cash; worked a few hours cleaning up the butcher shop at the Cheesebox; and on some Saturdays, I rode with the driver of a bread truck to help him deliver his goods.

I discovered that if you reached under the seat of our riding lawnmower, you could use the fingers on your right hand to override the throttle stop and give the engine a whole lot more gas. The lawnmower scooted like a go-kart when you did that! Once I discovered the machine was a bit of a speed demon, I named it "Big Wheel," a name I painted in silver script on one of the mower's red body panels. When the folks left me alone, I liked to fire up "Big Wheel" and take it for some fast spins around the back yard. Sometimes I let neighbor boys join in the fun. That stopped after John Overbee ran Big Wheel into a little tree Dad had just planted.

I had a lot of friends my own age. They were almost entirely boys. In eighth grade a cute girl named Pearson Marvin asked me to our junior high's Sadie Hawkins dance, but that was it, in terms of youthful romance. My best buddies were Bill and Terry from next door, Bruce from across the street, Phil from up the hill on Badgley, and Rick, maybe three quarters of a mile away, on Plateau Drive. In the 1950s, as youngsters, we learned to tie knots and cook over an open fire when we were Cub Scouts and then Boy Scouts. We tromped through the swamps and woods, catching snakes and turtles and shooting frogs with BB guns. Bill and Terry even trapped muskrats. In the summer, we raced around on our bicycles. It was great fun to start on the high end of Schaffer at Badgley Road, race down the hill, and then dart onto the smooth asphalt drive at my house. I'd push down hard on the coaster brake with my right foot and turn the handlebars. This kicked the bike's rear wheel out to the right, and the Schwinn went into a power slide and skidded to a stop.

We neighborhood kids played tons of baseball. Baseball was *the* game. In terms of official play, the boys of Summit Township played ball against the small towns around Jackson, like Spring Arbor, Parma, Concord, Hanover, and Horton. We started playing in the spring when our wool uniforms felt good against the evening's cool—and sometimes, even, against the evening's cold and snow flurries. We continued playing into the summer, when the same wool uniforms were too itchy and hot. I pitched tennis balls for hours at a rectangle chalked onto the back of our garage. To improve the accuracy of my arm, I threw balls up at the cupola surmounting the garage roof; if I missed, I had to go around the house and across the street to retrieve my errant toss. Rick and I played imaginary Tigers-Yankees games in the yard. One pitched, the other caught and called balls and strikes. Here was our one and only chance to strike out Mickey Mantle or Yogi Berra. The backyard at 1861 was big enough to play flies and grounders, especially if the batter stood a bit over into the Crossleys' yard. Flies and grounders got more interesting once the neighbor on the other side of my house put up a wooden fence. Now, you could be Al Kaline, patrolling right field in Briggs Stadium. It was a long fly ball. You raced back to the fence. You found it with your bare right hand, pushed off, leaped up, and robbed Moose Skowron of a home run when the white ball sank into your well-oiled glove.

Most often, we played pickup games of work up. You had batters and fielders. When a batter was out, he picked up his glove and rotated into the field. Meanwhile, a fielder went in to bat. We had a makeshift diamond right near our houses. We used our families' lawn mowers to cut the weeds on the large vacant lot at the corner of Badgley and Horton. The field was rough, to be sure, but big enough to throw down bases and play games. If we wanted a better field to play on, we rode our bikes a mile and a quarter to Ella Sharp Park and played on one of the beautiful diamonds there. More than once an angry groundskeeper chased us away with some nasty words after our feet scarred up a diamond he'd dragged and lined for an official game that evening. We didn't mean to cause trouble, but there was something simply irresistible about a grassy diamond with a tabletop dirt infield, all lined in white. In addition to hardball diamonds, Ella Sharp Park had one especially nice softball diamond, fenced and lighted, with stands, an announcer's booth, and concessions. I often went there in the evenings with Dad, especially when the Jackson Merchants were playing. The Merchants had some strong-armed men who jacked big homers, and on the best of nights, I served as their batboy and scored an old ball or cracked bat.

A couple of times, I saw Eddie Feigner play on this diamond. Feigner toured the nation as "The King and His Court." Feigner was the "King." His "Court" numbered only three additional players—a catcher and two fielders. They played against local all-star teams fielding a full nine men. The King and His Court always won, because Feigner was such an amazing pitcher. He was unhittable from the pitcher's rubber. He had too much dip and curve and blazing speed for the locals to handle. They'd have to start their swings early to have any chance of hitting Feigner's fastball. Sometimes, as a joke, Eddie only pretended to let go of the ball. The batter swung, the catcher thumped his mitt with his right fist, and the umpire proclaimed, "Steee-rike!" Next thing you knew, Eddie was pitching blindfolded from second base—and still striking men out.

On many summer evenings, a buddy and I slung our small golf bags over our shoulders and rode our bikes up to the golf course at the park. We'd get there late enough to sneak on without paying. On a good night, we'd get in seven or eight holes before the sprinklers and darkness arrived at the same time to chase us off. Over at Rick's, a backboard and net perched over the garage door, so we dribbled around the cement driveway, shooting baskets and playing "horse." In the fall, we played pickup football games, and some played for Frost Junior High's team. In winter, we rode sleds and toboggans down steep hills at Cascades Park, played pond hockey, and bowled in a youth league on Saturday mornings.

Life played out on a small stage for me and the other Schaffer Drive boys in the mid-1950s to the early 1960s. We had our homes and families, our neighborhood and friends, our teams and sports, our school, and family cars that took us out on Sunday drives or on trips to see relatives. Basically, we went day to day, having fun and building up a reservoir of pleasant memories. The kids did notice that there was another world out there, a more dangerous world, a more competitive world. On weekends, I often lunched over at Rick's house. His mom, Wilma, made white bread sandwiches and Campbell's tomato soup and popped open two Cokes, while Rick's father, Roy, inhaled deeply of cigarettes while sipping a Manhattan. Mr. Cosier was a perfectly affable and friendly man—a great suburban dad who doted over his son and went to Little League games—and yet you knew that a decade before he had been a captain in World War II, that he had flown fifty-five missions in the Philippines in his B-25 bomber, and that he had seen crew members shot up. Bill and Terry's dad had been in the war too. He served in the O.S.S. and never told his family what he did.

Enemies really did exist in this world. The Ella Sharp Park grade school had yellow-and-black signs carrying a circle and three triangles and the words "Fallout Shelter." That meant that somewhere in our school people stored dried food in barrels and kept water, in case of a nuclear attack. That's what the "duck and cover" practice was all about. If our teacher told us to, we'd hide under our desks to survive a nuclear attack. We sixth graders would all be safe.

While the nuke never came, something else did that enlarged my view of the world: Sputnik. On Saturday, October 5, 1957, I was having lunch with Mom at a Big Boy restaurant in downtown Jackson. I could see the newspaper box near the front door and cash register. The paper's headline announced that Russia had rocketed a "Sputnik," or man-made satellite, into space. To me, that seemed cool. The world expanded from Jackson all the way to outer space as first little satellites, then satellites carrying small animals, and then space capsules like "Vostok" and "Mercury," carrying men, went up into the heavens. There was a race going on here, and the Russians seemed to be ahead. All this stuff seemed so far away, and yet even as a seventh grader I knew I was somehow involved, because in my advanced math class at Frost Junior High, I had a new paperback textbook with a blue paper cover that came out of the University of Michigan. This was some kind of new math. It taught problem solving, and it taught stuff like base two, instead of just base ten. Nobody told the class just what this was all about, but I figured that my seventh-grade class, new math, base two, the space race, and communism were all tied together somehow. My learning took on a new purpose, it seemed: to boost America, as well as my own intellect.

Nuclear bombs and a space race registered in my consciousness, but, frankly, those things were distant and did not really seem to threaten 1861 Schaffer Drive as much as some adults seemed to think they did. Immediate, local events—those were a different story. They could rock your little world and its security. When I was in third grade, little Reed Crossley, a four-year-old next-door neighbor, went into a hospital simply to have his tonsils out. He died on the table, due to a reaction to the anesthesia. In December 1959, my father fell ill. It turned out to be leukemia. He was the oldest father on the block, yet he had been the best athlete of the bunch, a college football player in the 1920s. He spent more time with the neighborhood boys than any other dad, hitting us flies or teaching us how to punt. In September 1960, after nine months of quiet and hopeless suffering, he died.

That death spelled the end of life as I knew it at 1861 Schaffer Drive. My mother sold our house on December 18, 1961. She sold the big car, the 1956 Packard. In January 1962, Mom drove me in the little 1958 Hillman to Danville, Illinois. We moved there because she had family there. I finished junior high and high school in Danville. For a brief period of time, we had our own house again in Danville, one with a yard and a nice field behind it. But Mom's earnings as the dining room hostess at the Danville County Club couldn't afford it. So we ended up living in an upstairs apartment near downtown.

Later, reading books and listening to music, I learned that in the 1950s, the car culture had made possible an unfortunate proliferation of suburban housing in America. All those newly built suburbs were too ticky-tacky, too homogenous, too all-white, too stifling. They were "little boxes" that all looked alike, containing people who all acted and thought alike, if they thought much at all. Social critics, I reasoned, made some valid points, whether they were folk singers, sociologists, or historians. Still, I could never totally embrace their perspective, because I always recollected that 1861 Schaffer Drive had been a great place to grow up, while it lasted.

# 4

# WOMEN AT THE WHEEL

In the mid-1950s, I had seven living aunts, ranging in age from the mid-thirties to the mid-fifties. They lived in Grosse Pointe Woods, Pontiac, and Detroit, Michigan; in Kingman, West Lebanon, and Veedersburg, Indiana; and in Danville, Illinois. Three of them lived on farms at some distance from shopping and other amenities. None of them worked outside the home. If memory serves, only two of my seven aunts drove a car. Ruby Warburton, wife of Walt, a barber, raised two boys and a girl in Danville. She drove a Studebaker and then a big, green 1959 Chevrolet. She moved the bench seat all the way forward and controlled that large, tail-finned behemoth with the power assists that Detroit provided her.

My family had our version of "Thoroughly Modern Millie." My youngest aunt, Millie, born in 1922, was eleven years younger than my mom. She didn't have much Indiana farmgirl left in her and seemed at least a full generation apart from every other aunt. Living on Aline Drive in a new brick house in Grosse Pointe Woods, she seemed in tune with modern times. She did her hair, wore lipstick all the time, and enjoyed a good drink and a good laugh. Her husband, Darrell, co-owned a chrome plating shop with his brother in Detroit. I think Darrell must have produced parts for GM, because he always drove GM cars. They used to visit us, traveling in a sharp-looking 1955 red-and-white Buick. After Millie and Darrell adopted two young children, Cheryl and Mark, she did more driving around the Pointes, serving as shopper and chauffeur. After the Buick, I remember her driving a

Pontiac Grand Prix. I also remember that after the Detroit Riot of 1967, she never drove into that city again. Never.

On Emmett Street, when I was starting kindergarten, my sister was finishing high school. Our family had only one car, and Lynn didn't know how to drive it. Well, that's not exactly true. She had driven it once. When I was three and Lynn was sixteen, the whole family drove thirty miles to Adrian, where Mom and I got on a train bound for Danville, Illinois, where we visited with her family. After our early-morning departure, Dad and Lynn walked back to the car. Lynn was very mature for her age, and I guess my dad trusted her. He handed her the keys and said to Lynn, "You're driving." She had never driven before, but she made it back to Vandercook Lake, while my Dad slept in the passenger seat. After that nerve-racking maiden voyage, Lynn was happy to return to bicycle riding as her primary means of transport. Right after high school she married Ben, her high school sweetheart. She moved out of our house and into the house that Ben shared with his parents and his younger brother, Price. She soon had one child, a boy, and quickly followed with a second, a girl. At age twenty-two, with two children, she decided it was time to learn to drive one of their stick-shift cars.

Ben was an unabashed fan of small foreign cars. He felt no compunction whatsoever in the 1950s to "Buy American." His parents did; they always had big Oldsmobiles parked in the drive. Eventually, Ben would come around, buying a Dodge Challenger convertible, a Chevy II convertible, a Plymouth Barracuda, a Ford Bronco, and a Pontiac Fiero. But in the 1950s, he acquired a Nash Metropolitan convertible, an MG, a Morris Minor woodie station wagon, a Hillman convertible, and what he called his "dollar a pound car," a 1,700-pound Volkswagen that cost 1,700 dollars. Notably, none of these cars had an automatic transmission. Lynn had to learn how to shift.

Lynn learned to drive at the wheel of their Morris Minor. Learning how to juggle a clutch and an accelerator did not come easy. And teaching her did not come easy to Ben. He grew frustrated when Lynn could not smoothly pull away from a dead stop in the Morris Minor. After many failed attempts, husband and wife agreed that Lynn needed a new instructor, and they turned to Ben's brother, Price. Price was an affable, friendly sort, slow to lose his cool. He calmly got Lynn through the business of "give it some gas while you slowly let out the clutch." Lynn could now drive herself and her kids anywhere. After teaching Lynn how to drive, Price went into the Army and was stationed in England. He was killed in an auto accident there, far, far from home.

In my Schaffer Drive neighborhood, if a buddy and I wanted to go sledding at Cascades Park, we did not have to wait till Dad could take us. Bruce's mom, Pat, could drive. Bill's mom, Shirley, could drive, and so could Rick's mom, Wilma. My mother, Mary, shepherded us kids all around town for sports or movies. Among my friends, only Phil's mom, Ginny, did not drive. Since she didn't drive, Phil's family had only one car. Other families all had two: one for dad to take to work and one for mom to take to wherever she needed to go.

I have no idea when my mother learned to drive, and I can't remember any time when she didn't drive. For the other boys, it was the same. At maybe 105 pounds, my mom drove our large 1956 Packard with ease. And when it became necessary, she drove our 1958 Hillman Minx, and that was a bit trickier. It had a four-speed shifter on the column, and its shifting pattern was backward from the usual. Changing gears, when she moved the shifter in or out or up or down, the motion was the opposite of an American car. But she never seemed to have any trouble with that. She was a good driver who never had an accident or a traffic violation. When all the family was in the car, she was the secondary driver, the relief driver. Dad manned the wheel at least 90 percent of the time. But on trips to Indiana, sometimes Dad stayed home, and Mom drove three hundred miles on two-lane highways in something like seven or eight hours.

I doubt if my mother could change a tire. But she never had to try while I was riding with her, so who knows? She took cars in for servicing, like oil changes, and she had a strong say about what cars our family owned. She absolutely vetoed one of Dad's car purchases, an Austin-Healey Sprite. She disdainfully assessed his choice, condemned it as too small, and told him to go back and get another car. He did what he was told. About six years later, Mom went to a Pontiac dealer and purchased a car that was totally unexpected. God bless her, she had a mind of her own and used it.

I think the percentage of Schaffer Drive moms who drove was quite a bit higher than the national percentage of married women who drove in the mid-1950s. But that percentage was going up, as more women discovered they needed a car, and Detroit automakers did everything they could to get women behind the wheel. The more women who drove, the more cars they sold. In an era of suburbanization, more families *needed* a second car. Without a car, the suburban woman was stranded at home. With a car she was free to go where she wanted, heading off to a paying job or serving as family chauffeur and shopper. By 1960, eleven million American households had two or more automobiles.

The Ford Motor Company recognized the car as a catalyst of social change. In 1949, Ford ran a print ad in *Good Housekeeping* and *Better Homes and Gardens* that had at the top, "Woman's Place is in the Home." But the word "Home" was crossed out, and the word "Ford" was written in: "Woman's Place is in the Ford." The woman depicted in the artwork says, "I know because I'm at the wheel so many times every single day." The ad treats her like a paper doll. She is surrounded by different outfits, as if you were going to cut them out with scissors, lay them over her body, and fold back the little tabs to hold them in place. The doll outfits are labeled "chauffeur," "delivery boy," "nursemaid," and "glamour girl."

A Ford television commercial in 1956 followed the same theme. A woman talking on the phone in her kitchen makes a date to meet another woman at two o'clock. Then she turns to the camera to address all Americans:

> You know, three weeks ago I couldn't have accepted that invitation. Like so many people these days, we live in the suburbs and Dave needs the car everyday for business. When he was gone, I was practically a prisoner in my own home. I couldn't get out to see my friends, could not take part in PTA activities. Why, I couldn't even shop when I wanted to—I had to wait till Thursday night until after Dave brought the car home. But that's all changed now. Three weeks ago we bought another Ford—the new low-priced Custom Line Victoria. Isn't it stunning?

> Dave has it all to himself, and I now have the Ranch Wagon all to myself! It's a whole new way of life. Now I'm free to go anywhere, do anything, see anybody any time I want to.

Auto companies and their ad agencies did not forget about men altogether. A 1950 magazine ad, "Staunch Friends," showed two hunters recently arrived at a pond. The goose decoys are ready to be put out, and a black lab pokes his nose out the back window. The copy reads, "A fine gun, a smart dog, a boon companion or two, and the sportsman needs but one thing more to assure a fun-filled day afield—a stout car with Body by Fisher to transport him to and from his hunting area." While selling cars to men longing for happy days in the field, General Motor showed that its cars liberated women, too, just as well as any Ford. A *Good Housekeeping* ad depicted a man next to a 1955 Chevy, saying, "I think about women all the time. Not that I'm romantic—I'm a Chevrolet engineer. But the most demanding part of my job is seeing that the cars we design come as close as possible to a woman's ideal." Part of that ideal, as Chevy made clear in a series of 1955 ads, was to have a car perfect for taking a woman anywhere she wanted to go. Smiling women in proper attire (be it "jaunty boyish shorts," "a delicate silk dress," or "your Sunday best") were featured in ads with titles like, "You're Going to a Picnic," "You're Going out to Dinner," and "You're Going to Church."

In 1953, *Good Housekeeping* made the point that good car keeping was as important as good housekeeping: "Today, with your car so much a part of your everyday life—taxiing your children to school, shopping, meeting trains, enjoying a social life and vacations—it becomes quite important for you to be a good driver as a good home manager. Both roles require knowing the right way to do things, planning ahead, and of course, practice." To help women learn more about cars, for six years in the 1950s *Good Housekeeping* ran a monthly car column, "The Woman and Her Car," written by Charlotte Montgomery. Montgomery's columns often broached the same subjects that came up in magazines for men: how to winterize a car; how to drive on snow and ice; why and when to rotate tires; and the ins and outs of batteries, brakes, and protecting a car's finish. Still, no column of hers could have found its way, exactly as written, into a magazine with a male audience. She wrote from a woman's perspective. She thought readers should know that "women are . . . easing into that masculine world of automobiles." In a May 1955 column, she introduced them to Lucille Pieti, an automotive engineer working for a Big Three company, and to Betty Skelton, a test driver who tipped the scales at ninety-eight pounds. Montgomery was her own new woman. She never wrote an article like "The good wife's guide," which appeared in *Housekeeping Monthly*. That article came out the same month and year as Montgomery's column on women engineers and test drivers. It counseled a woman to know her place; be happy to see her husband come home for dinner; make her home a place of peace, order, and tranquility; and not greet her husband at the door with complaints and problems. In her columns, Montgomery hardly mentioned husbands at all. She wasn't interested in keeping men happy, but in keeping women and their cars happy.

Montgomery didn't expect women to keep up with the latest engines and transmissions: "To the woman driver these may seem pretty bewildering, especially since each manufacturer uses his own coined name—Gyromatic, Easamatic, Hydra-Matic, Dynaflow, etc. Women wonder what they all mean." She urged women to find a trusted mechanic for auto service needs: "Finding the right serviceman is as important to her car as finding the right doctor is to her family." Montgomery adopted a romantic metaphor when she advised women: "So make a date with your mechanic, and don't rush him on the job."

Montgomery thought joining the AAA (American Automobile Association) was more important for a woman than for a man, because, "after all, she is seldom properly dressed or equipped to change a tire or dig herself out of a ditch or sandbank." The AAA offered emergency road help and would "send a man to fix the car." Her columns demonstrated that men and women looked at the car, and used the car, in different ways. *Motor Trend* or *Sports Cars Illustrated* never advised men, in the event of an accident, not to cry. But Montgomery cautioned her readers: "If your automobile is involved in an accident, keep your head. . . . Woman's tears, reputed to be effective on so many occasions, should not now be in evidence."

Montgomery's column on taxiing children to school said a two-door sedan was better than a four-door, because Mom could "feel safer when children are in back, with no door handles within reach." Because of the wear and tear that young children could inflict upon upholstery, Mom should consider seat covers for her car. If taking a long trip alone, a woman had to concern herself with personal safety more than a man. She should drive during the day, if possible. If she had to drive at night, she should stay on good, well-traveled roads and carry a flashlight—as well as "a modest weapon," such as a heavy tool, kept on the seat beside her. A woman who read the column on "Automobile Manners" learned how to drive slowly and yet keep out of people's way. In "Dressing for Driving," Montgomery announced an important find for *Good Housekeeping*'s readers: "a group of smart fall clothes designed especially for the woman who drives." "These clothes," Montgomery wrote, "are appropriate and well cut for our automobile age. They won't fight the motions of your body as you turn, park, swing open a door, scramble out of the car to pick up a package, or hoist the baby into his safety seat beside you." The "easy-cut skirts won't ride up," and their fabrics "won't muss or show soil or grab at the upholstery when you get in and out of the car." In a column on taking a first long drive, she advised, "Your clothes should be selected with care—a girdle that supports and is comfortable through hours of long sitting, stockings that won't cut at the top, shoes that allow for a bit of expansion. . . ." In "Sitting Pretty behind the Wheel," Montgomery told readers, "Before you begin your trip by car, take extra thought to keep up your good looks and enjoy good comfort along the way." On a long trip, "You'll want to look pretty at all your stops and arrive at your final destination refreshed in mind, rested in body, with skin smooth, hair at its best, hands soft." In other columns she offered tips on starting school carpools and on traveling with a baby or a dog.

Montgomery told readers that housekeeping and car keeping demands were much alike: "Don't let your car be a dirt collector or a family catchall. Many of us who wouldn't tolerate a swirl of dust on the stairs or a spot on the living room love seat, close our eyes when our automobiles grow untidy and unsightly." A woman shouldn't let that happen, because only a "little regular effort" was needed to keep a car "as neat and pleasant to sit in as when new." "There's no reason why that handsome new car upholstery can't stay sparkling," she wrote, and then she offered tips on using vacuum cleaners, whisk brooms, liquid cleaners, and spot removers to keep "attractive interiors looking bright." Car keeping was important on trips, too: "Teach the children to be good housekeepers and don't let the car get littered. At least once a day fold maps, pick up playthings, and brush the car out."

The woman responsible for stocking the house with supplies—with foodstuffs, toilet paper, or towels—took responsibility for stocking the car too. When a car backed out of the driveway to head off on a trip, most likely Dad was driving, but Mom had set up the checklist of needed travel supplies: maps, first-aid kit, flashlight, tissues and napkins, sunglasses, bug repellent, camera, small pillow, hand lotion, and lip balm. For the mother of a young child, the car doubled as a nursery, and who besides mother would think about acquiring and packing "bottle warmers that plug in to the dashboard cigarette lighter"?

In the 1950s women not only went shopping *in* their cars—they went shopping *for* their cars. The woman, the main family consumer, did not wait for her husband to bring home a new car particularly well suited to him. As the 1950s progressed, she became more involved in the car-buying decision. In its issue of January 7, 1950, *Business Week* ran an article entitled, "Women Buy a Lot—But Not Everything." According to a survey conducted by the Bureau of Economic and Business Research at the University of Illinois, "women are a far less potent power in purchasing consumer goods than many marketers think." According to the researchers, they did not account for 80 percent of all family buying, which was the figure accepted by many economists. In terms of buying automobiles, men wielded 75 percent of the *influence* in buying a car, women only 25 percent. Mom made only 5 percent of all car purchases on her own, while Dad alone accounted for about 70 percent. Mom and Dad, shopping together, accounted for the remaining 25 percent of auto buying. Researchers a bit later credited women with wielding more influence, or doing more of the buying, in all things automotive. In December of 1954, *Business Week* reported that a Hearst

Magazine marketing survey discovered "that women influenced 56% of the purchases of gas and oil, handling 55.9% of the car servicing." Another magazine survey found that when car-buying decisions were being made at auto dealerships or around kitchen tables, women now "influenced 75% of automobile sales."

Seventy million drivers traveled America's streets and highways in the mid-1950s, and about a third of them were women. Companies took notice of their growing importance as purchasers of automotive goods and services. Stewart-Warner Corporation, in sixty garages across the country, offered hundreds of sessions of an "intensive training course for women drivers" called "Gas, Gaskets, and Glamor." The purpose was not just to educate women about cars but to convert them into customers who stopped at the garages for oil changes, lubes, and tires. Husbands did not want auto servicing to encroach upon their leisure time on weekends, so many delegated auto servicing to their wives. Some women felt they were up to the task, because their World War II work in "defense plants undoubtedly helped break down the historic female feeling of abject helplessness in the face of machinery. The whole feminist cult drives the women into new fields of conquest." Other women, though, read Charlotte Montgomery's car columns in *Good Housekeeping*, or took a course like "Gas, Gaskets, and Glamor," because they didn't want "to feel dumb" when going to a service station. Some signed on to prove their mettle to a domineering husband. A "pert blonde" signed up for the Stewart-Warner car course because, "My husband said women shouldn't know anything about autos, so I took the course just to show him." Regardless of a woman's motivation for taking Stewart-Warner's course, when she completed its six two-hour sessions, she received a diploma and an orchid.

To promote its 1950 model, Mercury launched print ads that marginalized women and did not put them in the driver's seat. As shown in artwork and text, women sat in the passenger's seat and went along for the ride. "Dollars to doughnuts," read one of these ads, "the *man* of the house takes the wheel . . . if it's a Mercury. It gives his ego a gentle boost . . . it feeds his need for a sense of power . . . it lets him know that *he's* in control."

In these Mercury ads, a woman didn't wrangle over who was driving—that was *his* rightful place, if he wanted it. Instead, she was supposed to want a Mercury for the little things. It had a glove compartment big enough for her stuff and his stuff. It had good flow-through ventilation, so there was no need to open a window, which would mess up her hair. The Mercury allowed for a truce to be called in the battle of the sexes over who controlled the windows. The wife didn't have to have her temper ruffled by an open window that ruffled her coiffure, and the husband didn't have to sit in stony silence with windows closed, barely tolerating a car's stuffy air. Mercury's ventilation system quickly and gently brought a fresh change of air into the car. This pleased both husband and wife and was "just one of the reasons why more and more smart 'happily-marrieds' are making Mercury their car."

In 1956, Chevrolet ran ads based on the theme of husbands, wives, and cars. The tagline running through these ads read, "Every woman needs a *second* love—a new Chevrolet." The automaker made it clear that the Chevrolet woman of 1956 had greater automotive ambitions than the Mercury woman of 1950. Instead of merely wanting a closed window and a big glove compartment, the Chevy woman wanted a whole car to herself. In these ads, no husband appeared. The ad showed how a wife's life would improve if she had a new Chevy of her own. In one, she is in front of her suburban house with three young children. A '55 Chevy sits in one bay of a two-car garage, while her new 1956 Bel Air Sport Coupe is in the drive. The ad copy tells women to "show this to your husband . . . when his mood is just right!" The woman is supposed to tell her husband, "I never thought I'd find a companion as good looking as you, dear. But I did—the new Chevrolet." It would be a beautiful and perfect traveling companion for her: "Wide, low seats give me more than enough room for my fullest skirt, tallest hat, and children and packages in assorted sizes." The husband could make his wife's "dream come true by making a date with our Chevrolet dealer tomorrow."

In another ad from the same campaign, a young woman is shown alone in front of a very modern home; she's reaching over the passenger side door to grab a few bags of groceries out of the front seat of her top-down Bel Air convertible. The ad copy reads, "If he complains about those last-minute dinners . . . put this next to his napkin!" As the man reads the ad, she is supposed to tell her husband, "You want me to come home from work and fix a six-course dinner? Fine! Then I want a Chevrolet of my own." The woman in this ad was no stereotypical stay-at-home mom of the '50s. She has a job of her own, and there are no kids in sight. She wants to please her husband, but she wants to please herself too. A Chevy would treat them both. The car would let her "get home in time to prepare a real feast" for him. At the same time, she would enjoy "the thrill of driving" her own high-styled Chevrolet convertible with "its sizzling V8."

Charlotte Montgomery told the readers of *Good Housekeeping* that automakers were catering to them. In 1953 she wrote, "Interiors are designed to be feminine, . . . with lovely new fabrics handled in the manner of your finest sofa." 1955 she told readers to "look out the window at the cars going by—cream, yellow, pale blue, pink. Open the door of a new car and look in at the mouth-watering colors and fabrics. Plenty of evidence that women influence car buying today!" In a *Time* magazine article of November 4, 1957, Ford's chief stylist, George Walker, confirmed Montgomery's observations and conclusions:

> Beauty is what sells the American car. And the person we are designing it for is the American woman. Only one out of every three women in the U.S. drives, but we figure that 80% or better of all car purchases are decided on by women. A woman is naturally style-conscious from birth—in her home, her clothes, everything she does. So when she and her husband go out to buy a car, she wants beauty on wheels.

While Walker, a car designer, credited beauty and style for capturing sales decided by women, an engineer could have credited new technologies for the same sales. In advertisements and commercials aimed at women and featuring women, Detroit pushed them both: the luxury of chic interior appointments and Jacquard fabrics, combined with mechanical luxuries such as Hydraglide power steering and Dynaflow automatic transmissions.

Many ads and commercials stressed the beauty of both women and cars. They often depicted stylishly dressed women, where the car served as a part of her ensemble. Cadillac adorned ads with heavily jeweled necklaces ("Jewels by Van Cleef & Arpels," or "Jewels by Harry Winston"). Other ads put a pretty, dressed-to-the-teeth, upper-class woman near the Caddy, in her "Dress designed by Hallie Carnegie" or her "Furs by Revillon." For men, the Chrysler Corporation assembled a group of aircraft engineers and designers to make positive remarks about the company's cars. For women, they assembled "7 top fashion designers," six of them women, to line up in front of a 1955 Chrysler product and declare that Chrysler's new "Forward Look" style was "a stimulating new concept of good design." Automakers trumpeted the news whenever their cars won fashion awards. Ford publicized receipt of its Gold Medal from the Fashion Academy of New York in 1950. An ad reproduced the Fashion Academy's letter to Henry Ford, II, which was full of praise: "In the new 1950 Ford, America's Best Dressed women will find for their personal transportation a more perfect expression of the most modern fashion dictates and a more flattering background for their individual style awareness." Similarly, in 1953, Studebaker won the Fashion Academy's Gold Medal and used the award to bolster its claim that it was "excitingly different," with a "European look."

The car companies plugged lingo from the fashion industry into their ads. In 1950, Ford offered "smartly tailored" upholstery, plus a "smart looking" newly restyled horn ring to "prevent snagging of . . . a lady's bracelet." Meanwhile, Dodge said that "Like a well-tailored Suit (which 'looks *Smart* Front or Back!') this year's Dodge is an even bigger value!" In 1951, Oldsmobile encouraged American women to "ROCKET ahead in Glamorous Style" and depicted a woman in a strapless evening gown and wrap riding a flame-emitting rocket. This was "Glamor in the 'Rocket' manner—glamor on the GO!" A television spot for the 1953 Chrysler intoned, "Driving some cars is like getting into a tight girdle. You take a lot of punishment for looks." But that wouldn't be necessary with the Chrysler, with all its roominess inside. In 1955, Dodge proclaimed its products to be "flair-fashioned . . . and alive with beauty." The ad copy spoke of the car's "sleek silhouette," while the artwork depicted the silhouette of a trim-waisted woman, stroking a Dodge rear fin with one hand and holding her white gloves in the other. In 1956, GM and Buick boasted of a great new automotive "Fashion First"—the advent of the four-door hardtop. The ad parked a two-tone Buick Century in front of the Cleveland Museum of Art at night, with a woman in a lace evening gown standing next to it. In 1957, some Pontiac ads featured a model who was wearing a gown that had a shoulder on one side but was off-the-shoulder on the other. Her dress symbolized the "Off-the-Shoulder Look" that adorned Pontiac seats that year. Instead of carrying a solid color all the way across, a seat back had one corner, or shoulder, upholstered in a contrasting fabric and color.

When they weren't selling style in the context of feminine attire, Detroit sold style in the context of home furnishings and decor. Automakers pitched their cars as nice rooms for women to admire, sit in, and even entertain in. GM's Fisher Body division ran an ad in October 1949 headed, "Guest Room—*and then Some!*" The copy led off with: "There's real hospitality in your smile when you invite someone to share those wide, sofa-deep seats in Body by Fisher. Comfort is fundamental with Fisher." In 1950, Nash offered "Daring Decorator Interiors"; all Studebakers were "smartly appointed and decorator styled"; while all Fords had "LUXURY-LOUNGE INTERIORS," which were "color-keyed to Ford's sleek, 'Fashion Car' exteriors." The 1952 Packards had been "Fashion-keyed by Dorothy Draper." Draper, an "internationally famous decorator and color stylist," graced Packards with "the magic of her color and fabric genius." Meanwhile, Lincoln broke with "the heavy décor of the past" and departed from "impractical frills and furbelows," to create a modern design for the modern era, one marked by "striking, relaxing interiors" and by "beauty—graceful, clean and alive, . . . devoted to the cause of comfort and the joy of driving."

Detroit's feminization of the automobile reached its peak in 1955 and 1956, when Dodge sold its most expensive two-door hardtop, a Custom Royal Lancer, with an option package that dressed the car in special livery and rebadged it the Dodge "La Femme." An advertising brochure said Dodge made the La Femme "By Special Appointment to Her Majesty . . . the American Woman." Here was "America's most glamorous Car—Designed with the ladies in mind!" In its name, exterior colors, interior fabrics, and accessories, the car was "distinctively feminine" and "in mood and manner a distinctive car for the discriminating, modern woman." That modern woman, incidentally, as drawn in Dodge's promotional literature, was a dead ringer for short-haired Audrey Hepburn, who had just starred in the films *Roman Holiday* in 1953 and *Sabrina* in 1954.

The 1955 La Femme model came in one two-tone exterior color combination that was also available on other Custom Royal Lancers, Heather Rose and Sapphire White. It had a gold anodized "La Femme" script on the sides of the front fenders. Inside, it had "richly woven Jacquard fabric in pastel rose with special tapestry design"—that tapestry took the form of tiny pink rosebuds woven into the cloth. Special storage compartments attached to the backs of the front seats held the La Femme accessories, which were color matched to the car's interior: a rain cape, hat, and umbrella, and a soft rose-colored leather shoulder bag or purse, which held a matching compact, lighter, and cigarette case. The 1956 La Femme came in "the warm, delicate exterior colors of harmonizing Regal Orchid and Misty Orchid," two "lovely new shades" exclusive to the La Femme. The option package included special fabrics and colors on interior seats, door panels, carpets, and headliners. Although the purse had been eliminated, the 1956 La Femme package still came with color-keyed rain gear and umbrella.

The Dodge La Femme lasted only two years. As few as 2,500 customers selected it. Two possible reasons come to mind for its lack of success, one from the male side, one from the female side. In an era when rugged heroes packing six-guns starred in western movies and television shows, suburban husbands may have discouraged wives from wanting a "woman's car," because they would feel uncomfortable if seen driving or riding in it. From the female side, there was no real need to buy this car. All manner of mid-1950s cars came in two-tone paint jobs incorporating pink, rose, and other soft colors, with feminized interiors using fabrics and colors like those found in the home on drapes, sofas, chairs, and carpets. A woman could find a car designed with her in mind in any dealership in the country, even if it didn't come with a matching bag. A year after the Chrysler Corporation killed the La Femme, it ran ads saying, "If ever a car were perfect for a woman, it's the 1957 DeSoto," with its "new look in high fashion" and its "jewel-case instrument panel."

Engineers had women in mind when they added new technologies to cars of the 1950s. A 1951 Chrysler Corporation ad, with a heading of "New Engineering makes cars easier to drive," showed an older woman parallel parking her car at the curb. "Grandmother passes parking test," the ad read: "In a busy Detroit suburb, Mrs. Dorothy Cooledge parks that Chrysler Imperial with only one hand—thanks to sensational new Hydraglide Power Steering." Detroit sought to create as many two-car families as possible, and the automakers wanted those second cars to be full-sized, six-passenger vehicles carrying the highest profit margin, like Mrs. Cooledge's Chrysler Imperial. They did not want to downsize their products to better fit the "little woman." They had no interest in creating suburban runabouts for moms or grandmothers. Instead, they added power assists and convenience features to their big cars. Detroit told American women—even the millions just learning to drive—that they could confidently handle four thousand pounds of car with no problem. After a full day of driving—going from home to school, to post office, to drug store, to downtown, to the new shopping center out by the highway, to the grocery, and back to home again—they could still look as fresh as a daisy, as if they had done nothing all day. The announcer in a 1956 Oldsmobile TV commercial met a returning wife at her door and complimented her, "You sure look lovely after a whole day of driving around town!" She gave the credit back to her new Olds: "It's so easy and comfortable to drive and I enjoy it so much."

In 1951, Buick ran a print ad entitled, "Hand of the Free." The artwork showed a man's right hand resting atop a steering wheel, because with Dynaflow Drive he didn't have to use it to shift. Down at the floor, his left foot was free too—free of "the physical strain of pushing a clutch pedal hundreds of times a day in crowded traffic." In the push-button culture of the 1950s, easy, effortless, and fun driving became an important theme for Detroit.

What made the 1951 Buick ad novel was that it showed the Buick making driving easier for a man. Ads and commercials almost always depicted a woman receiving the benefits of automatic transmissions, power steering, and power brakes. A 1950 ad for Chevy, "Now Driving can be *Fun*," showed a woman driver decked out with gloves and a corsage and declared: "All in all the new Chevrolet is the fulfillment of every woman's dream of easier, safer, smoother driving." The 1951 Packard Patrician ad showed a woman at the wheel, while the copy gushed, "What a joy it is to *handle*! Effortless steering—and effortless performance." A 1952 DeSoto television commercial showed a woman swinging the steering wheel left and right with one hand, while Groucho Marx says, "It's as easy as dialing a phone!" Rounding out the decade, a smiling Helen Hayes, in front of a 1959 Lincoln Premiere Coupe, says, "Easiest role I ever played on the road: Touring in my new Lincoln." The ad continued with the actress admitting, "I'm only five feet two inches tall. . . . Most big cars overpower me. But not the new Lincoln. It seems so gentle and easy, I could almost drive it through a display of crystal and not break a single glass."

In 1953, Montgomery told her readers that an automatic transmission added about $200 to the cost of a new car; power steering, another $200; and power brakes, about $50. Most women, she wrote, would never want to do without these power assists, once they had tried them. That same year, a television commercial for the "DeSoto Automatic" hailed the automotive trinity of power steering, power brakes, and automatic transmissions by filming "a typical housewife" on a quick trip to the store. "On this one short ride, she had to make twenty-two turns." Those turns would have tired her out in an ordinary car, but with DeSoto power steering she made almost 50 percent fewer turns of the steering wheel. She had to make seventeen stops—"and seventeen times is a job." But the DeSoto's brakes took half the foot pressure of ordinary brakes, so no fatigue set in. Also, with her automatic, she didn't have to shift. The commercial asked, "Worn out from city driving?" Then it answered itself, buoyantly, "Not anymore!"

Detroit introduced other devices aimed at the woman driver. In a 1951 Christmas season ad, Ford advised husbands to purchase the

"Ford Turn Indicator" for "the woman on your list who hates opening the window to signal." This new device was a "fingertip control" that mounted on the steering post and caused lights to flash both front and back to signal turns. The turn signal, then, was a labor-saving option and a safety device. The woman pictured in a '52 Dodge ad says, "I wanted a car that considered *me*, a *woman*." She's happy as a lark with her new car, because it has "a parking brake that sets easily and releases with a simple twist of the wrist." Also, the Dodge had no starter button. It had "one-hand, ignition-key starting." Men enjoyed these same conveniences, but in advertisements and commercials it was almost always a woman's delicate hand that tuned the radio, lowered the window, moved the seat, shifted, or signaled a turn with a mere finger's worth of effortless ease.

Especially from 1950 through 1956 or 1957, Detroit did about all it could to make cars seem inviting—in their styling, appointments, and ease of operation—to women. They targeted ads and commercials at women, showcasing not only the beauty of the car but the woman as driver—the woman behind the wheel by herself, taking her man for a ride, or taking her women friends or kids for a drive. Many women succumbed to these ads and became drivers. Charlotte Montgomery, in her March 1952 *Good Housekeeping* column about "Learning to Drive," reported that, according to the Automobile Club of New York, the average pupil at various driving schools was "a woman of thirty-eight, married, and the mother of two children." Montgomery's monthly column on women and their cars was aimed at these newcomers, whom she felt needed to be schooled on everything from driving manners to lubrication schedules, to packing for trips, to reading maps, to driving on snow. She also offered encouragement and incentives. She ended her "Learning to Drive" column this way:

> Have you been wanting to drive the family car but hesitating to tackle the task of learning? Don't put it off any longer; you'll know endless freedom and pleasure when you no longer have to wait to be driven by someone else. You'll enjoy saying to your friends, "Yes, let's go. I'll drive."

*Good Housekeeping* dropped Montgomery's "The Woman and Her Car" feature in 1956. It was no longer needed. The older women who needed to learn how to drive *had* learned to drive, and teenage girls in America, like boys, were seeing a driver's license as a rite of passage and enrolling in the growing number of driver education classes across the country. In 1958, instead of running a feature for women on how to clean out a car, *Good Housekeeping* ran a feature, "HOT-ROD *terms for teen-age* GIRLS." If girls, boys, and cars were going to all get along, the girls had to learn car lingo. Here, girls could learn about Moon hubcaps, drag slicks, Hollywood mufflers, Glass-Packs, Nerf bars, and Deuce coupes.

In less than a decade, women had taken their place behind the wheel for good. They saw cars differently than men did and used them differently. But use them they did, and the lives of women and their families changed, just as the car changed. For six or seven years, Detroit marketed to women by developing labor-saving technologies, by redesigning and refitting car interiors, and by pushing the feminization of the car. After Detroit succeeded in luring women into the driver's seat, advertising shifted in the late 1950s to other themes. The "car as woman friendly," "car as home," and "car as fashion statement" ads and commercials became less frequent, while the "car as jet plane" commercials took off. Detroit emphasized bedazzling fins and exterior chrome more than interior appointments, emphasized power (ever larger V-8 engines) and speed more than ease of handling, and emphasized size over almost everything else.

By the 1960s, high school girls had seen their mothers driving a car every day, and they wanted to obtain their driver's license at age sixteen, just like the boys. The car had become central to the lives of families. Dads, moms, sons, and daughters all seemed to want and need an automobile, not just for the mere transportation it afforded but for the freedom it allowed. The women depicted in car ads and commercials in the 1960s were not amazed by the easy use of power steering and power brakes, because they were long familiar with power assists. They were not going to the store, weren't hauling the kids to school, and weren't picking up hubby at the commuter train station. Not anymore!

According to Detroit, they now lived a much more glamorous and exciting life. Women dressed in elegant fashions drove or rode in Cadillacs, Lincolns, or Imperials, and they arrived at the country club, estate house, or sidewalk art sale. Women dressed in sporty, casual fashions arrived not at a supermarket but at a sports car race, golf course, ski resort, or place where you could go up in a hot-air balloon. Women in bathing suits and even wet suits arrived at a beautiful beach, perhaps at a surfboard rental store. Smiling, attractive women enjoyed romantic, adventuresome dates with equally handsome young men. If the vehicle happened to be loaded with family, that family would be headed out on vacation, not on a trip to buy school clothes or shoes.

Much of this was a fantasy America, for sure, created by auto companies and their advertising agencies. It was an all-white America, with no people who were poor, or old, or plain, or obese, or poorly dressed—or who lived in a downtrodden neighborhood. But there was a kernel of truth in this America-as-advertised. Life was supposed to be more youthful and fun in the 1960s, and sexier too. It was the decade, after all, of the go-go dancer. Chrysler tried to sell the 1961 Plymouth as a "young, escape machine." A young woman of maybe twenty posed seductively next to the 1967 Pontiac Firebird. Ford tried to sell its 1967 "White Hot" model Ford by using a white-hot model—a very attractive young blonde dressed in a white fur coat and white boots, who leaned against the car. In the middle of the 1960s, perhaps the most ubiquitous symbol of the new, youthful American female was the Dodge Rebellion girl—pretty, pert, dressed in white, posed next to or on a car, holding a flintlock pistol or a fused bomb, or firing a cannon. Sprawled over the hood of a 1966 Dodge Coronet, holding a long saber or sword that was more than a tiny bit phallic, the Dodge girl symbolized that change or rebellion had arrived in the mid-1960s, for both cars and women.

# 5

## SAFETY CRUSADERS

My mother, Mary Atkinson, attended small rural schools in Indiana. She finished tenth grade in 1927, and that ended her formal education. She left Indiana and moved by herself to Los Angeles. In 1940 she migrated back to the Midwest and settled in Detroit. In both cities, she worked as a waitress or hostess in higher-end restaurants. Married for the first and only time in 1945, she gave birth to me in 1947. From the time I was a young boy, I knew she had skimped on her own education, but she would never skimp on mine. Mom was smart and well spoken. She had a quick wit. She had an extensive vocabulary and used near-perfect grammar. She was a good reader—and she read books to me. She read me children's books every night, so many times that I memorized some of them. Due to her, I soon learned to read and began selecting my own books. With my mom's support, I began reading way above my grade level, as they used to say.

Representatives of the Landmark Books series came by my grade school, Ella Sharp Park elementary, a couple of times a year. Published by Random House, the Landmark Books were well-written histories and biographies up to two hundred pages long. When the sales reps came, they spread the books out on tables in our gym. I started buying Landmark Books when I was seven. Mom gave me money to buy two, three, or even four books at a time. I circled the tables, searching for interesting titles and subjects. They had many books on the American Revolution, settling the West, and the Civil War. I read books about Ethan Allen and the Green Mountain Boys, Lewis and Clark, Kit

Carson, Davy Crocket, and Daniel Boone. The Landmark Book *Gettysburg* made me hungry to learn more about that famous battle. One of the last Landmark books I read was *The Story of D-Day, June 6, 1944*. It's worth noting, I think, that at age eleven, I spent two days at the Gettysburg battlefield, and when I was twenty-one, I visited Normandy and Omaha Beach.

My mom regularly drove me to the Summit Township Library in Vandercook Lake. She waited patiently while I made my choices. Long before being assigned Mark Twain's books in school, I found *The Adventures of Tom Sawyer* and *The Adventures of Huckleberry Finn*. In this little library I advanced to adult reading. Westerns were all the rage on television, and I found myself picking out Luke Short novels, like *Raiders of the Rim Rock*, and a Zane Grey book, *Riders of the Purple Sage*. I saw the movie *The Caine Mutiny* and read the 494-page novel by Herman Wouk. I saw the movie *The Spirit of St. Louis* and read Charles Lindburg's 567-page autobiography.

As an adolescent, I stumbled across a series of books written by Henry Gregor Felsen between 1950 and 1960. Felsen's juvenile fiction included *Hot Rod* (1950), *Street Rod* (1953), *The Cup of Fury* (later retitled *Rag Top*, 1954), *Crash Club* (1958), and *Boy Gets Car* (later retitled *Road Rocket*, 1960). Felsen's car books went into thousands of school and public libraries, and bookstores regularly stocked his paperbacks, which had colorful cover art that made the union of boys, girls, and cars seem so appealing. The books went through numerous printings and sold upward of six million copies. *Hot Rod* remained on the best-seller list of juvenile fiction for over two decades. Felsen's books sold like hotcakes because he wrote not only *of* boys who longed for cars—he wrote *for* boys who longed for cars. Whether painted in dull primer or glossy black or bright yellow, the hot rods depicted in Felsen's mid-America provided escape, attracted girls, elevated a boy's status, ran fast, and emitted deep, rumbling exhaust notes. For his segment of the juvenile fiction market, Felsen wrote of nothing less than the car-borne American Dream, as envisioned by postwar teens.

Felsen had street cred when it came to hot rods. He dedicated *Street Rod* to "my fellow members of the Iowa Timing Association," a promoter of drag racing. The author knew souped-up engines and gear ratios. In *Hot Rod*, Bud runs an old Ford coupe with a chopped top, a dropped front axle, a bored-out Merc mill having a new manifold and three carbs, a three-quarter race camshaft, and a high-compression head.

Felsen wrote about the '32 or '47 Fords that boys picked up for only $25 to $40 and turned into street rods. He wrote little of new cars from Detroit. Felsen not only ignored modern American cars; he ignored modern life as being lived in American suburbs. He did not write of upwardly mobile families having two-car garages attached to new ranch houses. Instead, Felsen wrote of small, one-cop towns in the Midwest, fictional towns nestled somewhere in Iowa, where the schools were old, farmland was never far away, and block-long downtowns rolled up their sidewalks when the sun went down, leaving kids with nothing to do and nowhere to go. Just a few hints of modernity reached these places, and they emanated from the West Coast. The prettiest gals in town hoped a talent scout would discover them at the local drug store and whisk them away to Hollywood, while the boys read car magazines and dreamed of building hot rods or customs just like California kids.

Felsen's characters weren't playing with radios, like kids did in the 1920s. They weren't struggling through the Depression in the 1930s or fighting the Germans and Japanese in the 1940s. Instead, like many teens across the country in the 1950s, they felt alone and isolated as they struggled to find their proper fit in their families and communities. Felson faulted small-town culture in the postwar period, because it offered sixteen- to eighteen-year-old boys little to do. Almost out of desperation, they turned to hot rodding for entertainment and thrills. The car became central to their lives; it was, in many ways, their home. They went looking for themselves in cars. Too often, however, what they found was trouble and danger. Felsen warned that a seductive street rod might kill its youthful driver, turn him into a juvenile delinquent, or at the very least drain him of time and money.

As I was reading my first Felsen book, *Street Rod*, I grew fond of the protagonist, Ricky. He was a good kid who struggled through difficult times. He was likeable. He becomes popular and builds a nice hot rod. Things are looking up for Ricky, and in the final pages I was looking for a happy conclusion. Then BAM! Felsen killed him off in a tragic accident. I was stunned. But then I got used to it, because killing young drivers and passengers in the most horrific ways became a habit with the author. He wrote of dead little towns and hopped-up cars that killed too many boys and girls.

Felsen set *Hot Rod* in Avondale, a small Iowa town with a single business street, still unpaved. Every night, the town fell dark and dead, as only two lights remained on. Pop Higgins's poolroom stayed open but was off-limits to teens because it served booze. The other light illuminated Jake's gas station and garage, where Bud Crayne, a high school senior, worked. Teens and younger boys congregated at Jake's. LaVerne, a cheerleader and wannabe Hollywood star, went to Jake's because Bud was her boyfriend, and "the only real excitement in Avondale was speeding with Bud, and exulting in the knowledge that her boy could drive faster and better than anyone else." Walt, one year out of high school, frequented Jake's to escape his family farm, where he was "just wasting his life." Walt didn't want to "sit home alone and read about hogs," so he'd hop into his Hudson, race over to Jake's, and slide to a stop on its gravel lot.

Dellville, the setting of both *Street Rod* and *The Cup of Fury*, was bigger than Avondale, but essentially the same, a small town initially patrolled by one old, fat cop. Dellville was pretty, with "big houses, big yards, quiet streets, and nice people." It had a square at its center that was busy during the day, but Dellville died at dusk. The stores all closed, except for the Dellville Drug. There was a light in the jail and a light in the café, open until eight. Dellville was "a town asleep with its mouth open before it even got good and dark." The awake ones, driving "around the square and around the square and *around* the square," included Ricky in his '39 Ford, Link in his yellow Chevy convertible, Chub in his black Ford Tudor, Sherm in his Plymouth, and Jerry in his Merc. Leaving the square, they went off "to race each other, or go to Missouri and smuggle back fireworks, or to tangle with other drivers in other towns." The boys were proof that Dellville was "a wonderful town for children—until they became big children." Then they were on their own and in cars.

Raccoon Forks, the setting for *Crash Club*, was "one of ten thousand little towns in the Middle West where country people did their small shopping." This community had 150 houses, two hundred trees, and a "bleak, dust-swept 'business district' two sun-baked blocks long." Unlike Avondale and Dellville, Raccoon Forks seemingly had a chance at the future, because an electronics company was maybe going to put a new plant there, which would deliver more jobs and housing. With higher tax revenues, Raccoon Forks could build a new high school, and that school's labs could teach the kids better science, which, thanks to Sputnik, was suddenly a priority across America. The elite teens of Raccoon Forks, however, paid no attention to a looming space race. Their myopic priorities were on winning drag races on the way to school.

In *Boy Gets Car*, Felsen never assigned a name to his fictional town, thus making it Anywhere, USA. Its James Audubon High School had seventeen classrooms and 431 students. This town was another island community surrounded by agricultural land. Woody, the main character, works after school candling eggs at the local dairy. Like Felsen's other towns, this one was filled with teenagers and cars, from sixteen-year-old Woody and his decrepit '47 Ford, purchased for $37.50, to Dan, a high school senior, and the '32 Ford that he had tricked out.

In *Hot Rod*, Bud, a poor kid, lives with an uncle because both his parents are dead. For him, "happiness reached its peak when he could express it in terms of speed and roaring power, the pull of his engine, the whistle of the wind in his ears, and the glorious sensation of free flight." Whenever Bud is unhappy, moody, or feeling put-upon, he turns to his hot rod for release: "Not a day passed without Bud's taking time for a spin. . . . In some ways these daily sessions on the road were his hours of meditation, of true self-expression, the balm for his soul and the boast of his spirit. In these flying hours he had sought himself out, molded himself into what he was, and found his creed."

In *Street Rod*, young Ricky, just a few months past his sixteenth birthday, hates having to mooch rides from friends because he doesn't have his own set of wheels. "If I only had a car," Ricky says to himself, repeatedly. "If he had a car, he could escape. . . . To where? It didn't have to be to anywhere. Just to ride around and be free and equal and *know* he could go anywhere." As soon as he gets his car, Ricky is fulfilled, proud and daring.

In *Crash Club*, Mike hates his freshman and sophomore years of high school. The upperclassmen make him feel inferior athletically, and all the good-looking girls cling to the jocks, without looking at him. But before his junior year, things change. He gets older, bigger, and stronger. Now it is his turn to be a prominent jock. Also, he buys a little bronze coupe and hops it up. When school starts, Mike happily discovers that he now belongs to the "new ruling class in school." Mike is a varsity man in football, and "best and most miraculous of all," he has established himself and his coupe "as the top boy-car combination in the school."

In *Boy Gets Car*, Woody knows that in high school, "to be on foot was to be a helpless swimmer in shark-infested waters. There was only one way to be safe, and equal, and *somebody*, and that was to have a car." His dad downplays the importance of having a car at age sixteen, but Woody better understands "what a car meant to a boy in this day and age. It *was* the difference between being a boy and a man."

The first car, the hot rod, was so seductive because of what boys could do *to* it and *with* it. The hot rod gave them goals, plans, skills, pride, and self-expression. It brought them freedom, independence, and escape from their school, their dull town, and their parents. It brought them excitement, girls, and status. Maybe it even promised them a career in automotive engineering. Felsen laid all these prospects out, but didn't spin yarns full of endless teenage joy rides. He made it clear that the teenage hot-rodder traveled a road full of deep and dangerous potholes. He wrote morality tales full of warnings. He was, at his heart, a safety crusader.

In *Boy Gets Car*, Felsen warns that you'd best be careful of what you wish for, because you might get it. Sixteen-year-old Woody has made dozens of plastic car models, and now he is desperate to move up to the real thing. He doesn't want his folks' car; he doesn't want a good car. He wants an old car with mechanical and cosmetic needs, so he and his car club buddies can turn it into a gem. His dad argues that car ownership will cost Woody too much time and money, but Woody dismisses all warnings and buys a broken-down two-door '47 Ford.

Woody is euphoric for a while. He feels older and better about himself and his place in the world. "Things sure changed," he thinks, "when a guy owned a car." But slowly, a troublesome reality sets in. His car club buddies are of no help in fixing up this machine, and it needs plenty of fixing. Woody will have to throw much time and money at his Ford that barely runs. It needs a new clutch. New exhaust. New fuel pump. New brakes. New tires. Woody takes a second job at the dairy to earn money to pour into "Sidekick," but finds he has no spare time. He has stirrings for pretty Sandra but hasn't got the time for both girl and car. He finds out that he doesn't own his car as much as it owns him. Woody discovers that "working on a car is all right, but there's more to life than that." So, he sells his Ford to another car-hungry boy of sixteen. Suddenly he feels unfettered and triumphant: "He could be a boy again, try out for teams at school, spend some time with his girl when he wanted to, and live his life the way he wanted to." For the first time since buying a car, he is free.

For Felsen, the car presented other, far more serious problems to teens than the consumption of time and money. In *Hot Rod*, the author sent out a warning about and for teenagers: "Once they got in cars, on the highway, it was as though they had gone mad." They feared too little and raced too much. They exhibited antisocial behavior. They scoffed at traffic laws, saw no need to hang an arm out the window to signal turns or stops, had no respect for village cops or highway police, and chafed at parental concerns and controls. They loved the roar of their loud exhausts as they passed through town, and they cursed anyone who got in their way. They saw a world full of adversaries—including other hot-rodders—who must be put down. They were aggressive with their cars or fists. They verged on juvenile delinquency and sometimes crossed the line. Time after time, they gambled and took risks. They never learned anything or got any smarter, until some very high price was paid.

Felsen avoided the issue of teenage drinking and driving. For him, the pitfalls of teenage driving resulted not from six-packs of cheap beer, but from hormones and immaturity. Felsen also dodged the issue of unwanted pregnancies resulting from teenage sex in back seats on back roads. Interestingly, he did write a book, *Two and the Town*, about a high school couple that "goes too far" and she gets pregnant. But on their fateful night of passion, they were pedestrians and did it on the grass, not in some old Studebaker. Girls inhabited Felsen's car books, and the boys wanted them—but not in an overtly carnal way. The boys don't park their cars on Lovers' Lane, hoping to "feel up" some sweet young thing. The girls are comely passengers, pretty adornments, rather like raccoon tails flying from radio antennas or a set of chromed wheels. If a boy wanted a girl at all, it was more for status than sex. The exception to this rule was Link Aller, who first appeared in *Street Rod* and then again, a year later, in a sequel, *The Cup of Fury*. In the second book, aimed at a somewhat older audience, Aller has the misfortune of being caught in the act. He is atop sixteen-year-old Darlene in his yellow Chevy at 2:00 a.m. when her father, a brutal cop, shines a light into the car—and subsequently delivers Link a terrible beating.

Felsen was in his mid-thirties when he wrote *Hot Rod*, and he had a rather curious background for a prolific writer of juvenile fiction. He was an ex-communist and an ex-Marine. Maybe that background toughened him up when he wrote about social problems. He didn't write romantic tales. He entertained young readers fascinated with cars but informed them in a didactic way that the seductive hot rod culture threatened their lives. A boy reader didn't even have to get to page one to pick up on Felsen's safety message; it was right there in the front matter. He dedicated *Hot Rod* to the Des Moines Safety Council, and the front of *Street Rod* carried a to-the-point message:

> This manuscript is being mailed from Des Moines on Friday afternoon, January 16, 1953. . . . If the printing schedule permits, this book will be published sometime in July. Between the time it is mailed today as a manuscript, and read by the first purchaser as a book, perhaps 150 young people will have died in this state [Iowa] by the automobile, close to 500 been injured and maimed, and a thousand or more arrested, fined, jailed, or deprived of their licenses.
>
> Is there an answer, a way to reduce the toll of young lives that a motorized civilization collects as the price of transportation . . . ? There are answers, and there are ways. Some of them are written about here.

Boys reading *Hot Rod* and *Street Rod* would have been well advised not to get too emotionally attached to Felsen's characters, like I did at first, because few of them survived. In *Hot Rod*, Bud Crayne leads the pack of young drivers in Avondale. A gifted mechanic and a skillful driver, Bud is just too cocky and reckless as he races from town to town, outrunning the police and forcing other drivers off the road. Because of Bud, taking risks becomes part of the Avondale car culture. Bud preaches speed, and other kids embrace his sermon. At the garage he talks to twelve-year-olds Jimmy and Kenny, who worship him. Bud tells them, "Let me give you some advice kids, and you'll never go wrong." He delivers his secret to sharp driving: "Power, that's it. Nine out of ten people think about their brakes right away. Forget your brakes. The way out of almost any tight spot is power." Soon after learning that the accelerator, not the brake, is their salvation, Jimmy and Kenny find a new Buick outside Pop's poolroom with the keys in it. They hop in to take the Buick around the block, but soon they are out on the highway, seeing how fast Jimmy can make the car go. Jimmy tries to drive like Bud through a dangerous S-curve going under a railroad viaduct. The boys don't make it. The Buick crashes into a stone wall and is thrown back onto the road, which fills with "broken metal and splintered glass. The colorless fluid of gasoline, the thick black streams of oil, and the dark red rivulets of blood." Two are dead, with more to come.

Two cars full of teens play a game of automobile hide-and-seek one dark night on the highways and dirt roads outside Avondale. One car is given a five-minute start, and then the pursuer heads out. Can the first car return to town without being spotted by the second? The two cars lurk in the dark, listening for the revved-up engine of the other. The one starts up, the other joins in, and to hide their positions, both cars run with their headlights off. At a bend in the highway, the cars collide head-on at high speed. Eight teenagers die instantly. Felson describes the gruesome wreckage of bodies. Marge "looked like a limp, ripped-open bag of laundry hung half-way out of a rear window." The steering column speared Ralph, and "in the pile of mangled steel, wedged in between jagged sheet steel on one side, and red hot metal on the other, was what had been the shapely black head and dainty face of LaVerne."

Walt lay pinned inside his wrecked car, "beyond knowing that battery acid ran in his eyes. . . . Somehow the lower half of his body had been twisted completely around and hung by a shred of skin." A few days later, Avondale buried its dead and their dreams. Ralph was buried "with his dream of a college career in sports." LaVerne was buried with "her dream of escape to Hollywood." Avondale buried Walt "with his dream of getting away from the farm" and going to California. And the Plain Jane girl, Marge, was buried "with her dream of being popular."

In *Street Rod*, subtitled "A story of young America's passion for speed," Felsen kills off several more teens. Some deaths are incidental, in the sense that they do not happen to main characters—they just happen in the neighborhood. Mr. Madison picks up the paper one day, and the front page, along with a picture of a smashed car, carries the headline: "Teen-Ager Killed, Three Critically Injured in Wreck—Race on Country Road Ends Fatally for Farm Youth." Ricky Madison's father says, "There's a story like that almost every day. Won't they ever learn?" A bit later, the radio blares the bad news that a race on a gravel road has led to tragedy and a seventeen-year-old boy and sixteen-year-old girl have been killed returning home from a roller-skating rink.

Felsen saves the worst for the last few pages in *Street Rod*. Ricky Madison is a good kid. Before Ricky buys his car, his dad opposes it. "When boys your age buy old cars and soup them up, somebody gets killed sooner or later," says Mr. Madison. After Ricky goes ahead and buys his '39 Ford, his mother worries. "She did not believe in luck, yet she felt that it was bad luck, tragic luck that Ricky sought to revive a machine that belonged with the dead of its kind." She fears that when that old car goes on to die, it will carry Ricky with it. Ricky indeed goes through careless, reckless times with his old Ford, but then he changes. He launches a car club that promotes safety on the road. With the help of his girlfriend, Sharon, he turns his old clunker into a pretty street rod, pink and copper over a brown interior, that has a high-speed rear end and a souped-up engine with three carbs, Edelbrock high-compression heads, a race cam, and a high-tech ignition. Ricky's coupe wins first place at a car show in Des Moines, and he and Sharon are on cloud nine. He sees a bright future for himself, working with automobiles.

Just before Ricky leaves the auto show, his buddies from Dellville show up, accompanied by Link Aller. Link's yellow Chevy convertible always led the parade of cars at Dellville, and Link always put Ricky and his car down. On the ride back home, while Sharon sleeps next to him, Ricky sees lights gaining on him from behind. He is sure it is Link, trying to catch up with him to bump him or pass him by. Ricky has never been able to beat Link at anything, and now, finally, with his souped-up engine, here is his chance. He can't resist the old urge. He hits the gas pedal and races off. All he had to do was "run the wheels off Link for once and for all," and then "he'd never have to do it again." Ricky pulls away from Link and continues screaming like a dive bomber back toward town. Then his car drifts to the left, and Ricky is helpless to stop it. The coupe leaves the road and launches into the air. Ricky's head meets Sharon's with a bone-splintering crunch, and they are both unconscious when the coupe clears the low end of a bridge and drops into the black water, upside down.

Felsen just couldn't leave a happy ending alone. To press the safety issue, to again prove that "once they got in cars, it was as though they had gone mad," Felsen sent Ricky and Sharon to a watery grave. The ending of *Street Rod* shocked and saddened me and no doubt most of Felsen's youthful readers. We were blindsided by the death of a boy who had worked hard to have it all, only to lose it all by acting stupid one too many times.

The safety message continued in Felsen's later car books. In *Crash Club*, when Mike says that a little crack-up is nothing to get excited about, his dad says, "That's the kind of attitude that leads to forty thousand highway deaths per year." Near the end of the book, Dave "Outlaw" Galt—who had killed two passengers while he was driving—is himself killed, and decapitated, while a back seat passenger in a car-train accident. Felsen's safety crusade continues in *Boy Gets Car*, when Woody's dad passes along the information that "the peacetime automobile has killed more of our young people than all the enemy guns in all the wars we've ever fought." He tells his son, "You're not a child anymore. Your car isn't a toy. Every time you drive away, your life, the lives of your passengers, the lives of everyone you meet, are in your hands. Don't ever forget that, Woody."

Felsen wrote in an era when auto fatalities were steeply on the rise. Before World War II, fatalities reached nearly forty thousand per year by 1937, but that number dipped sharply during the last years of the Depression and throughout the war, falling to as low as twenty-four thousand in 1944. When the postwar era put more people and cars back on the road, a 50 percent increase in traffic fatalities occurred between 1945 and 1946. By 1956, the annual fatality rate again reached forty thousand; a decade later it was in the fifty thousand range. Americans in the postwar period recognized that auto fatalities and injuries had become a national problem, and individuals and institutions—the government, myriad safety councils, educators, and the insurance industry—started looking for solutions. In 1946, Harry Truman called to order the President's Highway Safety Conference, which drew two thousand delegates from forty-eight states. That conference developed an "Action Plan for Highway Safety." An important part of the plan was to provide high school driver education "as an integral part of the curriculum for students approaching legal driving age." Felsen's work was informed by the new safety movement, and he wove emerging safety programs into his novels.

In *Hot Rod*, teacher Guy Cole and police officer Ted O'Day strive to get driver education added to Avondale's high school curriculum. If young drivers learned good habits before being turned loose in cars, maybe they would never learn bad habits, such as aggressive driving and speeding. They would learn the "proper attitude" for driving, learn to always be courteous and thoughtful, which would help reduce "teenicide" on the highway. Driver education in schools had been around since the 1920s but really took off in the late 1940s and 1950s. Felsen pushed for driver education in *Hot Rod* just when this safety program was going into thousands of high schools across the country. In 1947–48, 3,055 high schools offered driver education. The number of participating schools rose to 8,218 in 1951–52; to 10,280 in 1955–56; and to 12,278 in 1958–59.

Felsen knew that hot rod culture had migrated across the country from California, thanks to car magazines and B movies like *Dragstrip Girl.* Many teenage males raced their hot rods on public roads. Parents, police, and driver education classes could not stop this behavior, so some advocated taking racing off the streets and moving it to drag strips. Felsen knew that real hot-rod clubs in some spots around the country had set up drag strips with the support of local communities and police. He thought enough of the idea to write about it in *Street Rod.* Eighteen boys organize the Dellville Timing Association (DTA), a car club "dedicated to sportsmanlike driving, courtesy, cooperation with the police, [and] observance of all laws." The DTA petitions Dellville's city council to close part of the road to Cosgrove once every week or two, so they can use that strip of asphalt to hold quarter-mile drags. The DTA makes a good case for a drag strip. Many boys "own automobiles that have been modified with speed equipment," and "it is well known that there is a good deal of fast and sometimes reckless driving in and around Dellville." The DTA members promise they will cease racing on public highways if they have a better, safer place to do it.

Felsen knew that this idea's time had not come in most communities. There was a growing generation gap in the postwar years. Older folks who had lived through the Depression and fought in World War II wanted to rein in teenagers and make them toe the line; they did not want youngsters to make the rules or enjoy too much freedom or the power of self-determination. The Dellville city council scoffs at the idea of turning a public road into a drag strip—and before the idea can come up again, Ricky, head of the Dellville Timing Association, is killed in his street rod.

Felsen was not alone in showing how undisciplined driving led to young, dead bodies on the highway. While his novels killed off fictional teenagers, the driver education films of Richard Wayman, projected in thousands of high schools across the country starting in 1959, tried to scare teens into driving cautiously by showing gory images of mangled cars and *real* dead bodies filmed, in color, along Ohio highways.

Wayman's work defined the blood-and-gore genre of the safety film at the end of the 1950s. A one-time accountant and amateur photographer, Wayman turned a creepy fascination into a business that traded in death. In 1954, he stopped at an accident scene in Ohio involving a train and a motorcycle rider. To help police document the accident, Wayman pulled out his camera and photographed the carnage. Over the next few years, Wayman regularly showed up to photograph the remnants of automobiles and people. In 1958, he put his disturbing still photos into a slide presentation, which he shared with Ohio state police posts and with local high school students in driver education classes. Having upgraded from a still camera to a sixteen-millimeter movie camera, a year later he released his first color drivers education film, *Signal 30*—the term police used over their radios to indicate a fatal accident. The success of *Signal 30* prompted Wayman and his small production crew to chase accidents and put out additional films, such as *Mechanized Death* in 1961 and *Wheels of Tragedy* in 1963.

There was nothing subtle about these films. They marched from accident to accident to accident. The films never blamed the road surface or car—an accident was always the driver's fault. An unsympathetic narrator, heard but never seen, lays out the causes: "The finale to the tragedy comes as the lad is placed in the rubber sack, a last offering to the great god, Speed." Speed kills, as does reckless driving, careless driving, scoffing at traffic laws, running stop signs, misjudging curves, haste, and inattention. "Death is forever. Take time to think!"

The narrator's words were matched by images of carnage: drivers or passengers crushed by a door, impaled on a steering column, or dragged lifeless from beneath an overturned vehicle and lifted onto a stretcher or put in a body bag. The bodies of two different men are pulled from demolished trucks that had burst into flames. On one blackened face, the remnants of a mouth appear contorted into a permanent scream. Here, the narrator's words are horrific as well: "So the sickening, stiffened charred mass that once was a man is removed." In one film the narrator speaks directly to the audience: "We're cruel, cold, and harsh, you say? You shouldn't be made to see and hear this? How could we give a better lesson on carelessness? See for yourself how sordid and sickening impending death can be." Students watching these films saw many corpses. Even worse, sometimes they saw *impending* death and *heard* accident victims in their death throes.

When approaching my sixteenth birthday, I had heard about these bloody highway safety movies. I think every kid had. But thankfully I did not have to watch them in my driver's ed course at Danville High. We skipped the gory movies and studied the rules of the road and received behind-the-wheel training. Our instructor, Mr. Mathiesen, took two or three of us out in a car, and each of us had a chance to drive while he closely supervised. Mr. Mathisen, in his early forties, stood six foot five and exuded positivity and calmness. He never got flustered when a student driver flirted with disaster. He always seemed to be in control of everything. I thought his imposing demeanor no doubt was born out of his athletic past. In the early 1940s he was a center for the "Whiz Kids" basketball team at the University of Illinois. He captained the team in 1942–43, when Illinois went 17–1, and he was an honorable mention All American.

As student drivers, we didn't immediately head to busy downtown or out to the Interstate. We started in a less challenging environment: a cemetery near the school. It had many curves to negotiate and many intersections where we practiced stopping, signaling, and left and right turns. In my first ride with Mr. Mathisen, I was taking the cemetery's corners at maybe ten miles an hour. Fifteen at most. But I was acting as if I was under tremendous g-forces. When I turned left, I leaned left and cocked my head to the left. When I turned right, I leaned right. "Larry," Mr. Mathisen said. "Just sit up straight! This is not a high-speed race!"

A few months later I found myself at the driver's license bureau in our town. The devil himself had located it where several streets intersected at weird angles. Nothing would be easy. My mom drove me there and waited while I took the written exam. How many car lengths should you stay behind a car in front of you if you are going fifty miles per hour? A yellow, triangular sign means what? Where do you stop when you come up to a marked crosswalk? I passed that test and moved on to the driving part. An examiner got in the passenger seat of the Hillman and directed me around town for maybe fifteen minutes. I worried about working the clutch smoothly. I worried about the complex intersection and about parallel parking when we returned to where we started. I pulled back and forth a time or two to get between two cars and close to the curb. I stopped and turned the ignition off. Mercifully, the examiner did not make me wait long, "Congratulations! You passed," he said. I drove my mom home.

I had a license! I had freedom, just like all the boys in Felsen's novels. I was unlike them in many ways. I didn't live in a tiny town that offered me nothing to do at night. I didn't go to a small school. I didn't feel that my future was dim or limited. I didn't flirt with juvenile delinquency. And I didn't buy an old Ford or Merc to hop up. I didn't have the money or skills needed to build a hot rod. No, as I drove out into the world, I was at the wheel of a five-year-old Hillman Minx.

In the 1950s, Americans became familiar with British cars, especially sports cars like MG and Triumph. Before the arrival of the German-made Volkswagen, these cars were the most popular imports sold in the United States. Hillman cars, however, were not sports cars, and Americans paid little attention to them, except for my family. My uncle, my brother-in-law, and my dad owned a total of four Hillmans—four of the twenty-seven thousand sold here in the 1950s. Our 1958 Hillman Minx was what the Brits called a "Saloon car." We'd call it a four-door sedan. It was by no means the least expensive foreign car. It had good chrome, a good two-tone paint job, and leather seats. At a time when American cars were getting lower, it had a very high top. The top was so high, in fact, that it made the front and rear ends look out of scale. Its ninety-one-cubic-inch engine produced fifty horsepower, transmitted to the rear wheels by a four-speed manual transmission mounted on the column. Its top speed was eighty miles per hour, and it went 0 to 60 in twenty-two seconds, which seemed like a lifetime to me.

I'd like to claim that the cautionary tales of Felsen's novels, the sorrow of "Teen Angel" and other Top 40 songs about dead teenage drivers, and the tutelage of Mr. Mathisen made me a cautious, careful driver from the start—but they didn't. Even the little Hillman didn't slow me down. I remember the day after getting my license, I raced the Hillman down a gravel lane toward the baseball stadium where my high school team was playing. Stones flew off the lane and into the grass.

At the parking lot, I skidded to a stop. I was so full of myself and my little car.

Just a few months later, racing around a curvy dirt road, I rolled my brother-in-law's Hillman convertible, wheels to wheels, with five sixteen-year-olds in it. Rick suffered a gash in his arm, but the rest of us miraculously came out without a scratch. The totaled Hillman gallantly crawled back to its owner's house, and then died in the driveway, never to see a road again. All brother-in-law Ben had to say to me at the back door was, "I thought Stirling Moss had retired from road racing!" The famous British race car driver Stirling Moss had indeed retired from Formula I racing just the year before—and I should have retired from fast driving too. I should have learned my lesson and been thankful nobody was killed. But sixteen-year-olds are prone to think fate will always be kind, prone to think they are immortal, and they often fail to learn their lessons, even obvious ones writ large.

The simple truth was that there was no way to make Americans, young or old, into perfect drivers. You could educate, berate, scare, and ticket people all you wanted—accidents would still happen. That being the case, safety advocates in the 1950s went beyond trying to modify the behavior of drivers. To cut the number of accidents and make them more survivable, they looked at building safer roads and safer cars.

In the late 1940s and early 1950s, engineers and highway building agencies began formalizing modern designs for expressways. The Federal Aid Highway Act of 1944 supported highway improvements and authorized the construction, once the war was out of the way, of forty-one thousand miles of a "National System of Interstate Highways." This act, due to a lack of funding, fostered little construction, but did lead to more highway planning on the part of the Public Roads Administration and the American Association of State Highway Officials (AASHO). In 1950, AASHO published *Policies on Geometric Highway Design*, which included the chapter, "Design Standards for the National System of Interstate Highways." These new roads, when built, were supposed to move traffic more quickly and more safely. Depending on terrain and congestion, they would accommodate a minimum speed of forty to fifty miles per hour, and a maximum speed of sixty to seventy. They would be limited-access highways and maintain grade separation at railroad and highway crossings. Curves would be gentle, sight distances would be long, hill gradients would be reduced, a minimum of two wide lanes with wide shoulders would go in each direction, and the lanes would usually be divided with a median.

After passage of the Federal Aid Highway Act of 1956, construction began on the National System of Interstate and Defense Highways. Begun during the administration of President Dwight David Eisenhower, the Interstate program at the time was the largest, most ambitious public works project ever undertaken in the United States. It also symbolized the nation's growing commitment to and reliance upon cars and trucks, moving over roads and burning fossil fuels, to haul a nation's people and its goods. This was big government at work, authorized to spend $25 billion to build forty-one thousand miles of modern Interstates over a dozen years, with funding from a Highway Trust Fund whose revenues came from taxes on gasoline and diesel fuels, lubricants, and auto parts and tires. On the Interstates, cars and trucks could travel at higher speeds than along earlier highways, most of which had two lanes, oncoming traffic, innumerable intersections, blind corners, and poor cambers. They traveled faster, yet safer. Because of their design, Interstates both prevented accidents and lessened their consequences. Taking gentle curves of large radius, a driver was less likely to send his car into a spin. But if he did, he was also less likely to hit a tree or an oncoming car.

With forty-one thousand miles of safer roads on the horizon, designers, engineers, universities, insurance companies, physicians, and car companies set their sights on making the car safer. In the late 1940s and early 1950s, when presenting their contributions to automotive safety, car companies pointed out the strength of materials used in their sturdy designs, plus a stable ride, safety glass, and good brakes. Notably absent at this time was any reference to features that protected passengers from colliding with their car, or being ejected from their car, once the car had collided with something else. Crash survivability was not on the radar.

That began to change by the mid-1950s. Researchers at UCLA

conducted crash tests to study deceleration rates and the damage done to the structures of cars and to test dummies riding inside them. In 1954, they concluded that "there has been no significant automotive engineering contribution to the safety of motorists since about the beginning of World War II." In 1955, the *Journal of the American Medical Association* published the article "Prevention, the only cure for head injuries resulting from automobile accidents," written by a noted California neurosurgeon, C. Hunter Shelden. The article's abstract noted that "physicians of this country are up in arms against the ever-increasing number of fatalities occurring daily in our streets and highways as the result of automobile accidents." Neurosurgeons saw innumerable accident victims, because "Head and neck injuries account for nearly 70% of all auto crash fatalities." According to Shelden, lessening fatalities and reducing the severity of survivors' injuries could be achieved only by redesigning the passenger compartment. His article did not mince words on the subject: "There is almost no feature of the interior design of a car that provides for safety. The doors, seats, cushions, knobs, steering wheel and even the overhead structure [door and window pillars and roof] are so poorly constructed from the safety standpoint that it is surprising anyone escapes from an automobile accident without serious injury." The doctor then prescribed improvements. Install recessed steering wheels, so the top of the steering column is substantially lower than the collapsing rim of the wheel. Use better door locks. Install roll bars and reinforce the roof. Equip all cars with retractable seat belts and passive restraints, like an airbag, and, to reduce whiplash, mount elevated headrests to the seats.

On the other side of the country, at Cornell University, engineers were thinking similar thoughts. In 1942, Cornell's Aeronautical Laboratory had started investigating the crash injuries suffered by pilots in aircraft cockpits. A decade later, the lab was researching the causes of automobile injuries and deaths, and how to better package and protect automobile drivers and passengers. With the help of the medical school and a new project called Automotive Crash Injury Research, Cornell collected data on real-life accidents and victims, while also conducting its own crash tests. Cornell, like Dr. Shelden, easily concluded that the secondary collision was the problem. After a car crashed, its occupants then crashed into the steering column, dash, windshield—or maybe the pavement, if the doors flew open. Most fatalities resulted from head injuries. In most fatal accidents, one or more doors opened. In about 20 percent of all injury-producing accidents, the car rolled over. In head-on accidents, the steering post was "a harpoon aimed at the driver's chest." Anything that projected out from the dash could cause injury to the body. One discouraging finding—the kind that would catch the attention of automakers, whether they wanted to learn it or not—was that in serious crashes, cars built in 1950–54 suffered a *higher frequency of fatalities* than cars built in the 1940s.

Safety researchers outside the auto industry in the 1950s had no trouble identifying the automotive design and engineering flaws that killed and maimed people. The problems were not hard to find, and the solutions, from one study to the next, were pretty much the same. Keep the shell of the car intact, and with new safety locks, keep the doors closed. Put in collapsible steering wheel rims that would absorb energy and help bring the driver to a stop before hitting the steering wheel hub or steering post. Pad dashboards. Recess controls and knobs. Strengthen pillars and roofs and maybe incorporate roll bars. Install seat belts. Cornell went beyond other safety researchers, and with the support of the Liberty Mutual Insurance Company, it built a safety car of its own (built around the chassis and skin of a much-modified 1955 Ford) that debuted in 1957 and had some truly novel safety features. It put the driver in the middle of the car, instead of on the far left. It took away the steering wheel and column and designed safety levers positioned where they would not impale anyone. It used bucket seats, rather than bench seats, because they better held passengers in place. And one seat, which a child might use, faced backward from the central portion of the car and had a head restrain to help prevent whiplash.

Cornell's safety car toured the country and was written up in magazines like *Popular Science*. The university's research and prototype safety car generated more interest in the relationship between poor automotive design and high death and injury rates. Coat-tailing the Cornell safety work, in 1956 many Detroit automakers debuted cars that would better protect occupants in a crash. Ford made a big deal of its new standard equipment and optional safety features. Other companies gave them a soft launch and said little or nothing at all about them in advertisements and commercials. Apparently, some marketing departments and advertising agencies were not sure if they wanted to remind consumers that car travel could be deadly, forty thousand times a year.

In 1956, Chrysler Corporation's advertising, for all its marques, heavily emphasized "aerodynamic" fins, "Forward Look" design, and push-button drive. Almost as an afterthought, a limited number of Chrysler Corporation ads mentioned new, standard-equipment "Life-Guard" door locks and the availability of optional "Safety Seat Belts." More often than mentioning seat belts, Chrysler ads listed the location of the new push-button drive as an important safety feature. It was located on the dash to the left of the steering wheel, where "*Only the driver can touch it*." No little tyke could punch the drive button or try to change gears once the car was in motion.

General Motors and all its various divisions played down the importance of automobile safety. A car shopper in 1956 would have had trouble finding information on new safety features found on GM cars, even though there were some. In 1956, Oldsmobile retained the safety-padded instrument panel it had introduced in 1955. Buick offered optional seat belts. Chevy certainly did not sell safety. Its ads screamed, "The hot one's even hotter!" Chevy in 1956 sold "youth, beauty, Chevrolet, *action*"—"dynamite action"—and the most important new feature, shared with other GM cars, was the four-door hardtop. Chevrolets came with safety door latches and optional seat belts, but Chevy ads stressed rapid get-up-and-go as a safety feature. When passing, "you can rely on Chevrolet's trigger-quick acceleration to surge safely past the other car."

Studebaker in 1956 offered safety door locks, padded seat backs, safety glass rearview mirrors, and optional seat belts. As one of the small independents, Studebaker surely had its own independent idea about how to sell safety. Studebaker advertised that the corporation would purchase and pay the premium for a $20,000 life insurance policy on the original owner "against accidental death occurring while driving and arising out of an accident involving his Studebaker." Another independent, American Motors (Hudson and Nash), pretty much bucked the new safety trend by not including seat belts as an option. Its vice president of automotive research and engineering, in the September 1955 issue of *Public Safety*, recalled that Nash had included a seat-belt option in its 1949 models: "However, the public did not accept them, claiming that seat belts were a 'nuisance' in ordinary driving." For American Motors, what didn't sell in 1949 probably wouldn't sell in 1956, so the company chose not to reintroduce seat belts.

The Ford Motor Company, more than other automakers, kept up with Cornell's safety work, and Ford donated at least $200,000 to support it. (Chrysler and the federal government also supported the Cornell program.) Prior to introducing its 1956 models, Ford undertook two years of safety research and crash testing on its own. At times Ford used a 167-pound block of wood to simulate an average driver's body impacting a steering wheel, and at other times it used more anthropomorphically correct dummies. In cooperation with Wayne State University's Medical School, and with assistance from the Air Force's Aero Medical Laboratory, Ford also tested impact effects on cadavers. Following this work, in September 1955, Ford held a National Safety Forum and Crash Demonstration in Detroit and Dearborn. The forum summarized the findings of the Cornell and Ford safety research, and up to 150 attendees watched the host company wreck Ford Fairlanes, equipped with crash dummies, in a pair of staged, two-car collisions. Then the participants were introduced to the package of "Life Guard Design" safety features to be offered on 1956 Fords.

The features Ford introduced at the Safety Forum, and later pushed heavily in advertisements, included deeply dished steering wheels and double-grip door locks, which were standard equipment, and padded dashboards, padded sun visors, and seat belts (front and rear), which were optional. The 1956 Fords had other "silent" safety improvements that weren't highlighted in ads: rearview mirrors that would pivot out of the way if struck by a passenger and were designed to prevent broken mirror glass from flying out of the frame; redesigned front and back seat supports to keep them from coming loose; and an optional child-proof safety-locking device for rear doors. Ford ads stressed the importance of Life Guard Design:

> At last! A car dedicated to "Safety First." . . . The '56 Ford! More than two years ago, Ford determined to find the causes of accident injuries . . . so a safer car could be built. It was found that most serious injuries were caused by drivers being thrown against the steering post, riders being thrown forward against hard surfaces within the car, or being thrown *from* the car. See how new Lifeguard Design gives you added protection from these hazards.

The Ford Motor Company pushed safety far more than any other automaker. When my dad and I went to downtown Jackson to look at new cars in the autumn of 1955, at the Ford showroom we saw a big banner that read, "'56 FORD *Lifeguard Design*—A FORD FIRST for *Safety First*." Ford sent out press releases to newspapers and magazines. It ran numerous Life Guard ads in national magazines. It produced a twenty-page sales brochure to help sell customers on safety. Interestingly, the Ford Motor Company did put limits on its corporate safety push. It used the "Life Guard Design" package and program only to help sell basic Fords. It did not use its Life Guard Design to help sell Mercurys, Thunderbirds, Lincolns, or Continental Mark IIs, even if those cars (especially Mercury) had some or all of the Ford safety features. While the corporation made safety door locks and dished steering wheels standard equipment, consumers had to pay more if they wanted seat belts, a padded instrument panel, and padded visors. Saving somebody's life didn't come for free; the bottom line counted. Ford didn't want to raise its base price, which would have made it less competitive with other cars in the low-price field, especially Chevy. If Ford spent more to make a safer car, it needed to recoup some of that cost by convincing customers to buy safety options.

At the National Safety Forum in September 1955, Benson Ford pointed out to attendees that it had "taken a lot of diligent and devoted effort and considerable expense" to research, design, manufacture, and install safety features and build safer interiors. Ford was not willing to give away a full package of Life Guard safety features to consumers, but it was willing to give away its safety research and knowledge to other auto companies. Benson Ford said, "We hope other companies will use it and, if they can, improve upon it. This is one kind of competition we want to help out." He continued, "I think if we can get this hard-hitting automobile industry to fight for safety leadership, we can achieve some really wonderful results." The trouble was, other car companies weren't ready to fight for safety leadership. They still wanted to fight for market share by selling fun on the open road, size, style, status, comfort, and power.

Ford's Life Guard Design program met with some success in 1956. It earned *Motor Trend* magazine's award for the year's most important car advance. Forty-five percent of new Ford buyers in 1956 ordered their cars with the optional padded dash and visors, and the company noted that, "No optional feature in Ford history caught on so fast in the first year." But the seat belt option did not fare nearly as well; only 10 percent of new Fords rolled out of dealerships with safety lap belts. Buyers, it seems, still thought of seat belts as a nuisance, particularly so, perhaps, because these belts didn't simply click together. Instead, the nylon fabric at the end of one belt had to be threaded through the metal buckle, with its gripping apparatus, and then pulled tight. Many complained that belts were uncomfortable, too confining, and too prone to wrinkle a woman's dress or a man's pants. Belts were a nuisance when not used too. Since they did not retract, they cluttered the seat surface and were uncomfortable to sit on. Car owners often got belts out of the way by tucking them down into the seat.

Ford hoped that Life Guard Design would prove popular in the marketplace, bolster sales, and strengthen its competitiveness vis-à-vis Chevy. But that didn't happen. There had been a rise in demand for new cars in 1955, when many of the models sharply contrasted with the older styling found on 1954 cars. In 1956, new car sales, instead of rising again, sharply dropped. Both Ford and Chevy sold fewer passenger cars in 1956 than in 1955, but Ford's decline was steeper. The calendar year of 1955 saw 1,764,524 Fords and 1,830,038 Chevrolets leave showrooms. In 1956, Ford sales dropped to 1,373,542, a decline of 22 percent. Chevy sales fell to 1,621,018, a lesser decline of about 11 percent. Put another way, in the calendar year 1955, for every 100 Chevrolets sold, 96 Fords were sold. But in 1956, for every 100 new Chevrolets put on the road, only 85 Fords rolled out. This decline of Ford's position in the marketplace caused wags to say that "Ford sold safety while Chevrolet sold cars."

In 1957, Ford's ad campaign based on Life Guard Design essentially disappeared. Instead, Ford ads stressed just how much bigger the new Ford was. The '57 was "*smarter*, longer, lower than anything in its field . . . livelier, too—with Thunderbird V-8 power!" Still, auto companies spread the safety features initiated in 1956 to more makes and models. The high-priced 1957 Continental Mark II got the safety offerings found on the low-priced Ford in 1956. Companies continued making safety improvements—they recessed knobs and controls on dash boards and designed better windshield washer systems and hood latches. To protect pedestrians, General Motors even put rubber tips on Cadillac's protruding, bullet-like bumper guards! Still, when communicating with the public, the companies eschewed putting a strong emphasis on safety. Ford's sales decline in the year of Life Guard Design seemingly convinced the auto industry that safety didn't sell, and perhaps it even scared people away.

In January and February 1957, the periodical *Public Safety* ran a two-part article on "Safety Features of 1957 Cars." The articles started with this: "The 1957 cars . . . show features tending to minimize the seriousness of injury if an accident occurs." Then the text went on, "Grateful as we all are for these advances, we must not forget that any substantial improvement in the motor vehicle accident problem rests with the individual—the driver as well as the pedestrian." Briefly, the American car's design and lack of safety devices had been seen as a major contributor to forty-thousand deaths per year and hundreds of thousands of serious injuries. Then the pendulum quickly swung back in the other direction. The companies had done their share, now the driver once again became the problem, and it would stay that way for about another decade, until the pendulum in the mid-1960s shifted back to faulting cars. A milestone here was the 1965 publication of Ralph Nader's, *Unsafe at Any Speed: The Designed-In Dangers of the American Automobile.*

Ford led the auto industry's flirtation with a safety crusade in the mid-1950s, and to its credit it did not give up without a fight. In 1958, Ford revived Life Guard Design advertisements, not in national magazines but in local newspapers. In April 1958, the same Ford ad ran in the Daytona Beach *Morning Journal*, in the Pittsburgh *Press*, and no doubt in many other cities. It depicted a young pigtailed girl saying, "We drive a FORD. It's safer! . . . Give your loved ones the extra protection of Ford's Life Guard Design." The ad noted that this 1958 Ford was even safer than a '56 or '57 because it had four headlights instead of the old two, plus large twin taillights, and safety glass all around. But customers still had to purchase the optional padded instrument panel and Ford safety belts. Safety was a commodity, a consumer good for the consumer's good. The motor company in its 1958 newspaper ads gave consumers the best reason for buying safety belts: "Experts say highway deaths could be cut 50% if all passengers used this optional safety feature." In terms of safety, Ford had a better idea than other auto companies, but at the time a large part of the public wasn't buying it. Most Americans didn't want seat belts and, rightly or wrongly, they felt safe enough in their big Detroit cars, thank you. Americans had a strong tendency to believe that big cars were inherently safe cars. The auto companies did nothing to dissuade them from this idea, and in the second half of the 1950s, Detroit sold Americans cars that grew bigger every year.

A study conducted by the Opinion Research Corporation, as summarized in 1958 by a writer for *Automotive News*, concluded that Americans suffered burnout when it came to the auto safety issue. They suffered "safety slogan fatigue," so when implored to "Drive Safely," the message meant almost nothing. Americans tired of "righteous warnings asking us not to kill ourselves." Death statistics and grisly images of mangled cars and bodies elicited emotional responses—but it couldn't be proved that they led to safer drivers. In America in the 1950s, citizens were not nearly as zealous about protecting their health and safety as they would become, starting a decade later.

In the 1950s, many American families used large amounts of lard in their cooking, ate chicken with the skin on, slept soundly in houses without smoke alarms, left their dogs chained outside to doghouses on cold nights, drank hard liquor, gave their young sons BB guns and knives, rode bicycles without reflectors, and walked barefoot behind gas-engine, rotary lawn mowers. NERF hadn't been invented yet, so hard baseballs occasionally nailed children in the face, bloodying them.

Families followed 1950s social norms when they got into their cars, whether going on a long trip or just down the road. They chose not to feel at risk. After a Little League game, I would jump into the open bed of a pickup truck with my friends to ride to the ice cream parlor for a treat. In our cars, Mom, Dad, and I never buckled up, because we didn't have seat belts. As a baby, I rode on Mom's lap or lay bundled up on the front seat. I never had my own safety or booster seat as a baby or toddler. I often rode standing up on the front seat, next to Mom. In the event of a sudden stop, Mom's right arm—which she immediately threw out in front of her little boy—was our most used child restraint, however ineffective. When I was a bit bigger, I roamed free in the car, restlessly clambering over seats, moving from front to back and back to front. I liked to lie on the shelf or deck above and behind the back seat, right under the rear window glass. Sometimes I opened a window and leaned out of the car as far as I could, before getting yelled at or pulled back in. Usually, when the car was underway, Dad, Mom, or both pushed in the cigarette lighter on the dash, and soon they puffed on Winston and Kent cigarettes. We drove through a smokescreen, and after the fags burned down, some butts went into the ashtray on the dash, while others were tossed outside through the car's wing vents.

Much of this accepted behavior in the 1950s would later seem callous or even abhorrent, but only after Americans had the time to slowly embrace new values, behavior, and safety standards. Culture couldn't turn on a dime, even when it was a matter of life and death.

# 6

# HEAD OUT ON THE HIGHWAY

In 1908, two men set out to blaze an automobile trail from Calumet, in the Upper Peninsula of Michigan, down to Chicago, a distance of 430 miles. Hanse and Jim suffered a rash of misfortunes as they traveled over a landscape not ready for automobiles. After one of their car's rear springs broke, the blacksmith at a copper mine hand-forged them a new one. The car was stuck in clay until a horse team pulled them out. They had to build their own bridge to cross a creek. They needed a second horse team to pull them out of a second bog. They found a place to sleep at Bruce Crossing when a lumberjack got up to go to work and gave them his warm bed. In the next room, they heard a priest giving a groaning man his last rites. When they awoke, they discovered he was the fourth lodger at this place to die of diphtheria in the past week.

Near Watersmeet, they sprang a leak in the radiator and broke the water pump trying to fix it. The magneto died. Again, a horse team came to pull the car, but the team ran away with the vehicle and tried to jump a log. The horses made it over but the automobile did not. They walked through Indian camps with snarling dogs to get another horse team. While pulling the car behind a wagon hitched to the new horses, they encountered a cyclone, which removed the car's top and windshield and left poor Hanse and Jim like "a couple of drowned rats." Finally, they got to Rhinelander. In a week they did 120 miles. That was enough of that. They rid themselves of the car and bought rail tickets to the Windy City.

As manufacturers improved the automobile, the country built, bit by bit, the infrastructure needed to support its use. Governments promulgated traffic laws and licensing requirements for cars and drivers, and they established state police posts to patrol the roads. Insurance companies wrote policies covering liability and collision. A vast network of paved and numbered state and federal highways crisscrossed the landscape. They were maintained by highway department garages, the keepers of sand, salt, plows, graders, rollers, trucks, and patching and paving equipment. Travelers could take both potty breaks and lunch breaks at roadside rest areas. On the fringe of a roadway stood posted speed limits and signs telling travelers what route they were on and whether it was a federal, state, or county highway or road. Other signs gave directions or warnings—watch out for a railroad crossing, a sharp curve, or a no passing zone.

Service stations were an essential part of the auto culture's infrastructure. They provided mechanics (often dressed in company uniforms), two grades of fuel (premium and regular), motor oil, tires and tubes (and the compressed air hoses for filling them), batteries, fan belts, radiator hoses, antifreeze and tow trucks. Gas stations provided snacks. They provided toilets. If near a lake, gas stations also sold fishing licenses, tackle, and bait. Travelers, like their cars, needed fuel. Often, highway intersections had restaurants sitting on two corners and gas stations on the other two corners. On long trips, travelers needed places to stay. By the 1950s, roadsides had accumulated thirty or forty years of different types of travelers' accommodations—campgrounds, tourist courts filled with little cabins, and newer motels.

Roadsides included attractions that made long rides more entertaining. Dad and I rode in our '56 Packard to visit Niagara Falls, the nation's capital, and the Gettysburg battlefield. Not all tourist attractions were so grand. Americans on vacation liked to visit the unusual, the kitschy. If not within range of the towering Washington Monument, perhaps they could at least drive to see the world's tallest doughnut (thirty-two feet high) standing on top of Inglewood, California's Big Do-Nut Drive-In. Small towns and local businesses—and sometimes historical and religious groups—built large things to attract tourists. If a family couldn't make it to the giant doughnut, maybe they could make it to the giant Coney Island Hot Dog restaurant, originally erected in Denver. Entering a hot dog to eat a hot dog was a novel opportunity; the building's bun was thirty-five feet long and its dog, forty-two feet long. Similarly, travelers on US-2 in northern Minnesota could walk into a fish to eat fish. The Big Fish Supper Club was inside the belly of a sixty-five-foot-long muskie. You entered by walking through the muskie's mouth and past its many teeth.

A roadside attraction relatively close to our hometown was at Indian River, Michigan, where religious or curious travelers could stop to see the fifty-five-foot-tall "Cross in the Woods Shrine," otherwise billed as "The World's Largest Crucifix." In Tulsa, Oklahoma, "The Golden Driller"—twenty-two tons of concrete and steel, standing ninety-seven feet tall, celebrated the local petroleum industry. To celebrate lumbering and to attract the curious, at least seven Paul Bunyon statues (some more than fifty feet tall and accompanied by Babe the Blue Ox) graced various roads in the 1950s. Paul Bunyon got around. He could be found in Bemidji and Brainerd, Minnesota; Castle Rock and Ossineke, Michigan; Bangor, Maine; Portland, Oregon; and Klamath, California. In Jamestown, North Dakota, tourists stopped to see the World's Largest Buffalo, twenty-six feet tall and forty-six feet long. Meanwhile, South Dakota claimed four very large presidents' heads, otherwise known as Mount Rushmore. It may seem improper to catalog Mount Rushmore as roadside kitsch, since it is a National Monument, but its original purpose was to attract tourists to a part of the country whose economy needed their dollars.

In northern Michigan, not far from the World's Largest Crucifix, Sea Shell City attracted tourists by putting up numerous road signs enticing them to stop in and see a "Man Killing Clam," weighing five hundred pounds. My parents were never keen to stop to see a man-eating clam, a really big Jesus, or the gravity-defying "Mystery Spot" alongside Route 2 in the Upper Peninsula. One time I did manage to talk them into stopping at the Call of the Wild Museum in Gaylord, Michigan, but we drove right past other tourist traps, like a prehistoric forest and deer parks. Some vacationing families welcomed attractions that broke a long trip into smaller bits and made travel more colorful.

My dad, however, tended to keep his eyes on the road and his foot on the gas, and he drove right past the tall Santa and Mrs. Claus greeting visitors to Christmas, Michigan. Maybe once a year Dad drove us on a pretty Sunday out to the Irish Hills, about twenty-five miles southeast of Jackson. It was full of touristy things to look at and do. Real dinosaurs never lived in Michigan, nor did cavemen, but fiberglass versions of them coexisted here. The Prehistoric Forest was a grand tourist trap, but it didn't trap us. Dad was in his mid-fifties, and to be blunt, I think he was too old for that nonsense. We weren't passing through there for kitsch, but to see lakes and woods and enjoy a drive up and down hills and around gentle curves.

My family encountered frequent surprises along highways, both good and bad. On any long drive, we commonly passed disabled cars parked on the side of the road. Many cars, especially those built before 1955, ran on bias-ply tires that had inner tubes, and these were more prone to blowouts or punctures than later tubeless, steel-belted radial tires. Overheating presented another peril, especially in summer's hottest months. Broken fan belts, leaky radiators, faulty hoses or thermostats, or low coolant levels could cause a plume of steam to billow out from around the hood, signaling the driver to pull over immediately, kill the engine, lift the hood, and let the engine cool down. Batteries ran down if the generator or its drive belt failed. If you missed seeing a red warning or "idiot" light on the dash, you could run the battery totally dead and simply have to pull over and wait for help. My dad commonly packed a box of tools and some water jugs in the trunk, just in case.

The highways we traveled in the 1950s were less predictable and repetitive than the roads of later decades, especially Interstates. You didn't know what you were getting into until you got there. Every restaurant had a different look, a different name, and its menu was unknown. A restaurant looks a bit shabby. Maybe it's a greasy spoon, like the one described in Vladimir Nabokov's novel *Lolita*, whose sign simply said "EAT," and whose interior exhibited a deer head, a rack of picture postcards, impaled guest checks, sunglasses and Life Savers for sale, a half chocolate cake under glass, and "several horribly experienced flies zigzagging over the sticky sugar-pour on the ignoble counter." To

The Big Fish Supper Club in Bena, Minnesota, was built in 1957. If travelers passing by hadn't been there before, how would they ever know if the walleye or perch was any good? (John Margolies, Roadside America Collection, Library of Congress)

pick a restaurant on the road, my family tended to look at cars in the parking lot. It seemed probable that the more cars, the better the food. We preferred family restaurants, purveyors of hot dogs and hamburgers; fried chicken; meat loaf; hot beef, pork, and turkey sandwiches; real mashed potatoes with gravy; and pies and ice cream for dessert.

Billboards along the highway advertised motels up ahead. Signs bragged that the mom-and-pop motel had phones, air-conditioning, and televisions, but this information did not speak about quality or cleanliness. Dad slowed the car so we could get a better peek at them: single-story, linear affairs (or L-shaped or U-shaped), twelve to twenty rooms stitched together, each with a single door fronting a parking lot, maybe asphalt, but often gravel. A lighted sign announced "Yes" if the motel had any vacancies, "Sorry" if it was full, and it gave the motel's name: The Pines, the Vagabond, Bel-Air, Candle-Lite, Oasis, Wagon Wheel, or the Dixie Land. We had no idea which one was best, or what they charged. Dad slowly drove by one, then another, and finally stopped at the third. The desk clerk quoted a reasonable room rate. Dad was ready to register, but Mom always made him go look at the room first. Check it out. Would it be clean, or have two dozen dead flies on the windowsill, a rust-stained wash basin, and a yellowed linoleum floor around the toilet? Would the carpet be threadbare, or would the room even have a carpet? Would the air stink to high heaven of stale cigarette smoke? He would turn on the TV. Did it give a good picture for at least one channel, or was the screen snowy for all channels? Was there a desk and chair, so you could sit and write postcards? If the room passed inspection, we had a place to stay. If not, we moved on down the road.

Most highways in the Midwest were only two lanes wide and had narrow shoulders. The highways seemed to follow, and not overwhelm, the landscape and its contours. Less earth had been moved in making them. Their hills were left higher, their valleys lower, and their curves sharper than on later roads. Maintaining a desired speed could be difficult due to steep uphills, which required more throttle, or steep downhills and sharp curves, which might require braking. Relatively few highways in the 1950s had a third lane in the middle to facilitate passing. Many drivers squeezed the steering wheel tighter, and sat up higher in the seat, leaning toward the windshield, when deciding if now was the time to try to dash around an Allied Van Lines moving truck going uphill at only forty-one miles an hour. My dad was pretty unfazed by slow traffic. The car had a passing gear and he wasn't afraid to use it. If you had to go eighty-five miles per hour to get by a truck, just do it.

Two-lane highways increased the risk of head-on collisions. Because they passed through innumerable intersections, they increased the risk of T-boning as well, where the front of one car smashed into the side of another. Highway intersections abounded in the countryside and in urban areas too. Many highways in the 1950s did not follow bypasses or beltways around towns and cities. They went right through them, on the same grade as the surrounding surface streets. The pace of long-distance travel in the 1950s had three speeds. On the open road, my dad hurried along at fifty to sixty-five miles per hour. When we encountered the smallest of communities, those without traffic lights or stops, he obeyed the speed limit signs and slowed to twenty-five or thirty-five and passed right on through. When we arrived at cities, progress became stop-and-go, measured in blocks, rather than miles. We ran a gauntlet of traffic lights, and worst of all, flashing red lights at a rail crossing sometimes brought us to a full stop for minutes while a freight train went by. I always counted the cars.

Unlike the mom-and-pop restaurants and motels lining the highway, gas stations, selling leaded regular for twenty-eight or twenty-nine cents per gallon, were mostly known commodities, recognizable from a distance. Several small oil companies operated local or regional gas stations in the 1950s, but they competed with major oil companies that had been branding their products nationally since the 1920s. Gas stations wore standardized livery, the attendants often had matching uniforms, and tall signs with familiar trademarks or logos beckoned drivers. Mobil gas had its flying red Pegasus. Gulf announced itself with a round orange sign with Gulf spelled out in big blue letters. Pure Oil stations had round white signs, trimmed in blue, with the company's name across the center and "Be Sure With Pure" around the perimeter. An oval sign with, from top to bottom, red, white, and blue horizontal stripes stood for Standard Oil, and "Standard," in blue letters, was spelled out along the white stripe. A Texaco station was a glistening white box sided with porcelain panels. The attendants dressed in green work shirts, and their visored caps carried patches that proudly showed off the Texaco brand. Coming into a town and in need of fuel, my dad often sought out a Shell station. It would not be hard to find among all the others, given its distinctive clamshell logo, done up in yellow and red, standing atop a tall pole.

Auto travel changed dramatically in the late 1950s and the 1960s. Vacationing families ate and slept in new places and rode over a new generation of highways, the Interstates. All this change did not come without costs. When new roads drew traffic from established roads, businesses (and even whole towns) along the older roads withered or died. If you were driving in the late 1960s and listening to a country music station on the car radio, you might have heard Johnny Cash sing "Cisco Clifton's Filling Station." Once, Cisco was busy. He'd pump gas, clean windshields, check tire pressures, fix flats, and give directions. Cisco and friends also played checkers inside his station. But then they heard the bulldozers that came to build an Interstate. Cisco hoped his kids would stay fed when that highway opened, because it bypassed his station. It went right past it, with no ramps on or off. Cisco knew the Interstate was too much to fight. He took a night job to make some money. He still opened his station at dawn and the checker games went on, while cars flew past on high-test gas.

Corporate America took over from mom-and-pop America and spread their brands across the country. The landscape became repetitive, and through their windshields, travelers saw a less diverse nation. In the first half of the 1950s, in many parts of the country, travelers went out and back hundreds of miles from home without seeing any two restaurants or motels that were alike in their architecture, signage, name, or food. Then chain or franchise businesses multiplied along streets, highways, and interchanges. The country, as sociologist George Ritzer wrote in 1993, underwent McDonaldization.

More and more, Americans fueled themselves with hamburgers from a bag, chili dogs nestled in plastic baskets, or fried chicken pieces piled atop one another in red-and-white buckets, washed down with vanilla or chocolate shakes, Coke, Pepsi, or root beer. To obtain this new "fast-food," Americans frequented drive-in restaurants. If you were getting hot dogs, nobody had to leave the car to be fed. You pulled in, parked in the lot under a canopy, and a young carhop—usually a high-school-aged girl—came to take your order. She'd return with food and drinks atop an aluminum tray that hooked over and cantilevered out from the driver's partially rolled down window. At other drive-ins specializing in hamburgers, you drove in, parked, got out of the car, and walked up to the service window, where you placed your order after scanning a plastic sign board listing menu items and prices. A teenager rang up your bill, took your money, and a few minutes later handed you a bag or two of food and drinks, which you carried back to your vehicle, because there was no inside seating. You sat in the car, used the dashboard as a table, and ate your burger, stopping between bites to corral some French fries into your mouth or suck up a soft drink or shake through a straw.

Several chain restaurants originated in the Model T era, but they operated few outlets and had limited geographic range. In 1919, Roy Allen opened a roadside root beer stand in Lodi, California. In the early 1920s, he opened additional stands, where he pioneered in offering curbside service to automobilists, who stayed in their vehicles and were catered to by "tray-boys." Allen briefly partnered with Frank Wright. Taking their last initials, they came up with "A&W Root Beer." Allen grew this brand by franchising A&W. The A&Ws did not have a standard look or menu, but they all catered to the car-traveling public and served the same root beer, made from concentrate. By 1933, 170 A&W franchises operated in the West and Midwest, and by 1950, 450 A&Ws dotted the American landscape.

The first White Castle hamburger joint opened in 1921 in Wichita, Kansas. After incorporating in 1924, White Castle branched out to other Midwestern states, and the company grew to 130 outlets by 1940. Architecturally, White Castles were not identical, but they followed the same motif. They looked like little fortresses, with buttresses, towers or turrets, and a crenellated parapet wall. Their surfaces were clad in white porcelain enamel and stainless steel, materials selected because they made the outlets look hygienic and appealing. Servers wore standardized white garb, including paper hats, and all White Castles served the same burgers, whose ingredients were provided by the corporation: a small, thin, square hamburger patty, punched with five holes to make it cook better, topped with grilled onions and served on buns baked to stringent requirements. These "sliders" cost a mere five cents. White Castle in several ways set the tone for later fast-food chains: its buildings were instantly recognizable, its employees dressed alike, and its food was utterly predictable in price, appearance, and taste. But unlike later chains in the 1950s, White Castles tended to be in center cities, not in suburbs or along highways. Most customers came on foot, not in a car, to eat their sliders.

White Tower, starting in 1926 in Milwaukee, mimicked White Castle's architecture and business plan. White Castle entered lawsuits against this copycat company. Eventually they settled their legal problems and literally moved in different (compass) directions. White Tower moved east of Milwaukee. At the company's peak in the mid-1950s, about 230 White Towers operated in fourteen states. White Tower put most of its outlets in inner cities along bus or trolley lines, and they, too, did a walk-in business, not a drive-in business. Only a few White Towers attracted car drivers by offering curb service and carhops. That strategy hurt the company after the mid-1950s, when other chains opened drive-in locations on the outskirts of cities, in the suburbs, and along highways.

By 1950, Howard Johnson's was the most prominent restaurant chain along American highways. In the mid-1920s, the restaurant's namesake operated a drugstore in Massachusetts that sold a lot of ice cream at its soda fountain. Later in the decade, Johnson opened beachfront concession stands along the Massachusetts coast, as well as his first restaurant. Howard Johnson's began franchising restaurants in the early 1930s, and it also owned many of its own, most notably those that served food along the Pennsylvania Turnpike, which opened in 1940. At the start of World War II, Howard Johnson's had 200 restaurants. That number declined during the war but rebounded in the postwar era and reached 450 restaurants in thirty-two states in the eastern half of the United States by 1954 and 600 restaurants by 1958. (That was the same year that I first ate at a HoJo's, while on a long trip to the east with my dad.) More than any other, this restaurant chain targeted the car-driving public. An ad in *Life* magazine for November 15, 1954, told Americans to "Look forward to Howard Johnson's on the turnpikes." It then specified that "you'll find these friendly eating places on the Pennsylvania, New Jersey, Maine, New Hampshire and Oklahoma turnpikes, as well as the Garden State Parkway and the Massachusetts Limited Access Routes. They are operated by the Howard Johnson organization, specialists in serving traveling millions for over 25 years."

Howard Johnson's was built for long-distance travelers. It was full service, and its breakfast, lunch, and dinner menus offered the same food and prices from one restaurant to the next. Besides selling twenty-eight flavors of ice cream (a carryover from its soda fountain beginnings) and fried clam strips (a carryover from its New England roots near the Atlantic), Howard Johnson's served traditional American fare in sit-down dining rooms. It offered a "Grilled Frankfort" for big kids and strained baby foods for little kids. Diners ate off real plates, drank from glasses or china cups, and used stainless steel forks, knives, and spoons. Howard Johnson's billed itself as the "Landmark for Hungry Americans," and it made sure Americans could find a HoJo's without looking hard to find one. If a restaurant had a big sign out front advertising twenty-eight flavors of ice cream and fried clams, and if the building had a safety-orange tile roof topped with a cupola and weathervane, you had arrived at Howard Johnson's. In my inaugural meal at HoJo's in 1958, I enjoyed my chocolate ice cream but passed on the fried clams.

The chain restaurant business exploded in the 1950s and 1960s, when new entrants into the field initiated a revolutionary fast-food model. Customers would arrive in their cars and eat in their cars (or they could take the food home to eat). The model was family friendly. If they had kids, Mom and Dad didn't have to worry about corralling Johnny, Barbara, and baby Stephen in a crowded restaurant, praying they would behave. Customers would only briefly interact with the person taking their order at the front window, they didn't have to wait to get their bill, and they saved money by not having to leave tips. They would have little choice of food, but that food would be sold at low prices (twelve- to fifteen-cent hamburgers, with the same prices, usually, for shakes and fries) and be served quickly. The corporate food would look the same, taste the same, and be packaged the same. If the customer stuck to the same chain, today's hamburger would taste like last year's hamburger and next year's hamburger, and the Miami burger would taste just like the Seattle, Phoenix, and Boston burgers. And every time the customer ordered a burger, the person at the point of sale would ask, not by accident but by plan, "Would you like some fries with that?" This model, best implemented by McDonald's, made the hamburger the culinary king of the American road.

In 1940, Dick and Mac McDonald opened a drive-in restaurant offering curb service in San Bernardino, California. The restaurant served hamburgers, barbeque, and a wide variety of foods. In 1948, they conducted a makeover. They limited the menu to fifteen-cent hamburgers, plus cheeseburgers, potato chips, soft drinks, milk, coffee, and pie. (The next year, they cut out potato chips and added French fries and milkshakes.) They did away with carhops and introduced self-service. Customers ordered their food at a window and took it back to their cars to eat. By 1952, the successful McDonald brothers operated seven restaurants, and in 1954 Ray Kroc, a salesman for the company that made the Multi-mixers the restaurants used to make milkshakes, visited them in San Bernardino. He wanted to see how this restaurant could be so busy that it needed eight Multi-mixers. Kroc saw a promising future in this hamburger business, and the McDonalds were interested in franchising. Kroc returned to his home near Chicago with the rights and agreements needed to start franchising McDonald's.

Kroc's first McDonald's opened in Des Plaines, Illinois, in 1955. He liked putting his drive-in restaurants on the fringes of cities, where they were easily accessible by car, and he used a company plane to conduct fly-overs to discover locations along busy streets and roads. Thanks to their architecture, the new McDonald's were instantly recognizable to nearly everyone, everywhere. Their red-and-white-striped buildings, fronted with glass, with two golden arches reaching up and over an inclined shed roof, stood out against any landscape and helped create a national identity. Within five years, McDonald's operated 228 locations nationwide; by 1965, it operated 700; and by 1968, 1,000. The corporation didn't count hamburgers sold by the dozen but first by the millions (one hundred million by 1958) and then by the billions (five billion sold by 1969).

Critics faulted—or even assailed—McDonald's on several counts. It became a symbol of a throwaway culture, because it didn't use permanent plates, glasses, or utensils. Burgers were wrapped in paper, fries came in little paper bags, drinks came in paper cups, ketchup came in disposable packets, and the whole order arrived in one or two paper sacks. Inevitably, McDonald's paper products ended up as paper trash, blowing around nearby streets. McDonald's adhered to rigid and repetitive sameness in its architecture, employee behavior, and food, but it slowly accepted change if it promised to bring in more customers. It moved away from its drive-in roots and in the direction of a family restaurant. In 1962, it added the Filet-O-Fish sandwich and for the first time put indoor seating in a new restaurant. In 1968, the double-patty

Big Mac arrived; in 1969, the corporation swapped out its original red-striped-and-golden-arched restaurants for a new "brick and mansard roof" design with enhanced inside seating and a larger menu. In 1975, McDonald's went back to the future. It returned to its drive-in roots in a new way, by adding drive-thru windows to its restaurants. Customers could get their food without ever leaving or shutting off their cars.

McDonald's had company in the fast-food hamburger marketplace in the 1950s and 1960s. Burger Chef, now defunct, once offered McDonald's keen competition. The first Burger Chef, featuring char-grilled patties, opened in Indianapolis in 1957. Franchising began the next year, and from eight Burger Chefs in three states in 1957, the chain grew to one thousand outlets in thirty-eight states by 1969. Burger King started in 1954 in Florida. By 1955, forty restaurants operated there, selling flame-broiled burgers, fries, soft drinks, and shakes. Its roadside iconographic figure was a cartoonish king with a gold crown, dressed like an American flag in red, white, and blue, holding a red-and-white-striped milkshake cup while sitting on top of a hamburger. Burger King sold small burgers for eighteen cents and in 1957 added its trademark "Whopper," a much larger burger topped with more condiments, which sold for thirty-seven cents. Flame-broiling, plus the Whopper, offered customers something that in heft and taste differed from McDonald's. Burger King began franchising in 1959 and had 274 outlets in the United States by 1967, making it the nation's third largest fast-food chain. Another hamburger chain went the beefier route, featuring a Big Boy "double-decker" having two patties, cheese, and condiments, stacked into a three-piece bun. Starting from California, Big Boy restaurants spread across much of the nation in the 1950s, while the company made famous its iconic statue of a chubby lad—a big boy, indeed—wide-eyed and smiling, hair combed in a swoopy do, wearing red-and-white-checkered overalls, and carrying an uplifted plate filled by a delectable double-decker. Every new restaurant chain had to have what historian Chester Liebs, in *Main Street to Miracle Mile*, called "architecture for speed reading." Signs, symbols, golden arches, or Big Boys in red-and-white britches—all "designed to capture the attention of an audience passing by at high speed."

Fast-food hamburger joints spread across the county. Millions of Americans liked the taste and price of fifteen-cent burgers and stood in lines to get them, along with some salty fries. There was an appeal to their squishy blandness. They were so easy to eat. Chewing them took no effort. Maybe there was not much to like about them, really, but at the same time there was not much not to like. Even if Americans lifted the bun top, looked down, and wondered, "Where's the beef?" they kept coming back for more. Americans demonstrated a liking for mass-produced goods, even food. At the same time, picky eaters eschewed the likes of McDonald's and Burger Chef. They claimed that in the 1950s and 1960s, Americans lowered their standards of taste as they consumed more bad burgers by the millions or billions than ever before in recorded history. God knows how many beef cattle died to produce the small, thin patties that sat in little buns, sharing space with an optional slice of cheese, a dab of ketchup and mustard, two or three thin pickle slices (often sitting on top of each other and not properly distributed), and six or seven little quarter-inch squares of translucent white that had once been, allegedly, an onion. After I got my driver's license, I, to be sure, ate my share of little burgers. But I knew there were some better burgers out there. Not all fast-food chains wanted to slug it out in the low end of the market, so some moved upscale, including Steak 'n Shake.

Steak 'n Shake started in 1934 in Normal, Illinois. Like White Castle before it, the company wanted to assure the public—especially middle-class diners—that its ground patties were made of the choicest cuts, and that the beef was pure and free of contaminants, including parts of a slaughtered steer you might not want to look at, let alone eat. Steak 'n Shake used shiny white wall décor inside and out, as well as polished stainless-steel surfaces and tiled floors to represent cleanliness. It offered curb service and interior seating, and thanks to walls of glass and an open floor plan, customers inside and outside could watch prime beef cuts being ground to make "steakburgers" (not mere hamburgers) and then watch their individual steakburgers being seared on the grill and assembled. Steak 'n Shake adopted the motto, "In Sight It Must Be Right," which it put on its signs to reinforce the image of being a clean place offering safe and good food.

Without a doubt, as a teenager my favorite fast-food joint was Steak 'n Shake, where I always ordered a double steakburger with cheese, dill pickles, and extra onions, plus fries, and an orange freeze milkshake. (Courtesy of J. Andre, www.electric-art-gallery.com)

Steak 'n Shake grew slowly to fifteen outlets by 1943 and twenty-four by 1954. Then its business accelerated. It operated five hundred Steak 'n Shakes in twenty-six states, running from the upper Midwest to Florida. The brand had staunch loyalists. I ate my first steakburger with cheese and a real slice of onion and two big slices of dill pickle in Danville, Illinois, when I was twelve. Cousin Jim and I, when at Uncle Walt's, often talked Walt into treating us for lunch. On the best of days, we talked him out of enough money so we could eat at Steak 'n Shake on Vermilion Street and not have to settle for Burger Chef on Gilbert Street. Another great fan of Steak 'n Shake lived about thirty-five miles west of Danville, in Urbana-Champaign. The late great film critic Roger Ebert, when he was about four, ate his first steakburger at his local Steak 'n Shake. Extolling the virtues of this chain as if he were extolling the virtues of his favorite film, Ebert wrote: "A down-state Illinois boy loves the Steak 'n Shake as a Puerto Rican loves rice and beans, an Egyptian loves falafel, a Brit loves bangers and mash, a

Finn loves reindeer jerky, and a Canadian loves doughnuts. This doesn't involve taste. It involves a deep-seated conviction that a food is right, and always has been, and always will be." For Ebert, the steakburger was right food, good till the end: "If I were on death row, my last meal would be from Steak 'n Shake."

What worked for hamburger chains also worked for purveyors of root beer and hot dogs, fried chicken, ice cream, and somewhat later, pizza and tacos. A&W thrived in the 1950s. Teenagers cruising the streets of my birthplace, Jackson, often stopped at the local A&W, opened about 1951. It had no inside seating and just a few stools at an outside counter, but it had fifty-five parking spaces for customers in their cars, who drank root beer from frosty mugs and ate chili dogs and free popcorn. Jackson boasted another root beer chain, Dog n Suds, which started up in 1953 in Champaign, Illinois, and operated up to six hundred units in thirty-eight states and Canada at its peak in the mid-1970s. Jackson's Dog n Suds was a classic drive-in with a long yellow canopy for cars to park under, trimmed with neon lights. Carhops brought the food and drinks to your car. Dog n Suds's iconographic bright-red-and-yellow neon sign stood nearby on a tall pole. It depicted a dog that resembled Walt Disney's Goofy, wearing a chef's hat and carrying a mug of root beer and a hot dog on a delivery tray held high. Another root beer stand in Jackson—and there was one just like it in Lansing—knew the value of instantly communicating its purpose to passing motorists on busy Michigan Avenue. The Tip Top's roof was topped with a ten-foot-in-diameter simulated root beer barrel emblazoned with the price of a mug, "5 cents."

In the early 1950s, Harland Sanders operated a gas station and restaurant in Corbin, Kentucky. In the late '50s, he learned that the new Interstate 75 was going to bypass his chicken restaurant, leaving him high and dry. In the name of self-preservation, he came up with the idea of selling to other restaurants his method of pressure-cooking chicken and his "secret recipe of 11 herbs and spices," which made his product "finger lickin' good." This idea soon morphed into Colonel Sanders creating Kentucky Fried Chicken franchises, which numbered six hundred by 1964. When I was in high school, I had a friend, Bob Snyder, who liked chicken as much as I did. About every other week, we decided to "Take it from the Colonel" and off to KFC we went.

In 1958, the pizza joint that eventually turned into Pizza Hut opened in Wichita, Kansas. By 1966, Pizza Hut had 152 franchisees, and by 1972, 1,000. Californian Glen Bell got into the restaurant business in 1946, when he opened his first hot dog stand. In the early 1950s, thinking outside the bun, he eschewed moving into hamburgers and opened a fast-food Mexican place, Taco-Tia, followed by others, called El Taco. Changing the name once again, he opened his first Taco Bell in Downey, California, in 1962 and started franchising the brand. Taco Bells numbered 100 in 1967, 325 in 1970, and 868 in 1975.

Those with a sweet tooth could also indulge themselves at modest cost. Dairy Queen first opened in Joliet, Illinois, in 1940. Franchising soon followed. The ice cream stand required little capital to start up, and there were 446 Dairy Queens in 1950 and 2,600 in 1955. On summer evenings, especially in small towns, Dairy Queen was the place to go for a treat and to meet up with friends. If not Dairy Queen, then Tastee-Freez, another major player in the fast-food dessert industry. Tastee-Freez, started in 1950 in Illinois, had nearly 1,800 locations by 1957. Personally, though, I preferred to get my soft-serve ice cream cone at the locally owned and operated Custard Cup in Danville. The product was good, and the server was a pretty girl in my high school class.

I think my family drove past more fast-food restaurants than most families. Dad took me to eat coney dogs at the Jackson Coney Island restaurant, which was downtown near the old train station. We both loved coneys—which I guess you could almost classify as fast food. I don't remember Mom ever going with us and eating a coney heaped with spiced ground beef, mustard, and finely chopped onions. I remember Mom eating at a Big Boy restaurant with me, and she occasionally had a steak burger from Steak 'n Shake—but I'm certain that Mary Lankton and Big Larry Lankton never once ate a McDonald's hamburger. They never ate out of paper sacks while sitting in our Packard. No way.

Mom's tastes were born out of her working for so many years at upscale restaurants. She preferred real plates and silverware and cloth napkins. She wanted a whiskey sour or a sloe gin fizz, not Coke in a paper cup. She wanted frog legs, not salty fries. She liked Chinese food, so she often took me to Jasmine Towers in downtown Danville. She had a sweet tooth, but instead of going to Dairy Queen, she took me to the Rose Room within the Field's department store, where we ordered cream puffs with vanilla ice cream, topped with the legendary Sanders chocolate sauce. Our family ate at Bill Knapp's and at Bill Cones, which had frog legs for Mom. Best of all, we often ate at the Regent Café, housed in an old brick building in downtown Jackson.

The Regent was about as far as you could get from new fast-food places. It had been in business for thirty years before I started going there with my parents in the mid-1950s. It was owned by Angelo Johns, a Macedonian immigrant, and his wife, Ida, the daughter of Polish immigrants. The Regent was open twenty-four hours a day. It had tables and booths for 170 diners. Here, my mom found the white tablecloths and napkins that she liked, as well as a skilled waitstaff. The waitresses all wore black skirts and white blouses. They handed out an impressive menu shortly after you arrived, with at least a hundred regular dishes and many daily specials. The food appealed to wildly varied tastes: lobster and filet mignon, chicken gizzards, sweetbreads, liver and onions, hamburgers, cold cuts—and frog legs. Even as a young boy, my personal favorite was an open-faced steak sandwich on toast. As we ate, Angelo, dressed in a suit and tie, always came by to say hello and ask if we liked our food. I ate many meals there with Mom and Dad, and after my dad died, Lynn and Ben took me to a movie and then to the Regent. I always remember the Regent with a smile.

After Mom and I moved to Danville in 1962, we had to find new restaurants to frequent. Since Mom drove and Mom paid, she made the selections. She often took me to the DeLuxe near the middle of downtown. The DeLuxe was not at all fancy, but the food was reasonably priced, with a menu of belly-filling food like open-faced pork sandwiches with mashed potatoes and gravy over everything. On Sunday afternoons, we often ate at Connor's on Main Street. Connor's had a big neon sign out front with the restaurant's motto, "Good food every time!" The sign told us that the place was air-conditioned and served cocktails. Mom got a very red sloe gin fizz and we enjoyed fried chicken, steak, or shrimp, with a good salad and bread on the side.

Our special place to dine in Danville was atop the Wolford Hotel. The Wolford, known as the finest hotel in its part of Illinois, was nine or ten stories tall, with 250 guest rooms, a coffee shop, a cocktail lounge, a ballroom, and a restaurant, the Regency Room. I don't know how much it cost, but Mom paid for a meal plan at the Wolford. We ate at the Regency Room once a month. Mom and I walked through the hotel lobby, entered an elevator, and rode up to enjoy as fine and formal a dining experience as Danville had to offer. I am pretty sure that the Wolford, built in 1926, reminded Mom of the Los Angeles and Detroit restaurants she had worked at decades before.

Fast-food restaurants changed the look of American streets and highways. They changed how, where, and what we ate. It was a revolution of sorts. By the time Mom and I ate at the Wolford, McDonald's already registered hamburger sales in the billions. But they sold none to my mom. In this revolution she was a conservative Tory, an opponent of change. Before I got my driver's license, I guess I was a Tory too. I went where Mom went. That changed after I turned sixteen and could drive to whatever fast-food joint I wanted to.

In 1984, I was out for a walk with my three-year-old son, David. He came to a quick stop and pointed to a tall sign up ahead on College Avenue. "Burger King," he said. Those were the first words he ever read to me. I was both proud and chagrined. Why did it have to be a Burger King sign, of all things? Indeed, the fast-food culture had won over the nation. As for Jasmine Towers, Bill Knapp's, Bill Cones, the Rose Room, the original DeLuxe, Connor's, the Wolford, and my boyhood favorite—the Regent—well, they were all dead, and in some cases, torn down to the ground.

# 7

## THE BEST SURPRISE IS NO SURPRISE

While the number of drive-in restaurants expanded exponentially in the 1950s, so did the number of motels. At the end of World War II, there were approximately 20,000 motels in the United States; twenty years later, in the mid-1960s, there were more than 60,000, and by 1972, there were 120,000. Initially, mom-and-pop operators fueled the expansion of the motel industry. They owned 98 percent of the country's motels in 1948. In subsequent years, however, chain or franchised motels took over the business.

Motels had a suspect or seedy reputation long before Janet Leigh stepped into her shower at the Bates Motel in the 1960 Hitchcock film, *Psycho*. FBI director J. Edgar Hoover warned that motels were sometimes "dens of vice and corruption" hosting "immoral and criminal behavior." They allowed almost anonymous entry. Somebody had to register, but companions could quickly slip from the car into a motel room, without parading through a lobby under the watchful eyes of a desk clerk. "No-tell motels" allowed for adulterous liaisons and teenage sex. Author Vladimir Nabokov used the motel's less than snow-white image to craft his less than snow-white novel, *Lolita*. Published in the United States in 1958, *Lolita* is set in 1947–48. In it, middle-aged Humbert Humbert, having taken an active sexual interest in his twelve-year-old stepdaughter, proceeds to drive her around the country in his car. Serving as the book's narrator, Humbert notes that on this journey, "I registered . . . at 342 hotels, motels and tourist homes." He goes on to say: "To any other type of tourist accommodation I soon grew

Christmas, Michigan, a small, unincorporated community in the Upper Peninsula, became home to the Christmas Motel in 1957. The single-story motel, of ten to twelve rooms, had prancing reindeer and Santa in his sleigh on the roof. Out front stood a neon sign in the shape of a Christmas present. (Collection of the author)

to prefer the Functional Motel—clean, neat, safe nooks, ideal places for sleep, argument, reconciliation, insatiable illicit love."

Law-abiding travelers in the 1950s who wanted only a clean, comfortable place to stay were wise to consult the Duncan Hines or American Automobile Association guidebooks that evaluated motels and gave the better ones an "Approved" rating. Many travelers, like my folks, personally inspected a room before booking it. Still others looked for chain motels they had stayed in before. Knowing what they were getting, they booked ahead with confidence.

Chain motels started in Texas in the 1920s, when Alamo Plaza Hotel Courts put up multiple units. These grew slowly to become twenty-two Alamo Plazas by the early 1950s. In that decade, Howard Johnson's and Holiday Inn became two bigger and much better known chains. Howard Johnson's had fifty "motor lodges" in 1958. Advertised as a "Landmark for Sleepy Americans," each motor lodge sat adjacent to a "Landmark for Hungry Americans." Motor lodge and restaurant

Only in America: a bat-wing 1959 Chevy pulled up at the Wigwam Motel on old Route 66 in Holbrook, Arizona. (Carol M. Highsmith Archive, Library of Congress)

shared the same orange roof and other architectural features and presented a package deal—food and sleep together.

By the end of the 1950s, Holiday Inn became the most important player in motel development. In 1951, Kemmons Wilson, who had risen from a poor upbringing in Arkansas to become a wealthy real estate developer and home builder in Memphis, loaded his wife and five children into the family station wagon and off they went to Washington, DC. That trip changed Wilson's fortunes—making him even richer—and it also changed the face of roadside America. Wilson recalled that on this trip, "It didn't take long to find that motels had cramped, uncomfortable rooms—and they charged extra for children. (A $6 room became a $16 room, when five children were charged at $2 each.) Few had adequate restaurants and fewer still were air-conditioned. In short, it was a miserable trip." Back in Memphis, he joined with Wallace E. Johnson, a builder of prefabricated houses, to plan and erect a better motel, which they named "Holiday Inn" after the 1942 film of that title starring Bing Crosby and Fred Astaire. In 1952, they opened the first Holiday Inn along US Highway 70 on the eastern fringe of Memphis. In the next year and a half, they built three more Holiday Inns on major routes in and out of the city. Once incorporated as Holiday Inns of America, the firm began franchising its motels in 1954.

Holiday Inns gave traveling Americans amenities that ordinary motels lacked. They dressed their rooms in modern furnishings and offered televisions, telephones, air-conditioning, ice machines, a restaurant, a pool, a kennel for family pets, baby-sitter service—and kids stayed for free. You could book ahead with the company's reservation service—or just pull off the road, park, and walk in. Finding a Holiday Inn was no problem. The company created one of the most iconographic commercial signs ever erected in front of a business. Holiday Inn's freestanding, two-sided "Great Sign"—done in green, trimmed in yellow—stood taller than the motels themselves. It had a star at the top, an arrow pointing right at the front door, and below the arrow, a big panel carrying "Holiday Inn" written in script. Below that, a theater-like marquee announced that this motel chain was "The Nation's Inn Keeper." Impressive during the day, the Great Sign dazzled at night, thanks to 1,500 feet of neon tubes and five hundred light bulbs.

Most early Holiday Inns served travelers in southeastern states. Before approving each new location, Wilson often flew over the proposed site in his personal plane. He studied traffic flows and traffic counts and noted if there were any attractions nearby (such as sporting venues) that might draw visitors in need of lodging. The chain's growth was modest through the mid-1950s and remained regional. In 1956, there were 26 Holiday Inns; and in 1958, there were 70. In that year, a motorist could have driven well-traveled routes from Michigan to Los Angeles without seeing a single Holiday Inn. But the chain's geographical spread soon increased. In 1964–65, the same Michigan traveler en route to California would have encountered many Holiday Inns. There were about 15 franchises in southern Michigan and a total of 587 Holiday Inns, with 69,880 guest rooms, across the country. Most built after 1958 incorporated a new two-story design, with a curtain wall of glass serving as the outside wall of each room. When I was in high school, Holiday Inn put one of those new-style motels on Vermilion Street in Danville, just north of the main business district.

Best Western originated in California in 1946. This company was

Holiday Inn's "Great Sign": a nationwide symbol of a nationwide chain of motels, where the best surprise was no surprise. (John Margolies, Roadside America Collection, Library of Congress)

a growing network of motels that banded together under the Best Western name and logo to create a more visible and respected brand. Corporate scouts traveled busier roads, visiting and evaluating motels along the way, and signed up the best of them to join this new chain. Best Western motels erected the same signs, bought the same soap and shower curtains, followed the same standards, took advanced reservations on a shared system, and benefited from common advertising campaigns. They were listed in a Best Western motel directory, which showed the locations of motels aligned one after the other on well-traveled highways. Best Western spun off Best Eastern, and in 1965 the two (later recombined under the Best Western name) had 881 motels across the country.

Other chains flourished in the 1950s and 1960s. Quality Courts Motels had 340 units in 1959 and about 600 by 1963. Ramada Inn had 24 motels in 1960, started franchising in 1963, and grew to about 300 motels by 1971. Budget motel chains came into being. They offered sparser accommodations and fewer frills, but at less cost. Motel 6, started in California in 1962, had 145 motels by 1973. Super 8 and Econo Lodge also dotted the American roadside, filling it with ever more look-alike signs, buildings, and parking lots.

The new Interstate highways played a key role in creating a look-alike America. Their physical attributes matched up well with national-brand gas stations, restaurants, and motels. The Interstates appeared repetitive due to the engineering standards and safety concerns that guided their construction. Each Interstate had a broad right-of-way that pushed back its surroundings, leveled out the land, and kept a driver's focus on the multilane, divided highway itself. Traffic lanes, shoulders, median strips, overpasses, bridges, exits, entrances, and signage all looked pretty much the same everywhere. Interstates improved the efficiency and safety of car travel, but at the cost, many believed, of diminishing the aesthetics of a cross-country drive.

Interstate travelers didn't see the same America they had seen on earlier roads. Instead of going through a city like old trunk roads, the Interstates raced through urban areas in new concrete canyons that ran where houses and shops had once stood, or they ran above the streets, perched on stilts. Motorists, instead of seeing a city up close, saw a city held at bay by the dominating highway. They no longer sat at a traffic light, watching the locals cross the street or looking into a department store window. Instead, they saw the uninspiring undersides of overpasses, one after the other after the other.

Near small towns and in rural areas, fast-moving drivers and passengers connected to the road, not to the surrounding landscape. On older highways, narrower and much closer to the passing scene, motorists could watch a fellow on a riding mower cut his grass, see a woman hanging clothes on the line, glance over at kids playing flies and grounders in a field, or read a drive-in theater's marquee, telling the world that tonight's features were the B-grade movies *Zombies of the Stratosphere*, *Tarzan and the Slave Girl*, and *I Married a Communist*. Seeing a sidewalk sale while passing through a small town, a motorist might stop and find some great end-of-summer bargains on summer clothes.

The new highways did what they were intended to do. In 1970, the Federal Highway Administration/US Department of Transportation put out a short report, *Benefits of Interstate Highways*. This was not a cost *and* benefit analysis, just a benefit analysis. It did not delve into the roads, communities, or businesses (like the US railroad industry) that the new superhighways had hurt. Instead, the report lauded their attributes and accomplishments. They carried a large volume of cars and trucks at a high speed. An auto traveler in the Interstate age could drive 500 miles per day, instead of the 350 miles per day on older highways. Distances traveled on vacations increased, and families headed off to farther-away destinations. Operating costs went down, largely because the new limited–access highways did away with traffic lights and lowered the grades on hills. Drivers saved money on fuel and oil costs and on tire and brake replacements. It cost the operator of a twenty-ton semitruck twenty cents every time he had to slow his truck down from fifty miles an hour to a full stop at a light and then accelerate back up to fifty. A study showed that Interstate travelers passing through parts of twelve states encountered 582 fewer stoplights and passed by 35,711 fewer intersections. The lack of intersections, combined with other safety features, like gentler curves, guard rails, median strips, and wide shoulders, resulted in a major reduction in fatal accidents. Compared to older highways, Interstates reduced traffic fatalities by 43 percent in rural areas and 15 percent in urban areas. The Interstates were the fastest, safest highways for Americans to travel on, and travel on them they did. They eschewed their older routes, got onto an entrance ramp, and motored 500 miles before getting off at an exit, eating at McDonald's, and sleeping in a Holiday Inn.

Author John Steinbeck knew his roads. His classic 1939 novel, *The Grapes of Wrath*, told the tale of the Dust Bowl family the Joads. They migrated from Oklahoma to the promised land of California in an old, heavily laden truck along Highway 66, "the mother road." In 1960, Steinbeck took a long road trip of his own in a pickup truck with a camper on it, accompanied by his dog, Charley. He wrote about his ten-thousand-mile-long journey in *Travels with Charley: In Search of America*, published in 1962. One new road he encountered was "a wide gash of a super-highway, multiple-lane carrier of the nation's goods," otherwise known as Interstate 90:

> The minimum speed on this road was greater than any I had previously driven. . . . Trucks as long as freighters went roaring by, delivering a wind like the blow of a fist. These great roads are wonderful for moving goods but not for inspection of a countryside. You are bound to the wheel and your eyes to the car ahead and to the rear-view mirror for the car behind and the side mirror for the car or truck about to pass, and at the same time you must read all the signs for fear you may miss some instructions or orders. No roadside stands selling squash juice, no antique stores, no farm products or factory outlets. When we get these thruways across the whole country, as we will and must, it will be possible to drive from New York to California without seeing a single thing.

Interstates created a world of their own. Seventy-five percent of the proposed forty-one-thousand-mile system followed new rights-of-way. In rural areas, they created new, small American "villages" along those many miles, which were quite different from the crossroads communities of old. These villages didn't have names; they had exit numbers. They didn't have town squares; they had on-off ramps and interchanges. They didn't have tall church steeples; they had tall advertising signs. They didn't have courthouses, schools, cemeteries, or homes—on the four quadrants of an interchange they had nationally branded gas stations, fast-food emporiums, motels, and maybe a shopping center. They didn't have village elders; they had gas station attendants, order takers, and desk clerks. They did not have permanent populations, but transient ones—people who left the highway, did their business, and then got back on the road again. People could spend days in their car, traveling hundreds or even thousands of miles, finding fuel, food, and shelter without wandering more than a quarter or half mile from the ribbon of Interstate being traveled. For many Interstate motorists, there was no "here" that mattered, only a "there"—the place they were headed to. Car travel became less a passage through places and more a seventy-miles-per-hour drive toward a final destination where the holiday would begin. Getting there was no longer half the fun.

John Steinbeck humorously wrote that "Roads change, increase, are widened or abandoned so often in our country that one must buy road maps like daily newspapers." This was especially true during the era of Interstate highway construction. The first eight miles of Interstate highway opened in Kansas near the end of 1956. The entire system was to be completed in twelve years, but that didn't happen. Still, about ten thousand miles of Interstates opened by 1960; twenty thousand miles by 1965; and thirty thousand miles of Interstates carried traffic by 1970. The more miles that opened, the more traffic the Interstates carried and the less traffic older US highways carried. A 1970 Federal Highway Administration report noted that traffic along many old highway corridors "dropped by 50 percent or more."

This loss of traffic on older roads and highways was not an unintended consequence of Interstate construction. Interstates were never meant to serve the small towns and businesses along older highways. They were built to capture the bulk of heavy traffic, especially long-distance trucking, and to serve the nation's larger cities. The big cities served by Interstates won, and small towns and businesses bypassed by

Interstates lost, as did the older highways that had been superseded. Some of the older roads were shortened, obliterated, or abandoned here and there and declassified as federal highways. US Highway 40, the old "National Road," once ran across the entire continent from Atlantic City to San Francisco. Interstate 80 took away much of US 40's traffic and in places usurped its right-of-way. By 1964, US 40 was decommissioned as a federal, signed highway in California, and subsequently eight hundred of the highway's westernmost miles were lopped off, leaving its western terminus not in San Francisco but about fifty miles east of Salt Lake City.

In 1960, Michigan became the first state to complete a border-to-border toll-free Interstate highway, I-94, running from Detroit to New Buffalo, Michigan, where it passed into Indiana and on to Chicago and beyond. Before I-94, two other highways had carried the traffic between Detroit and Chicago. A federal highway since 1926, US 12 connected Detroit and Chicago by running to and through many of southern Michigan's key cities, including Ann Arbor, Jackson, Marshall, Battle Creek, Kalamazoo, and St. Joseph. Another federal highway, US 112, ran from Detroit through Ypsilanti and then dipped closer to the Indiana border to run toward Chicago through smaller communities such as Saline, Clinton, Irish Hills, Somerset, Janesville, Coldwater, Sturgis, White Pigeon, and Niles.

US 112 had a storied history, and even a prehistory. Ten thousand years before Fords and Chevrolets rolled over this route, mastodons had taken this trail. Later it served as an Indian pathway known as the Sauk Trail. French explorers, fur trappers, and missionaries used it. In 1825 the federal government surveyed this route as a military road. That road, called the Chicago Road, was built between 1829 and 1836; much of it had a corduroy surface of oak logs. This route carried early pioneers westward into Michigan Territory. Many arrived at Detroit via the Erie Canal and a lake boat, and many left Detroit by road, traveling by stagecoach. Decades later, about ten years into the Model T era, Michigan created its first numbered highway system, and in 1919 the state signposted the Chicago Road as M-23. In 1926, M-23, now paved, became US 112. In the 1920s and beyond, more and more tourist sites and other amenities for travelers sprang up on the margins of this highway that carried serious traffic and yet was scenic and picturesque, especially in the beautiful, rolling Irish Hills area with its fifty lakes.

In the Irish Hills, two side by side (but rival) observation towers, sixty-four feet tall, went up in 1924. Tourists paid a nickel and climbed to their tops to get a bird's-eye view of the surrounding countryside and then ate a meal and gassed up at their base. Developed over forty years, the Irish Hills welcomed many motels, lakeside cabins, and tourist attractions: a go-kart track; a water park; Mystery Hill (which played tricks on gravity); Prehistoric Forest, with plastic dinosaurs; a western-style Trading Post; and an 1890s Stagecoach Stop that incorporated a saloon and restaurant, an ice cream shop, an exhibit of antiques, train rides, and regularly staged jail breaks and Wild West gunfights. Along the rest of the highway, Clinton had a small speedway, Sturgeon had its drive-in theater opened in 1952, and White Pigeon had The Tasty Nut Shop and Soda Bar. Historic sites included the 1831 Government Land Office, also in White Pigeon; the 1832 Walker Tavern; plus water-powered gristmills, built from 1836 to 1857, in Clinton, Buchanan, and Saline. Travelers passed beside well-maintained farms and straight through quaint two-story towns of brick and wood, spaced about fifteen miles apart, featuring Gothic Revival, Italianate, Queen Anne, and Romanesque architecture.

And then I-94 opened.

The new Interstate was routed to serve the major southern Michigan cities of Detroit, Ann Arbor, Jackson, Battle Creek, and Kalamazoo. It so closely traced the route of the original US 12 that it literally wiped that 1926 federal highway off the map. In 1962, while decommissioning old US 12, the highway system created a new US 12 by reassigning that number to US 112 to the south, which now had to compete with the Interstate for visitors and traffic. The new Interstate rolled 205 miles across Michigan at seventy miles per hour, without a stop; the new US 12 rolled 209 miles through twists and turns and down the main streets of some twenty small towns that, as attractive as they were, slowed traffic.

Roads changed and the people in cars changed. The Interstates quickened travelers' expectations, made them want to hurry from starting point to destination without tarrying in the middle. The route through the Irish Hills peaked in popularity in the 1950s and early 1960s. Thereafter, it declined, not precipitously, but slowly as one decade turned into the next and into the next, and fewer people wanted to slow down to go through picturesque towns or to see plastic dinosaurs or mock gunfights, or to climb a tall tower to have a scenic view of hills and lakes. Gas stations, motels, the famed observation towers themselves, and other tourist attractions closed. The area had once been "a mecca for tourists," "one of the state's most popular vacation stops." It became a derelict reminder of pre-Interstate travel. Attempting to revitalize towns and businesses along this route, in 2004 the state designated it a Michigan Historic Heritage Route, under the name of US 12 Heritage Trail. This highway is not about getting travelers anywhere fast. As the Heritage Trail website says, "This Road is Meant for Michigan Memories."

A far more famous highway, US 66, became a road meant for "National Memories." It suffered the same decline as US 12 because of Interstate competition, but on a far grander scale. In 1926, Route 66 became one of America's new, national highways. Its route took it from Grant Park, in Chicago, to the Pacific Ocean in Santa Monica, a run of over 2,400 miles that crossed parts of eight states (Illinois, Missouri, a tiny corner of Kansas, then Oklahoma, Texas, New Mexico, Arizona, and California) and passed through cities (St. Louis, Joplin, Tulsa, Oklahoma City, Amarillo, Albuquerque, Flagstaff, and Los Angeles) and innumerable small towns. When first designated a federal highway, only 800 miles of Route 66 were paved, leaving 1,648 miles to go, a task not completed till 1937. By the 1950s and '60s, Route 66 had become the most famous, romanticized highway in the country. It was "the mother road," as Steinbeck had called it, and the "Main Street of America." Bobby Troup immortalized it in his 1946 song "(Get Your Kicks on) Route 66," which was covered by such diverse performers as Nat King Cole, Chuck Berry, and the Rolling Stones. In 1960, the CBS network introduced a weekly television show, *Route 66*, that ran for 116 episodes and followed Tod and Buz as they motored around, always in the newest Corvette.

The two observation towers drew tourists to the Irish Hills for decades. Now, long closed to the public, they are a perplexing problem to the historic preservationists who want to save them. (Courtesy of Dave Lawrence Photography, http://davelawrence.photo)

For small businesses, Route 66 presented 2,448 miles of opportunities for mom-and-pop gas stations, motels, restaurants, drugstores, curio shops, tourist traps, drive-in theaters, mini golf courses, or anything else that might lure in motorists. A forest of signs stood in the margins of Route 66, including neon signs that lit its way through block after block of small, home-baked commercial enterprises. Route 66 was a kind of automotive amusement park, where cars and commerce resembled a carnival midway, interrupted by stretches where it passed through nothing but prairie or desert.

America became a less formal and more casual place in the 1950s, and travelers liked Route 66's commercial attractions precisely because they lacked pretense and sophistication. This was not a buttoned-up roadside culture but a popular, come-as-you-are culture. Route 66 married maximum kitsch with local history and the environment. When running the gauntlet of Route 66 towns, particularly in the southwest, happy travelers knew where they were. This was not McDonald's Land, for sure. It wasn't Howard Johnson's or Best Western's. You could see it in the names of its motels and other businesses: Pow Wow Trading Post, Tepee Curios, Wigwam Motel ("Have You Slept in a Wigwam Lately?"), Cherokee and Apache Motels, Arrowhead Lodge, Bow and Arrow Lodge, and Tonto Drive-in Theatre. Route 66 had Cowboy, Pony Soldier, Wagon Wheel, Palomino, and Lasso Motels, plus a Lariat Lodge. Add in Westward Ho, Frontier, Western Hills, Desert Hills, and Cactus Motels, and a Cotton Boll Motel too.

All was well along Route 66 until the Interstate highways planned in the 1950s came along. Parts of five Interstates (I-55, I-44, I-40, I-15, and I-10) linked up to take travelers from Chicago to Santa Monica, just like Route 66 did—but at higher speed and without stopping or getting slowed down in towns. As the Interstates were completed, one stretch at a time, traffic along Route 66 fell off. Seduced by a high rate of speed, by easy Interstate driving where you could always pass without worry, and by interchanges where you could get off, fuel the car, fuel the family with fast food, and lickity-split get back onto the Interstate, travelers whisked right by the attractions, businesses, and towns they had once frequented. The 2006 Pixar film *Cars*, in a fanciful and entertaining way, portrayed life and business in the bypassed, downtrodden Route 66 town of "Radiator Springs."

Scholars documented Route 66's decline by counting motels. In *The Motel in America* (1996), John Jakle, Keith Sculle, and Jefferson Rogers quantified the rise and fall of the motel industry along Route 66 (Central Avenue) in Albuquerque, which came to be supplanted by I-40, about two miles to the north. In 1940, 30 tourist courts and motels stood along Central Avenue. In the 1940s, they were joined by 59 more, and in the 1950s, by another 33. That was the end of the boom. By 1960, 8 motels had gone out of business, although 114 still operated. In the '60s, only 4 new motels opened on Central Avenue, while 21 closed. In the '70s, 2 new motels were added, but they were out by an I-40 interchange. Meanwhile, another 23 motels on Central Avenue had closed. In 1960, if you drove west of the Rio Grande for a bit less than two miles on Route 66 to Coors Road, you would have passed 36 motels. By 1980, more than half had disappeared, leaving only 17. Albuquerque lost guest rooms when mom-and-pop motels closed but gained guest rooms at I-40 interchanges where new motels were built by Holiday Inn, Howard Johnson Motor Lodge, La Quinta, Ramada Inn, Marriott Inn, Days Inn, Super 8, and Motel 6.

After a collection of five Interstates had usurped Route 66's route and purpose, the Federal Highway Administration declassified the old road in 1985. No longer a US highway, it lost its official signage, and US 66 disappeared from road maps. Some parts of the route were taken over and renamed or renumbered by city, county, or state governments. In other places, its road surface and bridges suffered the ultimate indignity of abandonment. Going west, the highway had once terminated in Santa Monica. Now it terminated in several places out in the middle of nowhere. Starting in the late 1980s, states, towns, business owners, and historic preservationists banded together to protect what was left of US 66. They formed Route 66 associations, began assembling and distributing tourist guides, put up "Historic Route 66" markers where real US highway signs had once been planted, got some of the route listed on the National Register of Historic Places, and made other parts into a National Scenic Byway. Twelve surviving motels over fifty years old in

Albuquerque got listed on the National Register of Historic Places. In 1999, President Clinton signed the National Route 66 Preservation Bill, which provided for $10 million in matching fund grants, administered by the Cultural Resource Programs of the National Park Service, to preserve American popular culture and landscape features along "the mother road."

As Interstates opened in the 1950s, millions of modern Americans showed they were not like American travelers of old. Unlike some Mormons, they did not walk from St. Louis to Utah while pulling a handcart filled with all their earthly possessions. They were not in stagecoaches, Conestoga wagons, or prairie schooners. They were not riding with Horatio Nelson Jackson, who started in San Francisco and drove his Winton clear across the continent in 1903. They were not along for the ride when Jim and Hanse left Calumet, Michigan, in 1908, bound for Chicago, and had to stop at one stream to build their own primitive bridge. In the late 1930s, they did not ride in the back of the Joads' overloaded truck as it struggled mightily, in Steinbeck's *The Grapes of Wrath*, to carry them from the Dust Bowl of Oklahoma to the promised land of California. They weren't even with my family in the mid-1950s, when we traveled three hundred miles over two-lane roads to visit relatives in Indiana and Illinois, kept getting lost in Fort Wayne, and ate at places we'd never heard of.

These modern travelers did not want to explore, take chances, or wonder what was ahead of them. They did not want to endure or persevere. They wanted to ride in large cars with all the creature comforts, from soft suspensions to radios, air-conditioners, and all the power assists that took the effort out of driving. They eschewed variety, unpredictability, and uncertainty, and embraced the sure thing and the familiar. They knew what to expect along the Interstates, including a fast trip, so they chose them over older routes. They knew how a hamburger would taste and how much it would cost at a McDonald's, so they ate there. They knew just what a Holiday Inn "Great Sign" looked like, so they hunted for one and pulled into the motel, knowing it had a pool and a restaurant, that kids stayed free, and that the furnishings would be clean and pleasant. The toilet seat would have a little paper belt wrapped around it, which would comfort guests by making it clear that somebody had carefully sanitized that place to sit.

In 1975, Holiday Inn adopted a new corporate slogan: "The Best Surprise Is No Surprise." Americans, most of them, seemed to have no argument with that, based on the roads they chose to travel and the places where they chose to stop. But some, like me, tend to stay off the Interstates and frequent old one-of-a-kind motels and restaurants. I suppose that's because when Mom and Dad took me on my first vacations, there were no McDonald's, Holiday Inns, or Interstate highways. I kind of liked it that way.

As adults, in a car or on a motorcycle, my wife, Rachel, and I have traveled out and back from the Midwest to the Pacific Coast five times. Once we came back from California riding a Honda Goldwing four hundred miles on Route 66, before it was decommissioned. Another time we drove Historic Route 66, or what was left of the original highway, from Illinois west to California. We stayed at the Munger Moss Motel in Lebanon, Missouri; the 1920s Campbell Hotel in Tulsa; the Cactus Inn in McLean, Texas; the Blue Swallow Motel in Tucumcari, New Mexico; and the Supai Motel in Seligman, Arizona. We avoided Interstates on our trips and ran long east-west distances on US 2, US 12, US 20, US 30, and US 40.

We have lived for forty-five years in Houghton, Michigan, where the closest Interstate highway is 250 miles away. To go visit my sister, Lynn, in downstate Jackson, we take two-lane highways 275 miles to the Mackinac Bridge, where we have no choice but to get on I-75 for about ten miles. We exit to get back on two-lane roads again: US 31, then US 131, and best of all, M-66—"Michigan's Route 66." M-66 carries little traffic as it passes through quiet countryside, up and down gentle hills, past farm fields and small towns, and only small towns: Smithville, Lake City, McBain, Marion, Barryton, Remus, Ionia, and Woodbury. We get off at M-57 and cut over to Jackson.

We take two days to complete this 550-mile-trip. At the top of Michigan's mitten, we stop overnight in Mackinaw City. The Chippewa Room at Audie's Restaurant is open only in the evenings. I want to eat there because it serves an old family favorite that is hard to find these days: frog legs.

# 8

## THE FAMILY CAR

In all of the automotive imagery put out by Detroit in the 1950s (and later decades, too, for that matter), no driver ever cussed out a grandmother for driving only half the posted speed limit. No one exploded into a fit of road rage. Traffic flowed over idyllic streets and highways, free of traffic jams, fender benders, and roadkill. Drivers and passengers smiled as they motored without a care in the world—and why not? They moved toward a pleasant destination. As depicted in magazines and on television, cars never took people to the factory, a dentist, a funeral parlor, or an IRS office.

Instead, cars rolled over pothole-free roads leading to heaven-on-earth places: the buttes of Utah's Monument Valley; deserts decorated with cactus; coastlines bejeweled with lighthouses and yacht clubs; and ski resorts adjacent snow-capped peaks. Picturesque roads meandered alongside rivers and streams. They passed through farm country and woods on the way to lakes and rustic cabins. They delivered young adults to golf courses, stadiums, polo clubs, parks, and swimming pools. Occasionally, history, culture, cities, and monumental structures came into view. Through their windshields, Americans saw Native American pueblos, Mount Vernon, Colonial Williamsburg, the Jefferson Memorial, Hoover Dam, art galleries, theaters, museums, modern architecture, elite hotels, city skylines, and long, graceful suspension bridges. This was the USA that Dinah Shore sang about on her 1950s television show, the one she wanted you to see in your Chevrolet. After following the open road through Detroit's version of the United States, how could you ever *not* believe that America was the greatest land of all?

The people who traveled the American road were just as great as the land itself. They were all white, even in ads that ran in *Ebony* magazine. The adults were mostly under thirty-five, except for some gray-haired grandparents and distinguished Cadillac, Lincoln, or Imperial owners. Most clearly represented the middle or upper middle class; some displayed even greater wealth than that. They lived in new suburban houses, or even in mansions. They dressed snappily and sometimes formally for whatever occasion awaited them, even if they were driving a low-priced Chevy, Ford, or Plymouth. They lounged under beach umbrellas, enjoyed picnics, hunted and fished, and found dogs and horses to be fine companions.

Americans liked a big car, a family car or a six-passenger car, even if just one person, the driver, was in it. An unaccompanied man or woman drove a big new car across a magazine page or television screen. If you favored freedom, peace and quiet, and privacy, what could be better than traveling alone in a car? Small wonder these drivers always smiled. For the lone woman driver, that empty car surrounding her symbolized her modernity, self-confidence, and competence. By mastering control over four thousand pounds of fast-moving machine, she earned her escape from husband, housework, and kids. She was at liberty to go anywhere. But why would she ever want to escape her husband? In ads and commercials, when the front seat was occupied by a man and a woman, they would never have a little spat, let alone a divorce, because they were so perfectly matched in age, trimness of physique, grooming, and dress. Romance still burned bright across America as couples went stylin' and smilin' down the highway, loving each other's company and without a care in the world.

But who sat on the car's long back seat? That spacious back seat, with room for three, made Detroit's cars *family* cars. In the 1950s, families flourished. Baby boomers by the millions arrived to occupy the back seats of America. (A good number of them were earlier conceived in a back seat.) For sure, most commercial snapshots of Americans and their cars deleted small back seat passengers. From the standpoint of advertising art, this was understandable. While Dad and Mom sat high enough in a car for their chests, shoulders and faces to be seen through the windshield and side windows, little tykes' heads, barely poking up to a car's beltline, would look incomplete, like mops of hair riding down the road. Children didn't buy cars, so Detroit naturally targeted commercial messages at decision-making adults with money, not their kids. Even in a time of unprecedented birth rates, ad agencies usually chose not to show children.

But there were exceptions to the rule. Besides selling fun, freedom, and romance, Detroit sold family togetherness implicitly, if not explicitly. Just by making nearly every car big enough to seat six people, and every trunk big enough to handle many American Tourister or Samsonite suitcases, Detroit presented itself as family friendly. For foreign automakers, the situation was different. Their vehicles' diminutive size symbolized cuteness, low purchase price, and high gas mileage. But the early postwar imports hardly shouted out "Family Car!" to suburban Americans. So, when introducing their much smaller cars to Americans, makers such as Renault, Peugeot, and Morris often showed a cluster of children in or around a small vehicle. The ads implied that a family could be happy with an import, even if it hardly resembled a large, traditional family car. Ad copy for the tiny Renault Dauphine tried to convince Americans that the car had an "Amazing amount of head room, foot room, kids room." Volkswagen had a different way to appeal to active American families. *Popular Mechanics*, in its July 1955 issue, put on its cover a VW camper—or "Camp Car," which was a well-packaged vehicle that could take a family from campground to campground and offered sleeping space for three adults and two or three children. Three years later, Volkswagen marketed a van, which it first called a "full of sun, full of fun Station Wagon." It would be "the growing American family's pride and joy—roomy as can be—and carefree as the whole outdoors with sliding sun-roof, skylights and big picture windows." In the ad, an American family of four stops the VW van out in the countryside to buy fresh, local produce.

The Big Three American automakers didn't have to push the family theme hard, because the sheer size of their cars said it all: Dad, Mom, and four kids could obviously fit into virtually any GM, Ford, or Chrysler product, save for Corvettes and Thunderbirds. The Big Three spent their advertising budgets trying to seduce customers into showrooms by selling them on the virtues of automatic transmissions, power steering, power brakes, fins, hardtops, wraparound windshields, and new colors. Occasionally, though, Detroit explicitly pitched its products to families, using images, words, or both. An ad for the 1950 Plymouth informed consumers on "How to select a good family car." New cars, the ad said, "like growing families, come in many different types and sizes. So, when you buy a new car—regardless of make, you'll want to count noses and see which model best suits the needs and nature of *your* family." Alongside the text, illustrations showed mom, dad, and three small children standing beside a two-door Plymouth, while another mom and dad sat with their four kids inside a four-door sedan.

In a 1951 ad, a dad holding his little daughter's hand approached a Mercury and said, "Full-family sized if I ever saw one!" In a 1954 Chevy two-door coupe ad, the car has just pulled up in front of a cabin in the woods. A young boy sprints away from the car with a cavorting dog. The daughter slips out of the back seat with a tennis racket in hand. Mom carries a box of supplies toward the cabin door, while Dad lugs a small outboard motor toward the lake. The ad copy notes that "The family . . . has everything it takes to enjoy a wonderful vacation—a fine place to go and a fine new Chevrolet to get them there."

A 1956 ad announced that "Nash Thought of the Children, too, in the World's Finest Travel Car!" In an era of big behemoths on wheels, the smaller Nash, like imports, had to work to sell itself as a family car. The ad depicts a family of four leaving an amusement park. The boy and girl, tired from their exhilarating day, are already asleep. The Nash sedan offered a fully reclining front passenger seat, whose back reached down to the rear seat cushion, making into a bed, or what Nash called "an instant 'nap couch.'" In the artwork, Dad drives, while Mom sits behind him, next to her peacefully slumbering brood. Such scenes of blissful family life on the road were entirely absent from ads and commercials for American cars on the opposite end of the spectrum from Nash. The potential purchaser of a Cadillac, Lincoln, or Imperial was shown as not interested in kids, Boy Scout troops, or picnics, but in social status and a sophisticated, cultured lifestyle. Standing second only to Cadillac in GM's pecking order of cars, Buick eventually tried to tap the family market in explicit ways. In a 1958 ad, General Motors presented Buick as "The First Big Family Car—with a Sports Car Heart." Dad, Mom, two teens, and two younger children were shown motoring through the American West in a Buick B-58. Buick was one of the two most expensive makes (Chrysler was the other) to sell station wagons. The Buick wagon carried the tony name of "Estate Wagon." The station wagon was Detroit's ultimate expression of family-friendliness in the 1950s and 1960s.

The station wagon originated in the mid-1920s not as a family vehicle but as a hack or taxi with enhanced space in the rear for carrying multiple travelers and their luggage to and from railway stations. Small, independent body companies outfitted many of the early wagons, mounting them on a production chassis built and sold by Ford and others. The bodies were framed and finished in wood (which led to the vehicles being called "woodies"); the top was often canvas, and so were roll-down curtains for the side "windows," which had no glass. By the 1930s, a host of Detroit automakers decided to build entire wagons themselves. Still, by 1940 the station wagon—still viewed predominantly as a truck-like, commercial vehicle—represented less than 1 percent of new vehicle sales.

That changed in the postwar world. Millions of new suburbanites with growing families felt they needed a big "family car-of-all-work," a family carryall "for everything from crates to cats, groceries to Great Danes." General Motors trumpeted the station wagon's roominess, ruggedness, and adaptability—all characteristics "of such particular importance to suburban family life." Automakers popularized the station wagon by erasing its truck chassis roots, wrapping it in a steel body with many glass windows, and making it as comfortable, stylish, and well-equipped as a regular car. To attract buyers with a penchant for nostalgia, for much of the 1950s, automakers, especially Ford, attached real or simulated wood panels to steel bodies to make modern station wagons look like prewar vintage woodies.

In the 1950s, at least sixteen American auto companies rolled out station wagons. All GM divisions, except Cadillac, made wagons, and GM's English arm, Vauxhall, exported wagons to the United States. Lincoln produced no wagons, but Ford, Mercury, and the ill-fated Edsel all did. Chrysler Corporation followed the same pattern. It did not "cheapen" its elite vehicle, the Imperial, by having it sell a family wagon. But Chrysler, DeSoto, Dodge, and Plymouth all made wagons. Independent automakers, struggling just to stay alive in the 1950s, targeted this growing market segment too. Crosley Motors built tiny four-passenger station wagons (yet one had the braggadocio name of "Super Wagon") in the first few years of the 1950s, before going out of business. Studebaker, Packard, and Willys built wagons. Nash produced station wagons, and after merging with Hudson to form American Motors Corporation in 1954, AMC built both Nash Rambler and Hudson Rambler wagons.

Manufacturers often gave station wagons names that reflected their utility, their roadworthiness, and the fun they could inject into your life. You could drive one across town or country, carrying anything. You could head out to the hardware store or, like a V-8 cowboy, head out to the wide-open spaces of the American West. Chevy made a Handyman, a Townsman, a Yeoman, and a Nomad. Studebaker Lark called its smallish example a "Play Wagon," while Oldsmobile had a Fiesta. Plymouth built a Suburban, Pontiac a Safari, Rambler a Cross Country, Mercury a Country Cruiser, and Ford a Country Squire, Country Sedan, and Ranch Wagon.

Carmakers treated station wagons as variants of the passenger car. Wagons came in several models to appeal to a broader spectrum of buyers. Models differed in trim levels, number of doors, sizes and configurations of engines (six cylinder or V-8), and number of seats. Four-door wagons were by far the most popular, because family or friends could load into or out of them with greater ease, but two-door wagons were bought by people who wanted a sleeker and more modern look that resembled a hardtop car. Wagons came with seating for six, with two bench seats plus carryall space in the rear, or with three bench seats, seating for nine, and less carrying space, unless the third seat folded down and out of the way. The two leading sellers of passenger cars also sold the most station wagons. In 1955, Ford offered five station wagons, which it characterized as "do-it-all beauties." In 1956, Chevrolet did Ford one better, selling six models—three two-door models and three four-door wagons. That model year, Chevy sold 192,772 wagons, representing 12 percent of its total passenger car sales of 1.57 million vehicles. In 1957, a down year for the industry, Chevy's wagon sales hit 220,062—or 14.5 percent of its total sales of 1.51 million vehicles. Between 1950 and 1960, annual sales of station wagons rose from 142,000 to 1,059,000, and by 1958–60, wagons accounted for 16 percent of all new car sales.

In the 1950s, Detroit depicted Americans on the road as living idyllic fantasies. Ads and commercials suggested that a large percentage of America's 180 million residents (in 1960) couldn't be found at home, because they were on vacation, visiting motels, restaurants, and tourist destinations. *Newsweek*'s issue of July 4, 1955, declared that "the nation, at mid-1955, was living in tall cotton." It was America's "most prosperous year." The article continued, "About $12 billion was being spent on recreation (an increase of $750 million). Another $55 billion for meals and beverages outside the home (up $3 billion), $28 billion for cars and their upkeep as against $25.5 billion in 1954." The whole country, it seemed, was traveling: "Millions . . . of Americans were piling the family into new cars and taking off for the national parks (50 million visitors expected this year), for mountain resorts, for historical sites, for California, Florida, or New York—and they weren't worried about the expense."

Large cars and station wagons brought nuclear families together to take Sunday drives or long trips. In 1960, GM espoused that "There's Nothing Like a New Car to Bring Families and Friends Together." Detroit took no blame for splitting up and spreading out America's modern, mobile families, but it did take credit for bringing them back together: "A new car standing in your driveway seems to say, 'C'mon, let's get moving. Let's explore. Let's go places and see things.'" Some of those "things" were relatives, and a new car encouraged "More Frequent Family Visits," in part because "the whole family is safer and more comfortable in a new car." Ford had sounded this same message earlier. In December 1952, it ran, as part of the company's "The American Road" series, an ad titled "Through the wood to Grandfather's house." On the left side of this two-page spread, a family glides toward grampa's in a horse-drawn sleigh; on the right side, a family arrives at grandfather's house in a brand-new Mercury station wagon. The copy read, "Once upon a time, . . . you only saw your relatives on certain fixed great occasions. Christmas day was such a time. . . . You had fine visits, but only a few times a year, because travel was too difficult. . . . Today, the automobile makes the family reunion convenient; people measure distance in minutes, not miles."

* * *

It seemed to me that everything fun started with a car ride. To be sure, I walked or hiked to my buddies' houses and to woods and streams close to my boyhood home on Schaffer Drive. I rode my Schwinn to Ella Sharp Park's golf course and baseball diamonds, a mile or two away. But beyond that distance, one of our two cars delivered me almost everywhere.

The car took me to downtown Jackson, five miles from home, where shops and stores sold everything you could possibly need, everything from a car or car parts to Craftsmen tools, baseball gloves, underwear and socks, groceries, wedding rings, prescription drugs, cameras, film, or an alto saxophone. At Field's department store, in December you sat on Santa's lap in the basement and pled your case for being good, then, thanks to Mom, you had a sundae or a cream puff upstairs in the Rose Room tearoom.

The family car delivered my friends and me, in 1955, to the Michigan Theater downtown, where we stood in a block-long line to see Disney's film "Davy Crockett: King of the Wild Frontier." All things Western were so big then. In 1955, I also traveled downtown to see Gene Autry, "the Singing Cowboy," perform live at the Municipal Auditorium. Just a bit removed from downtown, every summer I went to the Jackson County Fair to play games for chintzy prizes, eat cotton candy, ride the Ferris wheel and bumper cars, and see the animals. At the age of ten I attended my first custom car show at the armory. On these drives around town, I had a few in-the-car rituals or games. At every railroad crossing, I picked up my feet. When stopped to let a long freight train go by, I tried to hold my breath until the caboose passed. I also held my breath whenever we drove past a cemetery.

Other trips extended beyond Jackson's city limits. While listening to Van Patrick announce a Tigers game on the car radio, my family often went for a Sunday drive. After lunch we cruised the countryside, taking a ride just for the sake of taking a ride, passing by lake and forest, maybe stopping at an orchard. In 1956, we drove all the way to the top of Michigan's mitten to see the Mackinac Bridge under construction. What a magnificent structure, what a daring deed it seemed to be. During the winter of 1957–58, Mom and Dad took me to see the Ice Capades show in Lansing. The announcer informed the audience that Mr. Al Kaline was in the house that night. Al Kaline wore number 6 and played right field for the Detroit Tigers. In 1955, at twenty years of age, he hit .340 and became the youngest player ever to win the American League batting crown. Kaline had become my hero, and I carried his baseball card in my little wallet. During an ice-show intermission, Kaline autographed my card, which I knew I'd keep forever.

I saw Al Kaline play many times. A favorite trip for Dad and me—usually accompanied by another father-son combination—was to drive eighty miles into Detroit to catch a Tigers game, maybe even a doubleheader, at Briggs Stadium. On the way, we boys often played the alphabet game. We scanned license plates, car names, billboards—anything that had words on it—to see who could be the first to find an "a," then a "b"—all the way to "z." Sometimes we played a game particularly apt for the Detroit area—one boy counted Fords, one counted Chevrolets. The count was always pretty close and ran into some pretty high numbers. Once in the city, Dad parked the car near the corner of Michigan and Trumbull, and we climbed ramps up into the stadium. I liked night games best, because while the sky was so dark, the baseball field was so green and vibrant under the lights. After a night game, and after driving back to Jackson, it became a ritual for all the travelers to stop at the Jackson Coney Island restaurant. Eating a coney or two was a midnight treat to be savored, indigestion be damned.

On many trips, my family visited relatives. I made the acquaintance of many of my relations at family reunions in Michigan (Dad's family) and in Illinois or Indiana (Mom's). We occasionally drove to visit my dad's brothers—Glenn in Detroit and Clyde in Pontiac. More often, we visited Mom's family. At least twice a year we drove to Grosse Pointe Woods, where Mom's youngest sister, Millie, lived with husband Darrell and children Charlotte and Mark. Their brick house at 1821 Aline Drive went up in the mid-1950s. To squeeze in more houses per block, the developer put detached two-car garages at the back of the lot, reached by a narrow concrete driveway. In one stall in Darrell and Millie's garage sat a small 1947 Hillman convertible. It was purely a fun car, not meant for serious travel but for cruising the Pointes on weekends. The other stall housed a Buick or Pontiac, perhaps because General Motors sent work to Darrell's chrome-plating shop in downtown Detroit. Darrell was one of my favorite uncles, and Millie was a playful gal who loved to talk and laugh and party, but at the same time she was obsessed with keeping a spotless house. Millie covered all the living room furniture in plastic. In truth, I thought, it should have been called the "non-living room," because nobody ever sat in it, talked in it, or snacked or drank in it. Everybody just passed through it, on the way to somewhere else. The living room was just for show. Convivial get-togethers always took place in the kitchen or in the finished basement with its wet bar.

Millie and Darrell's house on Aline Drive represented the new suburban America, ten years into the postwar era. My other aunts and uncles on Mom's side still lived in a decades older world. The seven Atkinson kids had been born on a farm between 1893 and 1915, and four of them remained on farms in the 1950s. Nearly every summer, we drove down to visit them, traveling on two-lane blacktop highways that passed through the middle of every town or city that stood in the way. Dad always got lost by missing a turn in Fort Wayne, Indiana, but once that problem was resolved, we would reach our first destination and then spend a week or two driving from relative to relative, hitting little towns that time had forgotten, such as West Lebanon, Veedersburg, Kingman, and Yeddo, Indiana. The biggest stop on the tour was Danville, Illinois, just over the state line. We never stayed in motels on these trips; we stayed with Mom's sisters or brothers.

For me, driving down to west central Indiana was like driving down to a living history museum dedicated to rural, small-town life. In most of my relatives' houses, no televisions could be found, and in one or two, chamber pots were used till the inside toilet was finally finished. At Aunt Wannie's, dishes were washed after working a big lever up and down to pump water into the sink. And the milk was warm, having only recently come from the cows out back. Most of my relatives' closest neighbors were, in fact, cows, pigs, horses, and big old farm dogs.

Some relatives even had names that seemed old-fashioned to me. I never got particularly close to Uncle Elmer and Aunt Ada, who farmed near Veedersburg, maybe because they were the oldest couple and never had kids. I could never remember playing with them. Their farm, though, seemed to be the most prosperous of the bunch. On another farm, we visited Uncle Carol and Aunt Sybil, who lived near Waynetown in a modest house at the end of a very long dirt path. Carol stood out because he had lost a hand long before in a piece of farm machinery. But being one-handed never seemed to bother him. In summer, he wore faded blue overalls and a white undershirt as he went about his many tasks. Sybil loved to quilt and grow things. She kept an extensive garden outside and dozens and dozens of African violets inside. I remember walking their fields, encountering novel dung beetles that rolled cow manure into balls about the size of shooter marbles. I also remember walking into a barn when suddenly a hog, in a hurry, came running out. I scurried out of the way, dove under a barbed wire fence, which left me safe but snagged my brand-new shirt.

Aunt Wannie (or Waneta, but nobody ever called her that) lived on a farm right next to the railroad tracks running by West Lebanon, which was far too small to have a train station. If Dad was not making the trip to Indiana, sometimes Mom and I, after being driven from Jackson to Adrian, caught a Wabash Central train that accommodated us and stopped next to Wannie's farm and let us off. I thought that was pretty cool. As for Wannie, she was a plain, heavy-set country gal, but she still managed to snag five husbands. She had so many because they kept dying on her. Over time, as she added more and more last names, she became Wannie Stull Isaacs Jones Sackmire Lyness. In the years when I visited her farm, she was Mrs. Bert Jones. Bert not only tended the farm with its small dairy herd; he also ran West Lebanon's Shell gas station, right next to where the train dropped us off. I liked to hang out there. Bert was friendly and let me have as many cold pops and bags of chips as I wanted. And I always liked the smell of oil and gas that lingered in the service bay, with its one wall fully lined with tires, new and old.

Getting to Uncle Charlie's place near tiny Bloomingdale, Indiana, required negotiating many backcountry roads, unmarked by names or numbers, bending around the corners of fields, and always dusty in the summer. I wondered how Dad always got lost driving through Fort Wayne but found the way to Charlie's place without trouble. Charlie leased the farm and its two-story brick house, built about 1885, that had bay windows and gingerbread detailing. Charlie was a tall, gaunt veteran of World War II. If it hadn't been for the war, he would have seen extremely little of the world beyond Parke and Fountain Counties, Indiana. Most of Charlie's relatives lived within fifty miles of him, and the ones that didn't, like my mom, usually came to visit him. Only once did Charlie make the trip up to Jackson to visit. The war got him to England and Europe, and it also got him a woman, Agnes. Right after the war she came from England to the States to live with Charlie. They never married, but that never seemed to matter. Agnes was not universally loved by the family, yet they realized that Charlie was better off with her than without her. A farm was not a place to run a one-man show.

Throughout my childhood, I had bad allergies. Dust and pollen drove me crazy. My family's cars, in the 1950s, lacked air-conditioning, so in the summer heat we drove with the windows down. Traveling the dusty back roads edged with weeds to Uncle Charlie's, I suffered sneezes, itchy eyes, and difficult breathing before we ever got there. And sometimes, after we got there, things got even worse. One morning, out alone, I played in a corn crib. I'd scramble up to the top of the field corn and slide back down. Then severe allergies kicked in, and I crawled back to the farmhouse to be tended to. After that experience, I figured it was a good thing I hadn't been born on a farm around 1900, like Charlie, because I probably would've died.

Despite my allergies, I loved visiting Uncle Charlie's farm. Life there was so different: no neighbors; different smells and sounds; big animals; and unusual things, like tractors. Charlie, lacking kids of his own, really seemed to enjoy my company. When I was just two or three, Charlie playfully put me astride a huge black-and-white hog and held on to me as I took a porcine ride. Charlie took me for tractor rides across the fields. I would take an ear of field corn into the chicken coop and shell it by hand for the chickens to scramble after. At noon, when Charlie and Agnes ate their big meal of the day, I often helped eat one of those chickens. I learned the routine: kill and bleed the chicken, scald the chicken, pluck the chicken, cut up the chicken, flour the chicken, fry the chicken. Make gravy from the drippings, make a big bowlful of mashed potatoes, boil some beans, and have at it. I never met a woman relative from Indiana who didn't make the best fried chicken ever. Even Charlie's Agnes, transplanted from England, had learned that art.

The family always visited Aunt Ruby on these vacations. Ruby and her husband, Walt, escaped living on a farm. They married in 1922, and in 1925 moved across the Indiana state line to Danville, Illinois. Danville was a real city, not a tiny crossroads place like West Lebanon, Kingman, or Yeddo. You could always smell corn in Danville, thanks to the large grain elevators there, but at least it didn't grow in the streets. Ruby was a homemaker; Walt, a barber, whose shop was attached to their house. They had three kids, two boys and a girl, and these kids spent almost all their lives in Danville. The oldest child, Bob, graduated from Danville High in 1943, giving him just enough time to find his way into uniform before World War II ended. After his service in the Pacific, he came back to Danville to settle down. Bob married Joanne, and their first child, Jim, arrived in 1948, just a year after I was born. So, in Danville I had someone my own age to play pool and baseball with. Ruby and Walt had a big pool table in the basement, and they lived only a few blocks from Lincoln Park, which had a ball field. In June 1957, as a ten-year-old, I spent some time in Danville without my folks. I sent a postcard home: "Dear Mom and Dad—I've been playing a lot of pool down here. It's been hot all the time. Going to Uncle Charlie's place tomorrow. I've now got Boone and Kaline in baseball cards. Went to the park and played ball yesterday."

Besides pool and baseball, Jim and I played another favorite game: tormenting poor Uncle Walt by staging fake fights to get him agitated. Walt was easily riled, and when his blood pressure rose, cusswords and misidentifications spat from his mouth. It was one god dammit after another. Then he would shout out the names of the combatants to get their attention. But Walt always got Jim's name and my name mixed up with his own kids' names. He yelled out, "Bob, Bill—stop this fighting, god dammit!" When we boys finally broke out laughing, after a few more god dammits Walt finally calmed down, realizing he'd been had again. Then we tapped him for money to go buy some burgers and fries for lunch.

Aunt Ruby was a devout Methodist (indeed, she died during a service at Lincoln Methodist Church one Sunday), which seemed to make it more surprising that in Ruby and Walt's basement, I found a collection of sex education books. I could read *Boys' Life*, or *Sport* magazine, or *Baseball Digest* anywhere, but only in Ruby's basement could I gain my first scientific knowledge of female anatomy and reproduction. When not playing rotation or eight ball or reading about fallopian tubes, I did odd jobs for Walt, sweeping the barber shop floor or painting a white picket fence. The fence took a couple days to finish in the hot Illinois sun, but the job paid well, and I took my earnings to Weese's Sporting Goods store and bought a brand-new Rawlings Trapeze ball glove, which became one of my most prized possessions ever.

The road trip from Jackson down to Kingman or Danville ran about 300 miles. I took a much longer car trip in 1958 with Dad. For some reason, Mom didn't go on this adventure. I had never been to many states. I'd toured Michigan, and I'd seen where family lived in Indiana and Illinois. My only trip to Ohio was a quick in-and-out to see the Toledo Zoo. But this trip broadened my horizons. In our family car, the 1956 Packard, the fifty-five-year-old father and the eleven-year-old boy bonded as we motored 1,750 miles over strange and new highways to the east and back.

We traveled from Jackson to Detroit and through the mile-long Detroit-Windsor Tunnel. That was a new experience! We passed on through Ontario, Canada, to Niagara Falls. We viewed this natural spectacle from the top and then from the bottom, riding on one of the *Maid of the Mist* boats that took you in so close you felt spray in your face. For a souvenir, I acquired a small purple-and-yellow pennant that said "Niagara Falls, 1958." From Niagara we dropped down to Williamsport, Pennsylvania, which was not a tourist destination for many. But it was here that kids my age played in the Little League World Series. Even though it wasn't being played right then, I just had to see this hallowed ball diamond with its green fences, scoreboard, and stands.

From Williamsport, we rode in the Packard to some real hallowed ground—Gettysburg. This was the highlight of the trip. Dad and I visited the museums and watched how the Blue and the Gray armies maneuvered across the Electric Map of the battlefield. Dad hired a guide who got in the Packard and directed a tour of the major sites: Little and Big Round Tops, Devil's Den, the Peach Orchard, and the Wheatfield. Later, Dad and I drove around the battlefield again, stopping to explore and photograph state monuments and rows of cannon. Dad bought me a small Gettysburg pennant, like the Niagara Falls pennant, but this one was red and yellow. He also bought some books about the battle, so I could learn more about Pickett's Charge and about poor Wesley Culp. Culp had been born and raised in Gettysburg but left to take a job in Virginia. When the Civil War broke out, Culp joined the Confederate Army and served with the Second Virginia Infantry Regiment. On July 3, 1863, he was killed at Gettysburg; he died near an uncle's farm and a hill bearing his family's name. I never forgot Wesley Culp and his tragic story.

After Gettysburg came the nation's capital. After a day and a half spent at museums and the Washington Monument, we left and started heading back to the Midwest, traveling many miles along a route that was historic itself. US 40 was the country's first coast-to-coast highway.

In some of its eastern sections US 40 followed the route of the first federally funded national road, built between 1811 and 1818 from Cumberland, Maryland, on the Potomac River, to Wheeling, Virginia, (now West Virginia) on the Ohio River. The Packard passed through town after town on US 40 before stopping at Washington, Pennsylvania. Washington was Dad's stop, a place he wanted to go.

We went to the campus of Washington and Jefferson College. Back in the 1920s, Dad (born in 1903) played football. He played end on the Detroit Eastern High team that won the state championship in 1922. From there he went to Alma College in Michigan, where he played a few years (for sure in 1923 and 1924) before moving on to the College of the City of Detroit (now Wayne State University). According to the 1926 yearbook, my dad "playing his first year for City College, was a valuable man to the team. His running attack was not so powerful [he played fullback], but his punting was the best City College has had in years." After City College, he moved to play for Washington and Jefferson, a small college that, surprisingly, was a national power during the 1920s. In 1922, using only eleven players, Washington and Jefferson fought the California Golden Bears to a scoreless tie in the Rose Bowl, and the next season it won a 14 to 13 game against Lafayette College played before fifty thousand fans at the Polo Grounds in New York. John Heisman, namesake of college football's Heisman Trophy, coached for a year at Washington and Jefferson in the 1920s.

Dad never earned a degree, despite going to three colleges. He kept matriculating, it seems, mainly to keep playing football. How he ended up at Washington and Jefferson is anybody's guess, but that small school's football program, according to a 1929 report from the Carnegie Foundation for the Advancement of Teaching, had been and was being supported by large financial contributions from alumni and local businessmen. A slush fund subsidized football and gave paychecks out to some players. Dad was highly skilled in one thing—kicking—and maybe that got him to Washington and Jefferson. In 1958, when Dad and I toured the campus, we stopped in at the football office. The football equipment manager happened to be there—just like he had been there in the late 1920s. The two men, one in his sixties and one in his fifties, reminisced about knowing each other thirty years earlier. The equipment manager told me that my father was the best kicker he'd ever seen play for the college.

Pulling away from Washington, Pennsylvania, the Packard continued west on US 40, going through Columbus, Ohio, and Indianapolis, Indiana, before turning on to smaller highways and then dirt roads to get to Uncle Charlie's farm. Dad clearly had an affinity for rural life and for men who farmed. Raised in Detroit, the son of an autoworker at Studebaker, in the mid-1940s he lived in Moscow, Michigan, on five acres with a house, barn, chicken coop, and corn crib. He kept about five horses and two hundred chickens, and sold eggs to the country stores nearby. I knew my father as a foreman, tool and die maker, and draftsman—not as a would-be tiller of the soil. I first saw that side of Dad at the Jackson County Fair. While touring the horse barn, Dad took particular interest in one animal. He hunted down the owner, and sure enough, he had owned that horse while living in Moscow. What, a horse? I was very surprised and thought maybe I'd missed out on something. My father surely kept no horses in our new subdivision on Schaffer Drive. Dad had once lived a very different life that he didn't live anymore, but he could still visit it in Indiana. He clearly liked visiting Mom's relatives on their Indiana farms, more than he liked visiting his own brothers in Detroit and Pontiac.

We stayed at Charlie's for a few days. One day, a raccoon meandered into the farmhouse drive, and then just stood there, refusing to budge. Worried about rabies, Charlie didn't hesitate. He went into the house, got a rifle, shot the critter, and burned its carcass. The next day, Charlie, Dad, and I stopped in a bar in nearby Rockville. Afterward, for some reason, we all peed outside, behind the bar, rather than inside. Charlie talked about having blood in his pee, which was something I had never heard of before.

The following day, we completed our trip, driving eight or nine hours back to Jackson. A month later, I started seventh grade at my new school, Frost Junior High. For an early assignment in English, I wrote a paper on the Battle of Gettysburg. It came back to me with a "See me" note on it, and no grade. The teacher told me the paper was too good—obviously I had copied it. "You plagiarized it," she said, and she failed me. Nobody had ever made me feel as bad as I did right then. The next day I provided her with the books I'd read and with a note from Dad that told of the trip to Gettysburg and the guide who toured with us to all the major battlefield sites. My teacher dropped the plagiarism charge and gave me an A.

A bit later, on November 1, Uncle Charlie died of cancer. He had been far sicker in August than I was ever told. After nearly a decade of annual pilgrimages to see Uncle Charlie, trips to his farm were over forever. No more long dusty roads, no more chicken dinners at noon, no more riding on hogs or on the tractor. After the funeral, Mom delivered three things to me. One was a late-nineteenth-century lithograph that had long hung on a wall in Uncle Charlie's farmhouse, called "The Battle of Shiloh." It depicted Union troops holding the line at a dirt road passing through a forest. It wasn't Gettysburg, but it was close enough. I also received Charlie's Army hat and the flag that had draped the gaunt veteran's casket and was now tightly and perfectly folded into a triangle. He really did have a fondness for me, and me for him—I kept his things forever.

In the years since the 1950s, when grown up, I read scholars' debates over the effects of the automobile on families. Did the automobile bring family members together as they shared Sunday drives and vacations, or did the automobile, quite literally, drive families apart, especially after teenagers got their licenses and drove off without Mom and Dad? Obviously, the automobile did both. For me, the automobile in the 1950s drew my family together, not only my nuclear family, which spent hours together in a car, but my extended family that I reached by car. The car took me to my people, to their houses and even their graves. The vacation trip by automobile—far more than postcards, letters, photographs, home movies, or telephone calls—made people and their places real.

The car, and the city streets, asphalt highways, and country roads it traveled along, made me feel *connected.* Trips weren't made for nothing, for no good reason. Being on the road allowed me to learn about different people, like Millie, the fussy homemaker; Sybil, in love with

African violets; Ruby, the devout Methodist with sex education books in her basement; and Aunt Wannie, who outlived her first four husbands but not the fifth. I came to know people like Bert, who ran the gas station; Walt, who cut hair; Carol, the one-handed farmer; and Uncle Charlie, keeper of huge hogs, who was there in August and dead in November. The car took me, accompanied by one or both parents, to farms, small crossroads towns, historic battlefields, downtown Detroit, and the nation's capital. The car introduced me to a world that was bigger than myself. Car trips made me conscious of the fact that I was a part of a bigger family and a bigger place. True, when I got my own driver's license, the car took me out alone, away from my mom, as I started the move from adolescence into adulthood. But that's the way it was supposed to be. You became your own man, yet as you drove to new places, you carried memories of earlier destinations, and as you met new people, they shared space in your memory with earlier generations.

# 9

## WHO'S THE FASTEST OF THEM ALL?

After World War II ended, Americans felt a need for speed. Conserving gas, rubber, and other materials was no longer necessary. Auto racing resumed, and motorsport venues popped up across the country. New race cars came into being. Their drivers treated fans to exciting competitions that lasted from a handful of seconds up to twenty-four hours. Cars raced against the clock, against a single competitor, or against dozens of competitors. They ran in a straight line, on curving courses, on ovals, or on dry lake beds. A new generation of drivers became celebrities and received public adulation. They took risks. Sometimes they won and sometimes they died. At the Indianapolis 500 in 1955, the great Bill Vukovich, trying for his third Indy win in a row, got tangled up with several cars on the backstretch. His car rolled four and a half times, catapulted over the retaining wall, and came to rest upside down and in flames. One of Vukovich's dead hands reached out from beneath his charred, upside-down race car.

In California, gearheads and speed freaks created the hot rod culture. Shops and garages built hot rods that accelerated quickly, attained high top-end speeds, handled well, and stopped on a dime. The classic California hot rods were roadsters (cars without tops), sculpted from Detroit autos built in the '20s or early '30s. Two-seater Fords were very popular. Model T's, A's, and B's made great hot rods. They incorporated some old Detroit sheet metal, but there was nothing corporate or old-fashioned about them. Young hot-rodders built the individualistic cars *they* wanted. They took off fenders and running boards. They stripped the body of trim and lowered it. They put in a powerful V-8 engine with a loud, throaty exhaust. They rebuilt the suspension and added new wheels, tires, and brakes. They took their creations to dry lake beds in California or Utah to run at top speed, and they took them to drag strips, where two hot rods competed side by side over a quarter mile.

In January 1948, Los Angeles publisher Robert E. Petersen put out the first issue of *Hot Rod* magazine, which became the bible for disciples of hot rod culture. The magazine did not adhere to any strict definition of "hot rod." It did not have to be a roadster. It could be a coupe or a sedan. The magazine applied the name "hot rod" to almost anything that had been modified to go fast. If you put an Oldsmobile engine into a '38 Chevy coupe, that was a hot rod. You could even hot rod a '57 Chevy station wagon if you wanted to. *Hot Rod* reported on speed runs on the Bonneville Salt Flats; stock car races on short tracks; sports cars on twisty tracks; and the Indianapolis 500. *Hot Rod* was particularly known for lionizing drag racing on drag strips: 1,320 feet of asphalt or concrete with a flag-waving starter on one end and a timer and a finish line on the other.

The allure of drag racing was acceleration. Engines roared at one another as the cars were staged at the starting line. The flagman leapt into the air and vigorously waved his flag. Drivers punched their accelerators. Large rear tires called slicks (because they had no tread) briefly disappeared behind a cloud of smoke, while smaller front wheels and tires rose up, often leaving the ground. In search of traction, cars often sashayed left and right. Then they came under control and ran straight down the strip. The first car to cross the finish line was the winner.

Sanctioned by the National Hot Rod Association (NHRA) and the American Hot Rod Association (AHRA), in the 1950s the sport of drag racing accelerated nearly as fast as the dragsters themselves. Promoters turned abandoned US Army Air Force bases into drag strips. Some were permanent; others ran only one or two meets. Between 1947 and 1960, approximately 59 drag venues sprang up in California, over 80 in Texas, and in my state, Michigan, 15 drag strips opened between 1952 and 1961. My brother-in-law, Ben, took me to the Onondaga Dragway, just twenty miles from my house. In 1957, *Life* magazine reported there were 130 active drag strips in America, spread across forty states, and they attracted 2.5 million spectators per year.

If you walked through the pit area of a drag strip, you would notice that the people looked alike, while the cars looked very different. Drivers and crew members were overwhelmingly male and white, and many wore jackets embroidered on the back with their hot rod club's name. Participants were young, in their teens, twenties, or early thirties, and they came to the drags in clothes stained by grease and oil, dust and dirt. Meanwhile, their drag cars displayed diversity and unlimited mechanical creativity. Builders followed no ubiquitous blueprint. They worked with what they had, what they liked, and what they could afford. Much was trial and error. If it didn't go fast enough, they changed it.

Drag racers employed engines of all sorts: Ford flatheads, Buick straight eights, GMC straight sixes, Chevy small blocks, Chrysler Hemis (with a hemispherical combustion chamber), and Olds and Pontiac engines. Some used Allison piston aircraft engines, or even jet aircraft engines acquired cheaply from salvage yards. Some engines ran with traditional carburetors. Others were fuel injected and still others were supercharged and used belt-driven blowers to force more air into the combustion chamber. Some ran on gasoline, some on methanol, and the fastest, on nitromethane.

In the 1950s, the assembled cars at a drag strip bore little resemblance to those in an auto showroom. They were not big, heavy, or new. Drag racers sliced and diced small, old cars to build lightweight, fast machines. Some of these cars had once been common on American streets: cars like Fords, especially those built between 1925 and 1940. But other cars (especially car bodies) were rare on US streets before they became commonplace at drag strips. I don't think I ever once saw a Fiat Topolino cruising a street in Jackson.

My favorite drag cars were "gassers." A gasser retained its stock-looking body, with front fenders, grill, hood, and headlights left pretty much intact. But a gasser had new running gear, and its original engine had been replaced with a high-performance power plant, like a blown Chrysler Hemi. Willys cars built between 1933 and 1940 never sold well during the Depression. They were deemed too small and slow. But salvaged and resurrected as drag cars, the lightweight Willys proved to be fast and popular. I loved the lines of small Willys gassers, especially the coupes, which looked much like scaled-down 1936–40 Ford coupes. Drag racers made gassers out of other small coupes and sedans: American Bantams, Nash Metropolitans, Henry J's, Crosleys, Austins, Fiat Topolinos, and Ford Anglias. Other racers turned these small cars into "altered" coupes or sedans. They stretched the frames, moved the engine and driver back, and removed fenders and headlights. Still others grafted these small car bodies onto the back ends of long rail dragsters, enclosing the roll cage and creating yet another new class of competitors, called "competition" coupes or sedans. It was an extremely creative era, when drag car builders clearly had a lot of fun.

The fans of drag racing were thrilled with their sport's speed, colorful cars, smoking tires, and trumpeting exhausts. But in the 1950s and into the '60s, most magazines and newspapers gave scant coverage to the sport. Television, too, rarely broadcast drag meets. To attract more attention, drag racing created special events, built faster machines, and highlighted popular drivers. In 1955, the NHRA held its first national championship drag races in the center of the country in Great Bend, Kansas. The event, held on an old Army Air Force base, drew two hundred racers and fifteen thousand spectators. Although torrential rain halted the racing after three days, the meet was a success. The event was newsworthy enough that the following year's nationals were covered by a CBS program hosted by Erick Severeid.

In 1954 and 1955, Mickey Thompson and others—mostly Californians–developed a new type of drag vehicle. Some called it a "digger" or "rail job," but the name that stuck with most fans was "slingshot dragster." Over fifteen years, the slingshot dragster transformed drag racing and drove it to its highest levels of competition and speed. Thompson and others mounted small, bicycle type tires in the front. Lightweight rails ran from the front end to the back. They positioned a powerful engine far to the rear, so it sat right in front of the driver, who now sat just above the rear axle, or, even better, behind it. These placements improved traction. Ninety percent of the dragster's weight rested on the rear driving wheels. To achieve better directional stability, builders shortened the rear axle, putting the rear slicks closer together. This kept the front end from weaving left and right so much, which kept the dragster on a straighter track as it left the starting line.

A great distance from California, a young Floridian, born in 1932, took up drag racing. In 1954, he raced a Model T roadster powered by a 1948 flathead. It wasn't fast enough. In 1955, he took the Model T body off, moved the engine back, and placed his driver's seat behind the rear axle. In his version of a slingshot dragster, Don Garlits won his first NHRA event with an elapsed time of 12.1 seconds and a speed of 108 miles per hour. Within a few years Garlits was a professional drag racer who used his natural gifts to build improved slingshot dragsters for himself. He named each successive dragster "Swamp Rat," and appended a Roman numeral to it: I, II, III, and so on. Don Garlits became "Big Daddy" Don Garlits. If an American knew the name of just one drag racer in the country, it had to be Garlits. In 1957, he

Don Garlits won his first NHRA national title at Pomona in 1963. His Swamp Rat V ran an elapsed time of 8.11 seconds at a top speed of 189 miles per hour. (Courtesy of Don Garlits Museum of Drag Racing)

was first to top 170 miles per hour in the quarter mile; first to 180 in 1958; first to over 200 in 1964, and first to over 240 in 1968. He traveled all around the country and won dozens of national championships over his long career, competing in both NHRA and AHRA events.

In the 1960s, current-model cars from Detroit became popular at the drags. Just as the muscle car era showed up on American streets, thanks to cars like the Pontiac GTO, Chevelle Super Sport, and Oldsmobile 442, a muscle car era showed up at drag strips when Detroit produced a plethora of high-performance engines. Chevy's legendary 409-cubic-inch engine powered many drag cars. Pontiac got in the mix with its Super Duty 421-cubic-inch engine with dual four-barrel carburetors. Dodge and Plymouth contributed 383 and 413 engines, which by 1964 were upped to 426 cubic inches and included a new Hemi engine. Ford manufactured a 390-cubic-inch engine, then a 406, and in 1963, a 427.

In the 1960s, Detroit helped drag racers climb into Fords, Mercurys, Chevrolets, Dodges, Plymouths, Pontiacs, and other makes. In some cases, the auto factory turned race-ready cars directly over to racing teams. They *looked* stock. They had all their window glass, bumpers, and headlights. But their bodies, engines, transmissions, suspensions, and exhausts had been tweaked to make them lighter and faster. The glass was lighter plexiglass. Body panels and hoods were aluminum, as were the exhaust headers and bell housings. These "pseudo stockers" mostly ran in the Super Stock racing class, or some variant of that. Many drivers and owners went further to create a faster, lighter car. They took an engine that the factory typically put into its largest, heaviest car (such as a Pontiac Bonneville or Ford Galaxy) and put it into a smaller, lighter model: the largest Pontiac engine into a small Tempest, or Ford's biggest motor into a Comet. These drag cars often ran in the F/X class, or factory experimental.

Moving through the 1960s, once-novel slingshot dragsters became ordinary. Having minimal bodywork and similar structures, they all looked much the same. In terms of safety, though, they were making news. Between 1963 and 1966, fifteen drivers died in slingshot dragsters when their supercharged engines running on nitromethane blew up. The driver sat right behind the engine and essentially straddled it. Fuel, hot water, and oil sprayed the driver, and when engines "grenaded," blowers, clutches, flywheels, and bell housings exploded, sending automotive shrapnel into a driver, especially his legs and feet. In 1970, Don Garlits's transmission exploded, splitting the chassis in half, breaking his left foot and leg, and cutting off half his right foot.

In the late 1960s and early 1970s, several drag teams, including Garlits's, developed rear-engine dragsters. With the engine behind the driver, the new dragsters were safer than the old slingshots and just as fast. Others in the late 1960s created "funny cars." These were shorter rail dragsters carrying lightweight bodies over custom-built frames, many of which cradled a blown engine running on nitromethane. They were called "flip tops" because the bodies were hinged at the back of the chassis and could be lifted up from the front to allow easy access to the engine and other components. Funny cars only vaguely resembled stock Detroit products. A Ford funny car was a Ford in name only. There was no "driver's side." The driver sat in the middle, aligned with the engine. The shape of the fiberglass body was altered for aerodynamic purposes (to reduce drag) and to allow for changing the placement of wheels to achieve better weight distribution and traction. Funny cars carried colorful bodies and bold graphics and proved popular with racing fans.

I never liked funny cars. I had a strong penchant for authenticity. A thing should be what it really was. To me, funny cars were fake. But drag-racing fans who liked Ford Motor Company cars cheered funny cars masquerading as Mustangs, Comets, Cougars, and even Falcons. Those who followed Chrysler products cheered Dodge Charger, Dodge Dart, and Plymouth Barracuda look-alikes. As for GM, faux Camaros and Novas and even a faux Chevy Corvair ran at the drags. Funny cars became popular in part because they were fast. At the end of the 1960s, regular top fuel dragsters ran elapsed times of about 6.4 seconds over the quarter mile, at a speed of 230 miles per hour. Funny cars ran 6.9 quarters at 215 miles per hour.

Over twenty years, as drag racing spread from California to all corners of the country, many top drivers grew in popularity and renown. Big Daddy Don Garlits, the king, was joined by other stars and future drag-racing hall-of-famers, including Don "The Snake" Prudhomme, Mickey Thompson, "Dyno" Don Nicholson, Jack Chrisman, Art Chrisman, Tommy Ivo, and Shirley "Cha Cha" Muldowney. Top drivers crisscrossed the nation with their cars, hitting ever faster speeds and attracting greater coverage in the press and on television.

Drag racing and sports car racing could hardly have been more different—in terms of fans, drivers, equipment, and types of competition. Drag racers went head-to-head and straight down the course, a quarter mile at a time. A sports car race featured a field of entrants who made left and right turns to get around a meandering course. Both motorsports, however, became popular at the same time.

Historically, American car manufacturers ignored sports cars, seeing them as a fringe market. They preferred selling larger, more expensive cars that brought higher profits. In the late 1940s and early 1950s, more Americans sought out the sporty cars that Detroit ignored. As a young boy, I noticed that more sports cars were showing up on the streets of Jackson. I was particularly enamored with one red MG TD convertible I often caught glimpses of when it was parked on Francis Street. It was a small, low-to-the-ground, wind-in-your-face kind of car. Curvy fenders, a chrome radiator surround, louvered hood, and a convertible top over a tiny cockpit for only two passengers. This car came from England.

During the war, American troops stationed overseas encountered British sports cars—MGs, Austin-Healeys, Triumphs, and Jaguars. They were fun to drive and inexpensive. Veterans sought out these sports cars. British manufacturers shipped them to the United States because they could sell more cars here. Between 1947 and 1959, more than 85 percent of all British MGs produced were shipped to the United States, and in 1955, Jaguar and MG were the third and fourth most imported cars in America. This popularity spilled over into a keener interest in sports car racing. Several of the best-known drivers drove imports from England. Phil Hill won his first race in 1949 in an MG-TC, and Carroll Shelby began road racing in 1952 in the same

MG model. When Dan Gurney began racing in 1955, he rode behind the wheel of a Triumph TR2.

The Sports Car Club of America (SCCA), formed in 1944, began sanctioning races in 1948. It awarded its first national championship in 1951. Many early SCCA races ran on courses laid out on public streets or, like drag racing, on idled military airstrips. Neither presented an ideal venue. Airstrips were too flat and barren of visual interest, and street courses quickly raised the issue of spectator and driver safety. While running on the streets of Watkins Glen, New York, in 1952, a car went into the crowd, killed a seven-year-old boy, and injured ten to twelve others. Racing over public streets at Watkins Glen stopped, and a permanent, dedicated road-racing course opened there in 1956. Sports car racing began on a street course at Elkhart Lake, Wisconsin, in the early 1950s, but the competition moved to the Road America course in 1955. SCCA road races took place over twisting town streets and roads at Pebble Beach, California, from 1950 to 1956. In '56, a driver slammed into a tree along the course and died. In '57, the race moved off public roads when the Laguna Seca road course opened.

Other foreign makes, such as Porsche, Ferrari, Maserati, and Alfa Romeo, came to compete with British cars on American soil. Detroit took notice of the interest in sports cars, and Chevrolet began offering its Corvette in 1953. Ford, too, came aboard, but only briefly. It produced a two-seater Thunderbird in 1955 through 1957 but gave it a rear seat and snuffed out its sportiness after that. Sports car races, with more diverse entries, attracted more press. *Sports Cars Illustrated* (later renamed *Car and Driver*) started publishing in July 1955. Its inaugural issue carried a Jaguar roadster on the cover and an inside article, "Tuning the MG for Competition." The cover of *Sports Illustrated* for March 6, 1959, showed Phil Hill, "Sports Car Driver of the Year," sitting on the nose of the red Ferrari he'd race at the twelve-hour Sebring endurance race in Florida. Sports car racing was not the most popular motorsport, for sure, but in ten years it became a permanent fixture on the American scene. It had driving champions whose reputations and names lived on for decades, and major tracks on both ends of the country and in the middle.

The most popular auto races in the late 1940s through the 1960s ran on short ovals from one-quarter to three-quarters of a mile around. Most were dirt tracks (oiled clay), but some were paved. Hundreds of these tracks hosted races at county fairgrounds or on the margins of small towns and larger cities. To help pay the bills, short tracks often ran diverse programs on different days and nights. Tracks featured motorcycle races, quarter-midgets, midgets, sprint cars, and stock cars. The drivers and cars were local or regional, and small sponsors, like gas stations, bars, and restaurants, helped pay the bills. Tracks charged small admission fees and paid out small purses to winners. Nobody got rich. Then along came Bill France.

France, born in Washington, DC, moved his family to Daytona, Florida, in 1935. Daytona Beach had once been the focal point of land speed record attempts held on its sands. That ended when racers moved across the country to dry lake beds in California and to the Bonneville Salt Flats in Utah. Hoping to attract another breed of competitors who would bring money back into the local economy, in 1936 locals held the first stock car race on the Daytona Beach Road course. Stock cars ran part of a lap on a paved road, made a big turn, and returned on the sands. Bill France participated in this race, and after 1938 he became an organizer of stock car races at Daytona Beach. World War II temporarily halted the events, but after the war France again raced at small Florida tracks. Then he pivoted. Instead of driving stock cars, he promoted stock car racing.

Stock car racing in the south was a growing sport but it garnered little respect. Tracks set different rules about what a stock car was and what modifications were allowed to enhance performance. Promoters offered small purses and sometimes ran off without paying car owners or drivers. France wanted to grow the sport and run it in a more businesslike manner. In December 1947, at the age of thirty-eight, he invited drivers, owners, mechanics, and promoters to a meeting in Daytona Beach. The meeting led to the creation of an organization to oversee the operation and growth of stock car racing. Bill France and his family headed this organization and ran it with a firm hand. They called it the National Association for Stock Car Automobile Racing, or NASCAR. The word "National" was an overreach. The first drivers were almost wholly southern born and bred, and NASCAR ran races on tracks from

Florida up through the Piedmont region to the Carolinas. Incorporated early in 1948, NASCAR ran its first race on the Daytona Beach and Road Course in February of that year. The next year, NASCAR held its inaugural full season of races, and participants adhered to a set of rules regarding technical specs, insurance, and purses.

The "Strictly Stock Division" represented NASCAR's highest echelon of cars and drivers. The cars could not incorporate any major modifications. They were like cars found in dealerships that anyone could own and drive. Headlights could be taped over and hubcaps and mufflers removed. That was it. No major engine or suspension alterations. Additionally, a car had to be a "new model," not more than three years old, and in good condition.

The Strictly Stock Division held eight races in 1949—seven on dirt ovals and one on the Daytona Beach and Road course. A Plymouth won one race, a Lincoln won two, and Oldsmobiles, five. To keep up interest throughout the season, NASCAR awarded points to drivers after each race and tallied them up at the end to determine the Strictly Stock Champion. The champion for 1949 was from Alabama, Red Byron, driving a Lincoln. The year before, he had been champion of NASCAR's Modified Division, winning eleven races in a souped-up 1939 Ford. Byron was a World War II vet whom people could root for. He had been hospitalized for twenty-seven months after his B-24 Liberator bomber exploded, mangling his left leg. Because of his injuries, Byron required a special setup in his race cars: the clutch pedal bolted to his metal leg brace to allow him to shift.

In 1950, NASCAR renamed its top series the Grand National Division. From 1950 till 1960, six men won the Grand National Championship. Bill Rexford (a rare Northerner from New York) and Rex White (South Carolina) won it once; Herb Thomas (North Carolina), Tim Fleck (Alabama), and Buck Baker (South Carolina) won it twice: and Lee Petty (North Carolina) won it three times. In the 1950s and early 1960s, Darlington Raceway was paved, but of the first 221 Grand National races, 198 ran on dirt tracks, and many of them were short "bull rings," such as Virginia's Martinsville Speedway, only 0.526 miles around.

In 1959–60, two longer tracks were built that changed the face of NASCAR. In 1959, the 2.5-mile Daytona International Speedway opened, and the inaugural Daytona 500 took place without any caution flags coming out. Three cars raced to the end, and Lee Petty won in a photo finish. He averaged 135 miles per hour over five hundred miles, 33 miles per hour faster than any other Grand National winner to date. Contested before 41,921 spectators, the race ushered in a new era of stock cars racing on super speedways. In 1960, the first World 600 NASCAR race ran on the 1.5-mile, paved track at Charlotte, North Carolina.

It was fitting that the first decade or so of Grand National races ran mostly on dirt tracks. Those tracks, with cars power sliding around corners, mimicked the runs moonshiners had made, racing down dirt roads in the mountains to outrun revenue men. Prohibition ended in 1933, so it was legal for poor Southerners to make liquor. However, it was illegal for them to sell "white lightning" or corn liquor without paying taxes on it. To outrun revenue agents, while hauling a hundred gallons or more of hooch, moonshiners ran cars like 1939 or 1940 Fords that had suspensions stiffened with extra leaf springs and engines bored and stroked to produce more speed. These scofflaws were folk heroes in the South, where many held rebels in high esteem while disdaining the federal government and its agents.

A significant number of NASCAR Hall of Fame drivers had earlier careers careening down dirt roads in the dark in support of the illicit booze trade. The most famous of them all, Junior Johnson, was known as the best moonshine driver in Wilkes County, North Carolina, the moonshine capital of the South. Jackson, owner of an illegal still, went to prison for a year in 1956–57, just after starting his racing career. Then he went on to win 50 NASCAR races, including the Daytona 500, and when he retired as a driver he owned a NASCAR team that captured 132 NASCAR races and six championships. Author Tom Wolfe, a Southern boy who knew a good Southern boy when he saw one, wrote a 1965 article for *Esquire* magazine that called Junior Johnson "The Last American Hero."

NASCAR and I had the same birth year, 1947. So, we grew up

together. More accurately, we grew up apart. By the age of ten, I recognized all the cars and drivers I watched at Jackson Motor Speedway, and off the top of my head I could probably name twenty to twenty-five current or former drivers in the Indy 500, both living and dead. Once I moved to Illinois in the early 1960s, drag racing was never far from my mind, thanks to the ejaculatory commercials that ran on Chicago's WLS radio station: "SUNDAY! SUNDAY! SUNDAY! AT BEAUTIFUL US 30 DRAG STRIP!" the radio shouted—followed by the names of famous drag racers who would be running that weekend. But I didn't see, hear, or read much about NASCAR, not until the late 1960s and the 1970s, when drivers like Richard Petty, David Pearson, Bobby Allison, and Cale Yarborough showed up and more races were shown on television. Of the first-generation NASCAR drivers who started around 1949, most were unknown to me, even the champions. I recognized the names of maybe three drivers from the early era, Lee Petty, Fireball Roberts, and Junior Johnson.

Born and bred in the North, I learned little about NASCAR, but I did learn a lot about the South. In my young lifetime, before the Vietnam War, the biggest story in America, without any doubt, was the divisive, but righteous, civil rights movement. My generation grew up in an era of important court cases and important voting and civil rights legislation. We grew up in an era when ordinary people, both black and white, exhibited extraordinary commitment and courage when they fought against Jim Crow laws and segregation. They sat in at lunch counters. They marched. They rode freedom buses while boycotting Montgomery buses. They prayed. They endured physical and mental abuse, turned the other cheek, and kept on. They went to jail. They stood up to governors Orval Faubus in Arkansas and George Wallace in Alabama, who blocked doorways with their bodies to keep Black students out of Little Rock schools and the University of Alabama. They heard whites proclaim "Keep them in their place!" and "Segregation now, segregation tomorrow, segregation forever." The marchers responded by singing "We Shall Overcome." They endured the wrath of Big Bull Connor and clubs, fire hoses, snarling dogs, bullets, and the bombs that killed little girls at church on a Sunday morning. Still, they persisted and persevered.

While all this social turmoil was going on, NASCAR became immensely popular in the South. Stock car racing and racial issues and strife were not unrelated. During the civil rights era, Southern whites felt under attack from the federal government, from print and broadcast journalism, and from Northern liberals. They resisted change and wanted to cling to old racial prejudices and relations. NASCAR was something new: a sport to cheer for in a part of the country that didn't have many professional sports teams. But it was something old too. It was nearly an all-white business, from the mechanics to the drivers to the owners to Bill France's dominating family. With its heralded booze-running past, NASCAR celebrated rebels. By cheering NASCAR drivers to victory at tracks throughout the south, fans were cheering for their rural roots and cultural past. They were cheering for themselves. At a time when so much of the nation chastised or outright condemned the South, Southerners became fans of NASCAR and reaffirmed the cultural heritage they longed to cling to.

NASCAR, through names and symbols, facilitated the linkage between stock cars and conservative culture, Southern history, and racial supremacy. The Civil War seemed to be alive and well at NASCAR tracks, where confederate flags were flown at souvenir stands and by crowds in the infield. Darlington had the "Rebel 300" race, and for years NASCAR held it on the weekend of South Carolina's "Confederate Memorial Day." Strom Thurmond, the segregationist senator from South Carolina, regularly attended races at Darlington. Martinsville promoted its races as "Civil Wars." Other tracks promoted "Dixie 400" and "Volunteer 300" races. A character dressed as Johnny Reb presented Junior Johnson with a rebel flag in the winner's circle, and other Johnny Rebs rode on winners' hoods en route to the winner's circle. The ring presented to the winner of the big race at Atlanta Motor Speedway featured a Confederate flag, and programs for Darlington's "Southern 500" had covers emblazoned with the Stars and Bars.

Bill France rubbed shoulders with segregationist politicians and curried their favor. He brought favorable attention to them by posing for pictures or letting them ride in a pace car around the track. In election years, a NASCAR race resembled a political rally. In 1964, George

Wallace ran for president in Democratic Party primaries; in 1968, he ran as the candidate of the American Independent Party; and in 1972, he again ran in Democratic Party primaries. Bill France was known for featuring George Wallace at NASCAR races and for providing the candidate with free rides in private planes. France served as Wallace's campaign manager in Florida in 1972, and Wallace won that Democratic Primary. The mutual back-scratching went both ways. In 1968–69, Alabama politicians, from locals up to Governor Wallace, helped France build NASCAR's longest and fastest track, the 2.66-mile, high banked tri-oval known today as Talladega.

It was hard for me to ignore NASCAR's overwhelming political bias. Besides that, I never bought into NASCAR's version of stock car racing. They started with real Fords and Chevrolets and ended with fake Fords and Chevrolets, bearing the name only, running with decals instead of real headlights, and carrying ads for sponsors who had nothing to do with cars or racing. NASCAR seemed too corporate and too controlling. Its rules limited a racing team's freedom to develop the best car it could on its own. And I never liked what NASCAR competition looked like—thanks to drafting, the race was like a parking lot of cars all going around a track at 180 miles per hour. They were like dogs, sniffing each others' tail pipes till the end. In my life, I went to exactly one NASCAR race, and now I can't remember if it was at Trenton or Dover.

Before Daytona became synonymous with NASCAR and stock car racing, it was known for land speed record attempts on the sands. Over several decades, fifteen land speed records had been set there, the last in March 1935. Sir Malcolm Campbell, an Englishman, set the record at 272.46 mph. If drivers wanted to go faster than that, it was time to move to a place with more room and smoother and safer sands. For many, that place turned out to be the Bonneville Salt Flats in Utah. Campbell was not a young man (he was fifty) when he moved west to Utah. In September 1935, he set his last land speed record. He ran 301.337 mph, making him the first to crack the 300 mph barrier.

Land speed record attempts were similar to drag racing. A driver and a vehicle went as fast as they possibly could in a straight line. But while drag racers ran a quarter mile in one direction, land speed record cars ran a longer measured mile—and they had to do it in two directions, down and back. The cover of *Life* magazine for September 1, 1947, carried a picture of "John Cobb and racing car." The man wore a jumpsuit and cloth flying helmet, with his goggles and gloves at the ready. The sleek aerodynamic racer behind him was skinned in aluminum. John Cobb, like Campbell, was an Englishman. He was news because he was getting ready to run at Bonneville. On September 16, he climbed into his four-wheel-drive Railton Mobil Special powered by two supercharged aircraft engines. The streamliner went 385 mph going south and, after being refueled, ran 403 mph going north. The average of the two runs, 394.19 mph, was the official land speed record. But the return run was the stunner—it marked the first time anybody had ever gone over 400 mph on land.

Hundreds, even thousands, of hot-rodders ran their machines at Bonneville. They prepared fancy customs, ratty roadsters powered by flathead Ford engines, and coupes with modern Chevy engines. They climbed into belly tank cars built from teardrop-shaped supplementary fuel tanks from World War II airplanes, such as a 315-gallon belly tank used to extend the range of a P-38 fighter. They towed or trailered their cars to the salt flats and settled in for a weekend or more. Racers endured cold nights and mornings and very hot afternoons. Many, running cars on tight budgets, slept in tents. They came to experience the thrill of high speed and the pride of mechanical accomplishment. Land speed runs were not without risk. Between 1947 and 1960, exhilaration spun into tragedy when eighteen drivers died trying to go as fast as possible. Still, they kept coming.

In the middle of the century, Mickey Thompson was one of the most versatile hot-rodders in America. He designed and competed in novel dragsters. He raced off-road vehicles and sports cars. He sent cars to the Indy 500 and participated in land speed runs at Bonneville. In 1960, he took his streamliner named Challenger to the salt flats. Sponsored by Mobil Oil, the four-wheel-drive Challenger was powered by four supercharged Pontiac engines of 415 cubic inches each, coupled to four 1937 Cadillac transmissions. On September 9, Thompson piloted Challenger to 406.6 mph in one direction. Mechanical problems kept Thompson from taking Challenger on its return run, so he did not set an official record. Still, he became the first American to go over 400 mph.

In the mid-1960s, a half dozen drivers sought ultimate land speed supremacy at Bonneville, but two stood out from the others because of their head-to-head battles. Aside from their love of speed, they had little in common. Craig Breedlove was from Los Angeles. At the age of sixteen, when most kids were still taking a driver's education class, Breedlove raced his first hot rod across the dry lakes of the Mojave Desert, and a few years later he raced an Oldsmobile-powered belly tanker at Bonneville. Beginning about 1960, bitten by the land speed record bug, he designed and started building a racer to take to Bonneville. His creation had only three wheels, one in front and two in back. It was not driven by piston engines but by a used General Electric J-47 jet aircraft engine.

Back in America's heartland, Art Arfons helped operate the family feed mill in Ohio. Mechanically gifted, before he was a teenager Arfons tore down and rebuilt an auto engine. In 1943, at the age of seventeen, he went into the Navy and trained in diesel mechanics. In 1952, Art and his half brother, Walt, got into building and running dragsters. When finishing his first dragster, Arfons—true to his rural roots—painted it tractor green (think John Deere). A track announcer called it the Green Monster, and the name stuck. Arfons named all his subsequent racers "Green Monster," even if they weren't green. Arfons first used surplus piston aircraft engines for power, and then he started using jet turbines. By 1960, he had become one of the fastest drag racers in the country. At that point he decided to take a crack at setting the ultimate land speed record at Bonneville. He designed a four-wheeled lakester powered by a J-79 jet engine. Arfons turned to his barn and other storage spots to pick up some needed parts. He found a rear axle from a 1947 truck, a front axle from a 1937 Lincoln, and steering gear from a 1955 Packard. Art and Walt no longer worked together as a team—each pursued his own projects. Both were interested in setting the land speed record, so the half brothers from Ohio took two land speed racers to Bonneville.

At Bonneville, the 1960s were exhilarating and sometimes tragic.

Drivers set many ultimate speed records, sometimes one right after the other. But other drivers died at the start of the decade. In August 1960, Athol Graham died in a high-speed crash, and in September 1962, Glenn Leasher perished while driving his jet-powered machine. The drivers at Bonneville were cut from the same cloth as American heroes like Chuck Yeager, the first man to fly faster than the speed of sound, and Scott Crossman, the first to fly more than twice the speed of sound. They lived on the edge, and often beyond it—just like test pilots. In 1947, an Englishman set the land speed record on American soil—and that record still stood. American racers thought it was time to take the record back.

Breedlove called his racer "Spirit of America." A small American flag was painted on its tail. Arfons carried on the patriotic theme too. He called his racer, per usual, Green Monster—but it was painted red, white, and blue.

The ultimate land speed record of 394.2 mph stood for sixteen years. Then Craig Breedlove, Art Arfons, and Walt Arfons shattered the record many times between 1963 and 1965. Breedlove made his mark first. On August 5, 1963, he hit 388 mph on his first run and returned at a much faster speed of 428 mph. Spirit of America averaged 407.447 mph over its two runs. This was faster than John Cobb and faster than Mickey Thompson. Initially, the Federation Internationale de l'Automobile (F.I.A.), which sanctioned land speed records in different countries, failed to give the record to Breedlove because his vehicle had only three wheels and was powered by jet propulsion. But nobody cared about the foot-dragging F.I.A. The public accepted that the land speed record belonged to Craig Breedlove, an American.

In 1964, Breedlove and Art and Walt Afrons were all active again at Bonneville. On October 2, Walt Afron's "Winged Express," driven by Tom Green, hit 406 mph on its first run and returned at 420 mph. The average speed of 413.2 mph bested Breedlove's record speed of the year before. Three days later, on October 7, Art Arfons took to the salt flats in his Green Monster powered by a J-79 jet engine and broke his half brother's record, averaging 434.02 mph. Breedlove took the record back on October 13, averaging 468.719 mph. Two days later, Breedlove

Craig Breedlove walks away from his "Spirit of America" on July 31, 1963, after a trial run at Bonneville of 349.5 mph. Five days later he set the land speed record of 407 mph. (Courtesy of Bettmann)

beat his own record and averaged 526.277 mph. He was the first man to go over 500 mph. At the end of his second run, Breedlove released two drag chutes to slow him down. They separated from the Spirit of America. Breedlove applied his brakes, and they immediately failed. He went five miles past the end of the course, hit a small salt dike, and went airborne. He ran under a line of telephone poles and sheared one of them off. Then he rode into a shallow pond that had a deeper trench running through it. Spirit of America fell into the trench and started sinking. Luckily, the canopy had blown away, and Breedlove extricated himself from the cockpit and made it out of the water. His crew arrived soon and congregated tightly around a man they supposed would be dead but wasn't. Breedlove had cheated death, and he seemed crazy high on adrenaline. He hugged one of his crew and simply said, "I broke my car." Next, he said, "What was the time? Did I break the record?" Yes, he had. But just twelve days after the wreck, Art Arfons took the record back, running 536.71 mph.

Craig Breedlove went back to California and designed and built a more "conventional" jet-powered vehicle. This one had four wheels, an entirely different shape, and a more powerful General Electric J-79 jet engine. Breedlove dubbed his new machine Spirit of America Sonic I. While this streamliner was under construction, the spirit of America—the spirit of American society in the mid-1960s—took an ugly turn. Breedlove built his car in a shop about a mile from where a police stop of a young Black man escalated into the Watts riots. Over six days, thirty-four persons died and arson and looting added up to $40 million of property damage. Breedlove's crew carried on through all of this. One of his men, armed with a shotgun, headed out to get some needed parts and soon faced a gauntlet of protestors hurling rocks and insults at him. "Holy shit," he thought, "I'm driving a red, white, and blue pickup truck with 'Spirit of America' on the side in pretty big letters." He was scared to death but made it back to the shop in one piece. Everybody inside the shop felt threatened. To protect the building from arson, a shotgun-wielding guard watched goings-on from the rooftop.

Breedlove's crew took the new racer to Bonneville to run it in 1965. Art and Walt Arfons were there too. Walt's racer was unsuccessful in taking the record back from Art. On November 2, Breedlove had better fortune. He averaged 555.127 mph, a new record. Art Arfons went out five days later and ran 576.553 mph in his Green Monster, another new record. On November 15, Breedlove climbed into Spirit of America Sonic I again and averaged 600.61 mph. The land speed record changed hands three times in just thirteen days.

In 1966, Art Arfons returned to Bonneville again with a modified Green Monster. On November 17, he lost control of his racer and it cartwheeled at 600 mph. Miraculously, like Breedlove in 1964, Arfons survived his horrendous accident. The valiant battle between two men and their jet-powered machines was over. They had pushed the envelope time after time and sometimes scared themselves to death. By any measure, Craig Breedlove came across all those measured miles as the winner. He was the first man to set the ultimate land speed record of over 400, then 500, and then 600 mph.

Breedlove also won, as they say, the hearts and minds of the people. Meaning no disrespect, Art Arfons, born in 1926, was an older man from rural Ohio and a World War II vet. Craig Breedlove, born in Los Angeles in 1937, was only eight when the war ended, and he grew up in a city that perfectly matched his car-crazy career path. Breedlove acknowledged this in the first few lines of his autobiography: "If I had grown up in Montana or Iowa or Texas, or *anyplace* else, for that matter, I don't know what I would have been. . . . The fact that I grew up in Los Angeles in a period when drag racing was also getting out of the toddling stage meant only one thing—I was going to be a race driver." Racing was young, so was Breedlove, and they grew up together.

At the age of only thirteen, for seventy-five dollars Breedlove bought his first car, a '34 Ford three-window coupe. A young man named Roger Rourke lived across the street, and his house was the unofficial headquarters of the Igniters car club. Members worked on their cars there, and the place was cluttered with hot rod parts. Breedlove joined in, proved to be a quick learner, and he soon became an honorary member of a hot rod club before he was old enough to drive legally. In Los Angeles he had access to young hot-rodders and to speed shops. By the time Breedlove was sixteen, his seventy-five-dollar Ford had a supercharged V-8 engine, custom paint, and a custom interior. Its proud owner began drag racing his car and, a year later, he ran it over the El Mirage dry lake course and hit 148 mph. Jump ahead a few years, and Breedlove drove a belly tank racer powered by an Olds engine at Bonneville and hit 234 mph.

In high school Breedlove studied industrial arts. After graduating in 1955, he worked at a speed shop, at a Buick dealership, and then at Douglass aircraft in its materials and process engineering department. He met car-racing icons Mickey Thompson, Sam Hanks, Carroll Shelby, and Dan Gurney. He picked up valuable knowledge every step of the way. He then got a job at the Costa Mesa Fire Department. The shift schedule there left him more time to work on cars, and the downtime between fire calls let him study aerodynamics. By now he was aiming not just to win drag races but to set the ultimate land speed record.

While Breedlove was growing up, Los Angeles, the land of movies, music, and dreams, became an ever more important center of popular culture in America. Craig's dad created special effects for movies, and his mother was a professional dancer. The youth culture and car culture thrived in California, and Breedlove embodied those cultures. He was handsome, a quintessential Californian. He was about three or four years older than the young men who formed the most famous California groups known for car songs—the Beach Boys and Jan and Dean—but if you put him up on stage with them, he would have looked perfectly in place. Sponsors supported him. When he broke speed records, Goodyear tires, Shell jet fuel, Champion spark plugs, and even Classic car wax pumped out multiple ads touting his achievements. After Breedlove wrecked and Spirit of America was half underwater, a Shell ad ignored the wreck completely and ran this: "Young Californian drives 526.28 miles per hour. Shell's turbine fuel powers Craig Breedlove's car to new world land speed record." Given this young Californian's good looks, Dep for Men featured him in magazine ads for hair care products.

Breedlove made public relations tours and showed up on television. On October 25, 1964, he appeared as an unidentified guest on the highly popular quiz show *What's My Line?* Panelists asked yes-no questions to try to figure out what he did. Yes, he was in sports. The audience laughed when Dorothy Kilgallen asked a follow-up question, "Do you have to move rather fast at what you do?" The venerable Bennett Cerf finally identified him as the young man who had recently set the land speed record.

One tribute to Craig Breedlove was a musical one. In October 1963, the Beach Boys released a new album full of car songs. The album had a customized 1932 Ford three-window coupe on the cover, and "Little Deuce Coupe" was the album's title track. Other popular songs included "409" and "Shut Down." The album, released just two months after Breedlove set his first land speed record, included a new song cowritten and sung by Brian Wilson, called "Spirit of America." How cool was that? A kid from car-crazy California set all the speed records, and a band from California celebrated him. Craig Breedlove was, without any doubt, the fastest of them all.

# 10

## OFF TO THE RACES

In 1909, Carl G. Fisher, an Indianapolis businessman, talked three investors into joining him to build an automotive test track that would also host occasional races. Fisher's group built the Indianapolis Motor Speedway, paving it initially with tar and compacted crushed stone. Late in 1909, they repaved the 2.5-mile track with 3.2 million bricks, which led the speedway to be called "The Brickyard." In 1910, over sixty races ran at the track over three weekends. In 1911, rather than hosting dozens of events over multiple weekends, the speedway owners created a single, monumental race to take place on Memorial Day. The Brickyard guaranteed a purse of $14,250 to the winner of the first Indianapolis 500. An estimated eighty thousand spectators turned out to watch Ray Harroun win in his Marmon Wasp, averaging nearly 75 mph over the five hundred miles (two hundred laps).

The Indy 500 ran every year except in wartime. In 1946 the race picked up where it had left off in 1941. Driver George Robson won that year with an average speed of nearly 115 mph. It was the most attended, most famous auto race in the country. It was, as the Speedway immodestly bragged, "The Greatest Spectacle in Racing."

In the late 1940s through 1964, open-wheeled roadsters powered by the legendary four-cylinder Offenhauser (or "Offy") engine won every five-hundred-mile race at Indianapolis. Over that time, changes to cars and engines were incremental, and yet the cars got faster. In 1950, the Indy 500 took nearly four hours to complete; by the early 1960s, a half hour had been trimmed off that time. The pole sitter in 1950, over a four-lap, ten-mile qualifying run, averaged 134 mph. Pole speeds increased to 140 mph in 1955, and hit 150 mph for the first time in 1962. Renowned drivers raced at Indianapolis in the 1950s and 1960s. Bill Vukovich, a Californian, won in 1953 and 1954. Sam Hanks, born in Columbus, Ohio, but a resident of California since the age of six, won Indy on his thirteenth try in 1957. He first raced there in 1940, and prior to his win he had finished as low as thirty-third (last) and as high as second. The popular driver, at the age of forty-two, wiped away tears as he announced his retirement while in Victory Lane after his win. Rodger Ward, born in Kansas but raised in California, won Indy in 1959 and 1962. Parnelli Jones, born in Arkansas but raised in California, won in 1961 and came close in other years. The greatest of them all, however, was A. J. Foyt, a Texan from Houston.

Foyt first raced at Indianapolis in 1958. He was a fierce competitor who hated anything that stood in his way of winning, whether it was another driver, a pit-crew mistake, or a broken part. The combative Foyt gave no ground. He had a short fuse and always spoke his mind. He suffered serious injuries at Indy, a track that between 1950 and 1969 killed five men while racing and another seven men while testing or qualifying. Still, he motored on. If not endearing, he nevertheless demanded respect as the best race driver of his generation. When A. J. Foyt was at his peak as a competitor at Indianapolis, it is safe to say that public interest in that race peaked as well. He won Indy in 1961, 1964, 1967, and 1977. His career, by itself, shows how varied the auto racing world became after the war. Besides being the first driver to win the Indy 500 four times, Foyt won sixty-three other Indy car races sanctioned by the United States Auto Club (USAC), plus twenty-eight USAC sprint car races and twenty midget races. He drove to victory in forty-one USAC stock car races and in seven NASCAR Cup Series stock car races, including the Daytona 500. He drove or co-drove sports cars to two wins in the 24 Hours of Daytona, and he chalked up single wins in the 24 Hours of Le Mans and the 12 Hours of Sebring.

The famous drivers and cars running at Indianapolis in the 1950s garnered millions of fans who eagerly looked ahead each year to Memorial Day. I was one of those fans, starting at the tender age of six. In

May 1953, my family drove from Jackson down to tiny West Lebanon, Indiana, where we stayed in the farmhouse belonging to Uncle Bert and Aunt Wannie. This was pretty much an annual pilgrimage to the Indiana places where my mom had grown up, but this trip was different. The men in the family—my dad, plus Burt, Bob, Bill, and Russ—were all going to the Indy 500. The problem was, I wasn't going, and I pitched a fit. I wanted to hop in the car with them, end up at the most famous track in America, and watch the colorful open-wheeled roadsters zoom past. Dad was usually great at taking me along to experience all kinds of things. But this time he held firm and disappointed his boy. I stayed in West Lebanon with the women. Very early in the morning, the men drove down the dirt lane from the farmhouse, crossed over the cattle guard, pulled out onto the road right by Uncle Bert's Shell gas station, and headed off. I watched them go, and I never forgot my disappointment, my sense of being abandoned. That day was awful, and drinking lemonade under a shady tree and riding a pony around the yard didn't make it any better.

In following years, the men who left me behind that Memorial Day in 1953 reconnected at family gatherings. Their talk drifted back to that year's Indy 500. They had not been in the grandstands, but in the infield. Bill Vukovich won the race. He dominated it. His number 14 fuel injection special led for 195 of the 200 laps, finished the 500 miles in 3:53:01, and averaged almost 129 mph. But the thing the men talked about most was the heat and sun that day in 1953. It was the hottest Indy 500 ever. The mercury climbed to 93 degrees. Many drivers stepped out of their cars during pit stops and let relief drivers take over. Vukovich joked that if people thought the race day was oppressively hot, they'd never spent a July day on a tractor in Fresno, California, his hometown. It was clearly too hot for one driver, Carl Scarborough, who died that Memorial Day, not from a crash but apparently from heat exhaustion. No amount of cold beer kept spectators cool in the infield sun, and the men returned to West Lebanon sweat-stained and sunburned. They had gone to the race, but in the main they had survived a miserable day. I had a miserable day too.

There would be better Memorial Days ahead. We spent other race days in the 1950s at home, where radio connected us to Indianapolis. Memorial Day, nominally about veterans, wars, and the memory of sacrifices, proved mostly to be about yard work, grilling hamburgers or steaks, starting summer—and listening to the Indy 500. An extension cord ran out of the garage to the front or back yard, depending on where the family was mowing, weeding, or planting flowers. At the end of the cord sat the radio. First came the pre-race patter about favored and favorite drivers, their cars, and qualifying speeds. The fastest qualifier always sat on the pole; he had the inside position in the first of eleven rows of cars. Three cars occupied each row. The announcer ran down the entire field of thirty-three cars and drivers, leaving nobody out. Everybody in that race was a somebody from somewhere, and their neighbors back home wanted to know just how their heroes were doing. You heard about past winners, the best finishes other drivers had ever achieved, and the names of the rookies, the men who would soon be doing something for the first time that I thought must be terrifying: accelerating out of turn 4 on the green flag lap, roaring past the start-finish line, and then racing side by side by side in a pack into turn 1.

The Indy 500, even on the radio, went beyond spectacle—it was a ritual. The Speedway was the 1950s cathedral of the American church of cars, sponsoring companies, speed, bold men, beer, gasoline, oil, religion, and patriotism. The voice of the 500, Tim Collins, carried the race message out to the flock via the ever-growing Indianapolis Motor Speedway radio network. Collins called the race, ran down the leader board, described the scene (exhilarating competition or catastrophic accident), and cued the commercials. Often, instead of Collins, race fans heard the voice of track announcer Tom Carnegie over the airwaves. What Carnegie said to the assembled throng at the track, Dad and I heard in our yard a couple hundred miles away.

This Memorial Day ritual wasn't over in a flash but lasted for hours. Collins and Carnegie, together, moved the trackside and radio audiences from one ceremonial act to the next, from prerace, to race, to postrace. This was Memorial Day, so a lone bugler played "Taps" before the race to honor war dead. Other music was brighter than that and was played by the Purdue University marching band, nicknamed the

"All-American Band." This was the Cold War era of burgeoning patriotism, so the band played the national anthem while the crowd stood with hats off and hands over their hearts, and maybe "Stars and Stripes Forever" and "America the Beautiful" too. This was Indiana, so they played and sang the official state song, "On the Banks of the Wabash, Far Away," as well as the more popular "Back Home Again in Indiana." The last two songs surely had absolutely nothing to do with a racetrack, crowded parking lots, throngs of people, speed, technology, or competition. You could argue they had little to do with the mid-twentieth century. Both painted a pastoral picture of Indiana, one of rivers, fields, new-mown hay, homesteads, and moonlight. Nevertheless, it all seemed to fit in and contribute to the tradition and spectacle playing out in Middle America. When all of the music stopped, thirty-three men went racing and risked their lives, so a man of the cloth offered a benediction that blessed the drivers and spilled over to cover spectators, crews, and indeed, all Americans. Shortly after the benediction made its way heavenward, so did forty thousand helium balloons released by the Speedway into the prerace sky, thanks to the generous sponsorship of Terre Haute Tent & Awning.

The cars stood in their rightful positions on the starting grid, surrounded by their crews. The drivers climbed in, and then Speedway president Tony Hulman intoned: "Gentlemen . . . start your engines!" Crew members inserted portable starters into the noses of the cars. The starters whirred and engines roared to life. Crews retreated and race cars pulled out behind the pace car for parade laps. The pace car pulled off to the pits, the cars ran around the oval another time, and if they were lined up properly coming out of turn 4, the official starter, from his elevated platform, furiously waved his green flag in tight figure eights, and the announcer shouted, "They're off!" About three and three-quarter hours later, the same man furiously waved his checkered flag to the winner, who drove around the track a time or two, waving to the crowd, and then pulled into Victory Lane and came to a stop. He took off his helmet, received the big, silver Borg-Warner Trophy and a wreath of flowers for his neck, got a kiss from a beauty queen, and swigged milk out of a bottle.

In the 1950s, nothing was more All-American than the Indy 500. Earlier in the race's history, foreign drivers and foreign cars had sometimes done well. German-built Mercedes cars won twice in Indy, and French Peugeots, three times. An Italian Maserati captured the checkered flag in 1939 and in 1940, but in the postwar world, foreigners had no chance. Not in the 1950s. This was America's decade, if there ever was one. True, a Ferrari made the field in 1952, but it dropped out early due to mechanical problems. From 1950 to 1959, American cars paced every race. Every winning chassis and engine was American—and so was every winning chief mechanic and driver.

The auto company that provided the pace car for the Indy 500 received a tremendous amount of free publicity. It was an advertising coup for the car's manufacturer. In 1957, the president of the Speedway, Tony Hulman, along with United States Auto Club (USAC) champion Jimmy Bryan, appeared on Sunday night's *Ed Sullivan Show.* Sullivan and an auto executive touted the merits of that year's pace car. The Speedway made sure to spread this advertising benefit around to Detroit's Big Three. In the 1950s, GM ran at the head of the pack three times, with a Chevy, a Pontiac, and a Buick. Ford Motor sent two Mercs and a Ford. Chrysler Corporation also paced three races, with a Chrysler, a Dodge, and a DeSoto. Since three didn't go into ten evenly, that left one race to be paced by a smaller US automaker. Studebaker was a struggling company, but it was an Indiana company, so it got the nod at Indianapolis in 1952.

Open-wheeled roadsters dominated Indy in the 1950s and into the early 1960s. I loved these roadsters. They were beautiful machines, brightly colored. Gray, silver, and bronze machines, plus yellow and red ones. They wore several shades of blue, plus white, red, gold, black—and even pink. The top of the nose and both sides of the tail were emblazoned with large numbers of contrasting color, so they could be read by spectators even as the roadster flashed by at 140 miles per hour. Along with its number, each car carried its main sponsor's name along the hood and, in smaller letters near the cockpit, the names of the owner, driver, and chief mechanic. The Indy roadsters were not the gaudy billboards that later NASCAR racers became—their skins were not dominated by large advertisements for laundry detergents, tobacco companies, paints, beers, banks, candies, soft drinks, fast-food restaurants, and, ultimately, pills to raise you up from the despair of erectile dysfunction. The Indy promotional stickers or decals were small and added bits of color to the machine, while they promoted sponsors that universally had something to do with cars, such as Mobil gas (with the flying red Pegasus), Champion spark plugs, Perfect Circle piston rings, Wynn's Friction Proofing, Bowes Seal Fast brake fluid, Raybestos brake linings, and Monroe shock absorbers.

The roadsters were long and their bellies ran low, close to the track. In profile, the top of the lengthy hood ran flat and straight to cover the engine bay and large radiator. In front of the radiator, the nose dipped down for better aerodynamics, to lower wind resistance. If you looked at the nose head-on, it looked something like the mouth of a shark, all the better to suck up a sea of cooling air.

Behind the hood, a short, clear windscreen fronted the leading edge of the driver's cockpit, which had no top and, instead of being centered between the wheels, was often offset a bit to the right. The high tail behind the driver carried the top of the roll bar and the fuel-filler cap. The tail curved downward from right behind the driver's helmet till it reached a low push bar at the very back of the machine. Suspension pieces on the four corners of the Indy roadster glistened with their chrome plating. On many roadsters, a chrome four-into-one exhaust pipe ran from the engine outside the bodywork. It kicked upward gracefully near the back, where it ran between the driver and the left rear wheel. The driver's cockpit was taller on the left side, the exhaust side, than on the right. The roadster's bodywork came nearly as high as a driver's left shoulder. But on his right, the bodywork dipped much lower, literally giving him more elbow room to wrestle his large steering wheel, whose diameter seemed about right for a city bus. Like the steering wheels, the tires and wheels on these roadsters were large in diameter, making them a dominant feature of the overall architecture. As he roared around Indy, a driver rather looked like he was sandwiched between tall, narrow rear tires that were as high as his shoulders.

Despite being high-powered racers, the roadsters exhibited some of the commonplace. They were accessible. They were a kind of an understandable, mechanical "everyman." For starters, although bigger and faster, Indy cars were similar to quarter midgets, midgets, and sprint cars being run at tracks across the country. They didn't look like airplanes on wheels, dominated by wings and spoilers and ground effects. Like the everyday passenger car, they had engines in front and rear-wheel drive. They all ran on Firestone tires with raised white letters that spelled out the brand name. These tires had squiggly tread on them; they weren't fat racing slicks. The Indy cars burned gasoline like a Hudson or Ford, and not some special racing fuel like methanol. The cars tended to go faster each year, but over the decade they changed only incrementally in design and technology. They symbolized American tradition in open-wheel racing, rather than rampant innovation.

The drivers exhibited "everyman" characteristics too. They didn't fly into Indy from Brazil or Europe, accompanied by tall, lean women dressed to the nines. They were all-American boys become men, who came from short tracks across the country and who enjoyed their beer and their fans. They were clean-shaven white guys. They did not strut across the infield in fancy high-tech racing suits made of fire-retardant DuPont Nomex, dotted with sponsorship patches. Instead, they often wore jeans and T-shirts. Drivers' faces did not disappear into full-face helmets. Instead, they buckled up shorty helmets with leather earflaps. With goggles over their eyes, they went racing. In their cars, the drivers sat almost upright, with their heads, shoulders, and hard-working arms (that muscled the car through eight hundred left turns) visible to the crowd.

Many drivers came from the heartland; they were the favored sons of small towns in Indiana and around the Midwest. But only a few from the heartland won in the 1950s: Sam Hanks from Ohio and Rodger Ward from Wisconsin. One winner, Lee Wallard, hailed from New York. Most winners came from the West and South, including Troy Ruttman from Mooreland, Oklahoma, and Jimmy Bryan from Phoenix. Four drivers from the Golden State won half the decade's races: Johnnie Parsons and Bob Sweikert from Los Angeles and Pat Flaherty from Glendale each won once, while Vukovich, from hotter-than-blazes Fresno, won twice.

In the 1950s, American culture tilted away from the East and toward California. World War II played a major part in this, introducing changes in the 1940s that rolled on through the 1950s and beyond. The war encouraged a large migration to California and expanded its industrial base; aircraft companies and others grew to meet the demands for war planes and other war materiel. In the boom days of the 1950s, California seemed to be the place to go—just ask the New York Giants and the New York Dodgers, who moved to San Francisco and Los Angeles, respectively. Or ask Walt Disney, who opened Disneyland in Anaheim to lure in the tourist trade.

The Indy 500, all-American event that it was, reflected the mid-century flowering of California. It was like a pivot point in the nation's middle, just where the weight of Eastern influences declined while California's grew. California drivers won half the races in the 1950s, but that wasn't all. California produced the four-cylinder "Offy" engines that won all the decade's races; these power plants were named after Fred Offenhauser of Los Angeles. All the winning and highly competitive roadsters rolled out of California shops run by Frank Kurtis, A. J. Watson, Lujie Lesovsky, Quin Epperly, Eddie Kuzma, and George Salih. And for over a decade, all the winning chief mechanics at Indy hailed from California too. The race belonged to Indiana, but the cars, and the men who designed them, set them up, and drove them, belonged to a state far from the banks of the Wabash.

In the 1950s, aside from being there, listening to the radio was the only way to keep up with the live race. After the fact, you might catch pieces of the race in newsreels, or find photos and stories about it in newspapers and car and sports magazines. You might see some of the exciting action (the start, the finish, an important pass or two, an important crash or two, and smiling faces at Victory Lane) on television. But compared to the full-length radio broadcasts, early television coverage in the 1960s was terrible. It did not do the race justice. The race was a marathon, a test of the endurance of men and machines. The heavily condensed and edited version of the race shown on ABC's *Wide World of Sports* ruined the race's continuity and epic nature.

My father made amends for going to the 1953 Indy 500 without me. He took me to the races at our local short track, Jackson Motor Speedway. From 1953 throughout the rest of the 1950s, if Dad went to Jackson Motor Speedway, so did I. These weekend races highlighted my youthful summers.

Short-track racing, on dirt or on asphalt tracks usually a quarter to a half mile around, became extremely popular all across the country in the 1950s. It was certainly popular in Michigan. In the mid-1950s, Fred Wolf, a pioneer in sports broadcasting on radio and television in Detroit, announced televised races from the Motor City Speedway. Dad and I used to watch them on Channel 7. Across southern Michigan, in the 1950s at least fourteen short tracks offered racing programs. Drivers and crews towed or trailered their race cars from place to place. They ran races on different nights of the week in a host of cities or small towns: Hastings, Galesburg, Ionia, Hartford, Grand Rapids, Marne, Lansing, Detroit, Owosso, Milford, Flat Rock, Adrian, and Quincy. The Jackson track was a favorite of many drivers and attracted the fastest and the best. It was built and opened in 1948 as a high-banked half-mile dirt track of oiled clay. It ran a limited schedule in its first two years, and then in 1950 went to a full schedule of twenty race days. To make the track safer, and to make it easier to get through turns 3 and 4 coming off the back straightaway, in 1953 they cut the oval down to three-eighths of a mile, with corners 1 and 2 steeply banked at twenty-five to thirty degrees and turns 3 and 4 banked at six to eight degrees. On a typical night, races at Jackson attracted about fifty cars, but special races (of up to one hundred laps) ran on weekend afternoons and sometimes attracted over one hundred cars. Many drivers were local, so scattered across Jackson, modified stock cars sat outside gas stations, garages, or houses. Jackson Motor Speedway was very popular. A single race day might draw in four thousand fans. One year, the racing season drew forty-seven thousand.

Admission charges at the speedway were about a buck and a quarter for adults, and you always got your money's worth. First, every car ran a timed qualifying lap to set up a ranking of cars, from slowest to fastest. Then ten cars at a time ran heat races of eight to ten laps. Then ten of the best cars ran an Australian Pursuit race, starting with the fastest cars at the back. Any time a car passed another car, that car was eliminated and withdrew to the infield. Then they often ran a four-car dash. The top four qualifiers raced each other for four laps. Then came the B-main, or the twelve- or fifteen-lap semifinal for cars that hadn't qualified for the main feature. The four best finishers in the B-main were put at the back of the pack of the twenty fastest cars of the night, and the twenty-four cars ran the final race—the main feature of twenty-five or thirty laps. The cars created a cyclone of wind and noise as they raced by the grandstand.

Mom never went to the races at Jackson Motor Speedway (JMS). This was a father-son affair. Sometimes another father and his boy went along, or my friends Phil, Bill, or Rick tagged along. Sixty years after the fact, Phil remembered going to the races with us, and my dad paid Phil's admission, because his family "didn't have much money then." Trips to the track were never taken for granted. We often went to the races, but not every Saturday. I was always ready with a quick "Yes!" if Dad asked if I wanted to go that day, and soon we'd be in the car and on our way. After passing through town, Dad would turn left off US-127 onto Clinton Road, go only a little way, and turn right into the big field where everybody parked. We would walk up to the ticket booth, pay to get in, and then walk to the grandstand of wooden bleachers.

I liked to stand at the foot of the grandstands, where cars raced by only a couple feet away. A wall of vertical railroad ties, sunk firmly into the ground and surmounted by a catch fence, protected fans from a loose tire and wheel or a careening car. To watch most races, Dad and I sat at the very top of the grandstand to get a better view of the entire track and its corners, which at first carried no walls or guardrails. Cars often collided. They lost traction, spun out, or flipped over. Some went up and over the top edge of the curve—and literally disappeared. God knows what happened next, after they went out of sight. I was there when one driver died going up and over a curve at JMS, one of the six drivers who died there. A track photographer, struck and killed by an errant race car, was the first to ever die at the track. As part of his funeral procession, a hearse carried his coffin around the dirt oval.

We always arrived early at the track, while it was still light, so we could watch all the time trials. As the race card progressed, day turned to night. Floodlights atop tall poles illuminated the track and attracted huge swarms of summer insects. The races had a rhythm to them. There was a great rush of speed and noise, then the race ended and activity paused. Then came another great rush of speed and noise, then another pause. Between races, adults went for beers while the kids walked down the grandstand's steep steps to go to the concession stand to get a Coke and maybe popcorn or a hot dog. During another break in the action I might do a little nervous dance while waiting in the long line outside the restroom, which was little more than a linear shack with an entrance on one end and an exit on the other, and an inclined trough running along an inside wall. Once I made it to the trough, always wedged between two big guys, I tried to hold my breath until I was done and out the door. This was not a pleasant place.

When Dad and I started going to the track, we watched modified stock cars race. The cars were cut-down versions of Detroit products from the 1930s or 1940s. All glass had been taken out, interiors had been gutted, and fenders had been totally removed or cut way back. Hood panels on the side were removed to open up the engine bay and give the motor more cooling air. Suspensions were altered and, importantly, engines and transmissions could be changed. Newer-model engines from one manufacturer could be put in a car built by another company. There weren't many hard and fast rules for building an "unlimited modified stock car." An entry form for a one-hundred-lap feature at JMS spelled out some of the basics. A car's chassis, body, and engine had to be American-made. All bodies had to have steel tops. All cars had to have suitable roll bars and safety belts. That was about it. In the parlance of the time, "You run what you brung."

There was a lull in the action before the feature races, and the crowd—even an eight- or nine-year-old kid—could leave the stands and go down to the infield and mingle with drivers and mechanics and take a closer look at the cars, which by now were covered with grime from the oiled track. Drivers looked track-worn too. I loved to run down the steeply banked front straightaway to the pits, struggling to keep up with my own feet as I accelerated down the steep slope. As a kid, getting so close to all the cars and drivers in the infield was one of the most fun parts of going to the track on a Saturday night.

In the late 1950s, JMS attracted a new class of cars and a new generation of drivers. In racing, jalopies had given way to stock cars, stock cars to modified stocks, and then modified stocks gave way to supermodifieds. The supermodifieds that came to run at Jackson were not cars built on a Detroit-produced chassis. Narrow, short, and low to the ground, these open-wheel cars were one of a kind. Generally, they had shop-built welded frames, snug driver's compartments and roll cages, and minimal sheet metal bodies. They ran the most modern and powerful engines a race team could afford. A new owner of JMS facilitated change by paving the track with asphalt. The last races run on the old dirt track took place on September 14, 1958. The track was then paved, and four or five race cards took to the asphalt before season's end. They proved that supermodifieds ran far faster laps on asphalt than on dirt.

I really liked supermodified racing on the paved track. The new drivers who showed up to run supermodifieds were truly impressive. They included Nolan Johncock, Nelson Ward, Art Bennett, and Dick Slade. All these drivers became early inductees to the Michigan Motor Sports Hall of Fame, although two of their racing careers were cut short. Nellie Ward died in 1963 while racing in New York, and Nolan Johncock was killed in a racing accident in Ohio in 1971. Two of the very best new drivers at Jackson were Dick Good of Mishawaka, Indiana, and Gordon Johncock of Hastings, Michigan. Good won an amazing thirteen features in 1959. That prompted the track to put a bounty on him as a promotion—the track would pay an extra two hundred dollars to any driver who could beat him. On the last feature of the year, Gordon Johncock beat Wood to the checkered flag and claimed the bounty. Johncock went on to become a track champion at Jackson in the early 1960s, and he won a total of eighteen features there. Going on to bigger and better things, he won the Indianapolis 500 in 1972 and 1983.

In the late 1950s, Gordy Johncock became one of my racing heroes. But another driver at Jackson loomed larger for me. When you are a kid, I think your first hero sits atop all the others who follow. In baseball, my first and everlasting hero was Al Kaline, right fielder for the Tigers. In football, it was Joe Schmidt, linebacker for the Lions. Interestingly, they both started playing in 1953, the year I, as a six-year-old, started going with my dad to Jackson Motor Speedway, where we watched a young race car driver named Ralph Donaldson. Donaldson became the first driver I would never forget.

Ralph Donaldson and I had one thing in common. Our dads took us to races when we were young. Donaldson's dad worked in a shop that ground crankshafts, some for racing engines. He started taking Ralph to the small track at the Jackson County Fairgrounds when the boy was just five or six. Ralph got the racing bug and kept it. He wrote stories and drew pictures of race cars in school. On May 9, 1949, at the age of nineteen, he began his racing career—and almost ended it at the same instant—at the half-mile dirt track at the Allegan fairgrounds. The first race hadn't started yet. He was warming up on the track. After one and a half laps, he lost control, spun out, and rolled. His seat belt broke and he was thrown out of the car, coming to rest forty feet from it. He spent many weeks in the hospital recovering from a severely lacerated leg, broken ribs, and head injuries. Once out of the hospital, he almost immediately "got back in the saddle." He went to the Galesburg Speedway and talked a car owner into giving him a ride. He drove Bill Treats's car for the rest of the 1949 season and in 1950.

In 1951, Donaldson drove for a Jackson car owner, Art West, and he ran regularly at JMS for the next six or so years. He drove for various car owners and a number of sponsors, who paid to have their names painted on his cars: the El Dorado Bar, the Show Bar, General Automotive, Jackman's Gulf gas station, and Max Sweeny's Drive-Inn Restaurant. Donaldson apparently had a thing for nines; he drove cars numbered 9, 19, and 91. The most successful car he ran at Jackson was number 91, a 1939 Plymouth body and chassis powered by a new Chrysler Red Ram Hemi engine. Dinky Donaldson, showing a sense of humor, had Dopey, one of Snow White's dwarfs, painted on his car. The Disney

Ralph Donaldson stands next to his modified stock car, a 1939 Plymouth with a Chrysler Hemi engine. Car 91 carried him to the track championship at Jackson Motor Speedway in 1956. (Courtesy of the Donaldson family and Michigan Motor Sports Hall of Fame)

movie *Snow White* had been re-released in 1952 in the United States, and it was all the rage. Dopey was the one with big ears, and Dinky and Dopey shared that physical characteristic.

Donaldson in the mid-1950s was at the peak of his career as a Michigan dirt-track racer. He had good equipment, and a crew chief and three mechanics worked to get him wins. But nobody got rich off this. The purse paid out to a winner was split, 40 percent to the driver and 60 percent to the owner. Donaldson raced from April through November, but with a wife and young son, he needed to supplement his racing income by driving a fuel tanker truck in the offseason. During the racing season, he drove from track to track to enter races on different nights of the week. He was successful wherever he went. In 1954 he was the track champion at Capitol City Speedway in Lansing; Tri-City Speedway in Auburn; and the Owosso Speedway. He was champion of the Toledo Speedway in 1955, Jackson Motor Speedway in 1956, and Mt. Clemens Speedway in 1958 and 1959.

Ralph thoroughly enjoyed being a winner and he carried himself well around the track. For all the aggressiveness he showed during a race, he had an easy manner when outside his car. He had the look of an all-around good athlete. Handsome, he stood a slender but strong six foot one. He wore everyman racing garb—a colored cotton shirt, white cotton pants, moccasins on his feet, and a satin jacket with a body and raglan sleeves of contrasting colors and a knit waistband and cuffs—much like what a softball player wears to a game. On race days, he wore a St. Christopher's medal around his neck. Donaldson saw four drivers die in accidents at Jackson, and he wasn't taking any chances. Before getting into his car, he donned his shorty Cromwell helmet with leather earflaps, goggles, and gloves. Unlike many drivers, he did not wrap his lower face in a kerchief or have hardware cloth installed where his car's windshield had once been. His face caught the dirt and the stone chips that came through. The right side of his face returned to the pits dirtier than the left side, because when going around turns the right front tire kicked up more track debris and threw it at him. Still, some young women at the track didn't seem to find track grime too offensive. They slipped Ralph matchbooks with a name and number written inside and the message "Call me." Sometimes, when the track had pretty much cleared out, he convinced a young lady to take a stroll with him under the bleachers.

Ralph Donaldson was king of the Jackson track when I was eight and nine years old and he was twenty-five or twenty-six. Donaldson won well over twenty feature races between 1952 and 1956. Many a night the feature race ended with Donaldson taking a victory lap around the track, holding the checkered flag out the driver's side window in his left hand. The capstone probably was the special Sunday, end-of-the-season race card in 1956 featuring a one-hundred-lap "Race of Champions." JMS attracted 105 race cars that day, at least nine track champions from Michigan, Ohio, and Indiana, and over three thousand fans, including me and Dad. In the concluding main feature, the thirty-three fastest cars roared off with the dropping of the green flag. In the first half of the race the lead changed hands many times. Then Donaldson got out in front of the pack on lap 57 and never looked back.

Ralph's career at JMS peaked when he won the track championship in 1956. After that year, he won more races elsewhere than at Jackson. Ralph at heart was a dirt-track racer, and when they paved Jackson's track near the end of the 1958 season, that was pretty much the end for him. Ralph focused on other tracks and, ultimately, on driving a different class of race car. He drove a sprint car with an Offenhauser engine for many years and was successful running at tracks in Michigan, Ohio, Wisconsin, Missouri, Kansas, and Iowa. He was named the Midwest Sprint Car Champion in 1961 and 1962. But sometimes he paid heavily for his success. He was racing a sprint car on August 26, 1961, at the half-mile dirt track in Belleville, Kansas. Ralph was fastest in time trials that day. He won the first heat race. He won the four-lap trophy dash. During the fifteen-lap feature, he slid high on turn 2 and flipped three times. The race was red flagged as he went to the hospital. Donaldson lay unconscious for ten days. The accident put a hurt on him all over—head, ribs, hip, arm, legs, and back. "I broke everything but my dick," he later said with a laugh.

All told, by the driver's own count, over his career he won seven track championships, ninety-nine feature races in stock or modified stock cars, and forty-five features in sprint cars. Dinky Donaldson ended his racing career at the age of thirty-five on June 28, 1965. While running a sprint car on the half-mile dirt track at Hartford, Michigan, he noticed he was slow getting off the throttle going into corners and slow getting back on the throttle when leaving. Other drivers were clearly quicker at this. Donaldson finished seventh in the race. After he pulled the sprinter to a stop, he climbed out and never raced again. For Donaldson, racing had not been a money sport. It was a love sport of speed, exhilaration, and keen competition. He lived to be the best and fastest driver around and to hear people in the grandstands cheer him on. He missed that when he retired and became a full-time trucker. When he was sixty years old, he walked into his employer's office and complained to the secretary, "It ain't the same, Sandie. It just ain't the same! I go into a bar, and NOBODY knows who I am!"

Ralph Donaldson was just a footnote in the history of auto racing after World War II, but for some, for a while, he was a memorable giant on dirt tracks. Before making a trip across the Mackinac Bridge in 2014 to visit my sister and brother-in-law in Jackson, as a sixty-seven-year-old man who once watched many races at Jackson Motor Speedway, I wondered—could my old hero Ralph Donaldson still be alive? Did he still live in Jackson? I found a phone number on the computer, dialed it, and after a few rings, a man answered. "Are you the Ralph Donaldson who used to race at Jackson Motor Speedway?" I asked. "Yes," the man said. Immediately, it was like two old friends had found one another. After an hour's conversation, I promised to visit Ralph on my trip to Jackson.

In the middle of May 2014, I arrived at Donaldson's small house tucked away off Flansburg Road. The landscape was not impressive, a mix of rural, commercial, light industrial, and scattered houses. Dorothy, Ralph's longtime girlfriend and nurse, when needed, answered the door. Ralph stood up, he and I smiled and shook hands, and the old race driver settled back into the corner of his couch. He livened up when he told stories of his career, the wins, the losses, the tracks, the wrecks. At one point he said, "Women love winners, and I was a winner!" Dorothy got out Ralph's scrapbook so we could see the collected photos and newspaper clippings. I didn't think Ralph looked frail, yet he still looked all of his eighty-four years. Turns out, not long before my visit, Ralph had beaten a rare form of throat cancer. We chatted and drank coffee while Ralph smoked his cigarettes.

After two hours, it was time to go. It was hard to tell which man had enjoyed the visit more. For me, Ralph had been an important part of my life as a kid. Now, I was an important part of Ralph's life as an old man. I was there, I remembered, and he had a great and real appreciation for that. Before leaving, I promised to come again when I could.

I returned near the end of September, 2015. As I entered the house, Dorothy pulled me aside. "He's dying," she said. Ralph did not appear in street clothes, like last time, but in pajamas and a robe. He had bowel cancer and stuck to his couch the whole time. Now he appeared terribly frail and very thin with a hollow face. He did not make jokes or tell stories this time. Instead, he said, "I don't want to die." I recalled that I had not sat by a man getting ready to die like this for a long, long time—not since I was just a boy and the terminally ill man was my dad. I paid my respects to Ralph and after a short visit I left. Dinky Donaldson died three weeks later on October 14, 2015, fifty years after he climbed out of his race car for the last time.

# 11

## VROOM! VROOM!

I grew up in an era of cowboys and cars. Half the time I was shouting "BANG! BANG!" while pointing a toy six-shooter at some innocent victim, who, playing the game, would grab his chest, let out a moan, and say, "You got me!" The other half of my time I was down on my knees, running a toy car back and forth on the floor to wind up its friction motor. Then I'd let it go with a "VROOM! VROOM!" The little car whirred as it raced across the floor and, much to my delight, invariably crashed into a chair leg or wall. I'd crawl over to the toy car, retrieve it, and do it all over again.

By the time I was three I had a complete cowboy outfit: vest, chaps, boots, spurs, holsters, and cap guns. I had everything needed to make me a cowboy except a horse in the garage and tumbleweed in the yard. But cowboys and guns weren't the only things that mattered. Things that moved, things with wheels, things like cars—these mattered too. While my Western fascination finally faded, my interest in wheels and motion carried on. Bang bang did not last as long as vroom vroom. As I moved closer to age sixteen, I knew that a horse was not in my future—but I was going to get a driver's license. It was only a matter of time until vroom vroom would be replaced by the revving of a real engine.

By the age of three, I had four kinds of wheels to move around on. A neighbor boy had a dogcart, rather like a miniature horse-racing sulky—and a stout black dog. The dog got harnessed to the cart, I got on its seat, and the dog took me for rides around the yard and neighborhood. I also rode around in a red Radio Special wagon, thanks to some willing adult, like Uncle Darrell, who pulled me around when he visited from Detroit. I got to move myself around (and *steer*!) by pedaling either my tricycle or my pedal car, or, in this case, my red-and-white Murray pedal fire engine, equipped with short ladders and a platform behind me for a second child to stand on. In an old family photo, I am left standing while Mom is in the wagon, my sister, Lynn, is on the trike, and Aunt Millie is atop the fire truck.

Children learn by watching and imitating what adults do, especially their parents. We baby boomers rode in cars and watched our parents drive all the time. We couldn't drive the family Ford downtown, of course, but we could replicate it as best we could by getting into our pedal car and taking it for a ride. The pedals in front powered the wheels at the back, using reciprocating levers connected to a crank or, in some cases, a chain and sprocket, like a bicycle. It was fun and safe on level ground, but pedaling uphill was hard on young legs.

Pedal car manufacturers clustered in the Midwest, in places like Kenosha and Sheboygan, Wisconsin, and Toledo and Murray, Ohio. These companies built steel wheels and parts for Detroit auto manufacturers, and they also used their tooling to fabricate pedal cars. After World War II, America's strong economy and the purchasing power of baby boom families supported the mass production of these kid-powered sidewalk racers in many styles and colors. The late 1940s to 1960 became the golden era for pedal cars. The Garton Toy Company sold an estimated one million of them, a figure probably approached by other companies.

Pedal-powered little vehicles weren't all cars. I had my fire engine. Other boomers pedaled station wagons, Jeeps, airplanes, tractors, boats, and even dump trucks. One manufacturer offered a "Dragnet" pedal car, like the one driven on the popular cop show of that name. It had a microphone and loudspeaker. Others were dead ringers for 1955 Buicks and Chevrolets. A very popular model was the "Kidillac," a knockoff of mid-1950s Cadillacs dressed in mid-1950s colors, like a black-and-gray two-tone job. A four-year-old boy enjoyed riding in his own status symbol, a mini-Caddy.

Parents tend to do the most for their children when they are very young. They nurture, dress, shelter, hold, protect, and cuddle them. They change diapers and, in the 1940s and 1950s, wash those diapers. The children, later in life, remember absolutely none of this. I had a wagon, a tricycle, and a pedal fire engine. Kodak snapshots captured all of them. But I do not know if they were Christmas presents or birthday presents, or if Mom or Dad stopped at a hardware store, saw a cute trike, and brought it home on a random Tuesday. Maybe Uncle Darrell and Aunt Millie gave me my fire truck on one of their visits from Detroit. I have no idea.

I have no strong memories of anything until I was about five. At five and a half, on Christmas, I received a toy car from Mom and Dad. Like many postwar toys, it was plastic, not metal. A convertible about fifteen inches long, the toy did not look like any specific automobile, but clearly it was in the Buick/Oldsmobile class. The body was light blue with cream trim. This toy did not have a friction or windup motor. To move it, I had to push it along. But it had other assets. Its front wheels could be turned. The hood opened, and inside was a plastic engine. The trunk opened, too, and held two tools: a small jack and a wrench. I used the tools repeatedly, loosening a wheel nut, taking the wheel off, and then putting it back on. The little car (with Dad's help) taught me the axiom, "righty tighty, lefty loosey." Another life lesson learned, thanks to a toy.

Three years later, Christmas of 1955 brought me clothes and other goodies, like a telescope. The big present that year was a tabletop electric football game that had a green field with yard markers, goalposts, and two teams of little plastic players who stood on nylon "feelers." Plugged in and turned on, the field vibrated, and suddenly the little players started dancing around and confronting each other. When a defensive player collided with the ball carrier, the play was over.

When I got this game, I was nuts about football and particularly crazy about the Detroit Lions. My father and I played electric football against each other and watched the few Lions games that were televised. We listened to the others on the radio. The Lions were the best in the 1950s, and they've been nearly the worst ever since, until recently. They won NFL championships in 1952, 1953, and 1957. They finished second in 1954. I knew the players at every position, their names and numbers, even offensive linemen like Lou Creekmur and Harley Sewell. Who could forget the all-time-great middle linebacker Joe Schmidt, running back Doak Walker, and the great quarterback bad boy Bobby Layne? One of the greatest games I ever saw on television occurred on December 4, 1960. In our den I watched alone, because my father had died in September. It was a back-and-forth game between the Lions and the Colts, being played in Baltimore. Baltimore led 15 to 13 late in the fourth quarter. Earl Morrall came in to quarterback the Lions, and on the very last play he threw a sixty-five-yard pass to tight end Jim Gibbons. Touchdown! Game over! I exploded, jumping off the couch and yelling like crazy. I wished Dad had lived to see that play, one I never forgot.

I got another toy car the Christmas of 1955, a Ford Crown Victoria that looked like the real thing. It was black on the hood, top, and trunk and yellow on the sides. This toy was a first for me. It was battery-operated. I held the controller. Out of it snaked about six or eight feet of wire that ran to the car. By manipulating little levers, I could make the car turn left or right and go forward or backward. It whirred and ran fast over the linoleum in the kitchen. It was not so swift on carpet.

In the 1950s, I had an infinite number of toy cars to choose from. American companies like Marx and Ideal sold toy cars, from old Model T's to new Corvettes. Many toy cars came from Britain, Germany, and, especially, Japan. After the war, the vanquished Japanese restarted their economy with the help of American occupational forces. The Japanese saw the United States as the wealthiest buyers of all things automotive, from real cars down to toy cars. Japanese companies produced a giant number of tinplate or stamped tin toy cars, often styled after Detroit's latest. The Japanese put out Chevrolets, Buicks, Chryslers, and millions of Fords. For some reason, these toys never found favor with me. I can't remember ever spending my weekly allowance on a Japanese toy car—and I rarely bought any tiny toy cars—the ones that were maybe two inches long. Only occasionally did I buy a Dinky Toy, Tootsie Toy, or Matchbox die-cast metal toy car, and only if it was one I really liked. I liked one Matchbox toy car so much I slid it into my pocket at the Toy

House in Jackson and left without paying for it. The fun of acquiring the little car was trumped by my guilt for stealing it. I confessed my grand theft auto to Mom, and she drove me straight back to the Toy House, where I handed the little car and its box over to the manager and apologized for stealing it.

Another gift I unwrapped at Christmas in 1955 was a Revell model kit of a World War II B-25 bomber. I had been building models for the last couple of years, and my folks figured I could handle the B-25 kit, which was not all that simple to assemble. Building models was a hobby I thoroughly enjoyed. I liked its attention to detail, the care you had to take to do a good job, and the sense of pride I felt when a completed model looked good. The hobby shop or toy store was a neat place to visit, mostly with Mom, to pick out the next project and acquire brushes and colorful Testor paints in small bottles, spray paints in small rattle cans, body putty, glue, and fine sandpaper. Aisles were usually small, hedged in by shelves full of model kits, stacked one atop the other. The boxes always carried an illustration of what was inside.

I built some models all on my own, without a kit—like a Viking ship about a foot and a half long that I built as a school project, made entirely of balsa wood. I also made a couple of balsa airplane kits. Gluing the fuselage and wings together out of parts the size of matchsticks was painstaking work. I covered the plane with tissue and then carefully painted it with dope to stiffen the surfaces. I was never sure what this dope was, but it sure smelled.

World War II was not far in the past. I watched war movies in theaters and on television and built models that captured the war on a small scale. Besides the B-25 bomber, I built the Navy Hellcat fighter, the Navy hospital ship *Hope*, and the battleship USS *Missouri*. But by far, I most frequently built scale-model plastic car kits made by AMT, Revell, Monogram, and Jo-Han. I preferred car model kits over preassembled toy cars, because of the fun of building them myself.

To build a model, out came the card table. Mom made sure I covered it with a couple layers of newspaper to protect its top from glue and paint. A small piece of thin plywood went on the table too. The plastic car kits were injection molded. My father taught me about injection molding; his company used the same technology to create the outside bodies of circuit breakers. When I took the model parts out of the box, they were still connected to plastic "trees" that had carried the flowing plastic through the die or mold. Smaller openings, "sprues," carried plastic from the trees into the mold cavities that, when filled in, formed half an engine block, an intake manifold, or some other part. To get things started, I separated all the parts from their trees. I could simply twist them off, but that often left a rough edge. Instead, I laid a tree on the plywood and used an Exacto knife or single-edged razor blade to cut the parts off.

Parts then had to be glued together using model cement in a tube. When performing delicate work, sometimes I put just a tiny drop of cement on the end of a toothpick and transferred the cement to the small parts to be matched up. Many subassemblies had to be painted by brush or with spray paint before being put together to turn a bunch of parts into a car. Sometimes, if a model had an engine and a hood that opened, to make it more realistic I glued little pieces of red thread from the spark plugs to the distributor. Most models came with a sheet of decals, showing a license plate with numbers, ever-popular hot rod flames, fancy pin striping, Mobil Oil's Flying Pegasus, or ones reading "Moon Equipped," "Iskenderian Cams," or "STP." If I wanted to use a decal, I soaked it in a bit of water, slid it off its backing, and placed it onto the model, making sure it was perfectly lined up.

Most of the car models I assembled were 1:24 scale, meaning they were about seven to eight inches long. I built a Stutz Bearcat, an MG TC (one of my favorites), and an Indianapolis 500 roadster. I assembled models of a 1958 Oldsmobile and 1958 Buick (both over-the-top expressions of American automotive excess) and of a Chevy El Camino pickup. Fords captured my attention, at least old ones. I built models of the Model T, the 1932 Deuce coupe, the 1936 coupe with a rumble seat, and the 1940 coupe. The '36 and '40 Ford coupes had some of the best body lines ever. I always thought they were beautifully shaped.

The Boy Scouts of America, in the early 1950s, launched the Pinewood Derby program to introduce youngsters to an "automotive" pursuit. Cub Scouts purchased construction kits, and once they finished their model cars, they raced them down an inclined track. My Cub Scout den never got involved in making these gravity-powered racers, but thousands of boys built them from a kit that included a block of pine 7 inches long, 1.75 inches high, and 1.375 inches wide; four plastic wheels; and four nails that served as axles. Each builder used knives or saws to shape the wood block into a racer that when finished and fitted with the wheels weighed no more than five ounces. Scouts could polish the nails/axles to reduce friction, and they could apply a dry lubricant like graphite powder, but they could not use any oil lubricants or bearings. Aerodynamics counted, even on a small scale, and a well-constructed, well-designed slippery pinewood racer was more likely to roll down the track and finish first.

The Boy Scouts encouraged participation in a second model-building competition, the Fisher Body Craftsman's Guild. Schools, newspapers, and General Motors dealers also supported the Guild. Fisher Body, part of General Motors's collection of car-making companies, started the Guild in the 1930s. Teenage boys from the United States and Canada joined the Guild and learned how to design and craft a model. Model builders could earn substantial awards on state, regional, and national levels, based on the style and craftsmanship of their work. This model-building competition, started during the Great Depression, handed out college scholarships and awards up to $5,000 in both junior and senior divisions. The Guild was a philanthropic endeavor, to be sure, but it was aimed at more than that. It taught skills, patience, and discipline. It taught the rudiments of automotive design. It also brought General Motors positive recognition among teenagers who would become car buyers—and it created a body of college graduates who just might go to work at Fisher Body or General Motors. In the 1950s, Fisher Body employed over two hundred Guild "graduates," and at General Motors's Styling Division, headed by the famous car designer Harley Earl, 35 percent of the employees had been active in the Guild.

Through 1937, participants in the Guild showed off their skills by building a model of Fisher Body's trademark: a horse-drawn Napoleonic coach. From 1937 until 1948, the coach makers were invited to submit a second entry if they wanted, a model of a futuristic car of their own design. Under the influence of Harley Earl, after 1948 contestants no longer built the old coach model; they strictly designed and built model concept cars, which were supposed to be 18.75 inches long, with a width of up to 6.75 inches, a height of about 4 inches, and a wheelbase of up to 10.5 inches. Earl and his staff encouraged participants to follow good styling (meaning graceful, light, fast, and flowing) and to avoid bad styling (slow, boxy, heavy, and squared). The Guild distributed a pamphlet, *Designing and Building a Model Car*, that gave guidance on how to paint a model and build windshields, interiors, moldings, headlights, taillights, and bumpers. It showed how to make clay, wood, and plaster models. Each year, until the Guild ceased operations in 1968, the models were well publicized and exhibited around the country. In many instances, models built in the 1950s resembled real cars built in the 1960s.

While I was growing up, my hometown of Jackson had several claims to fame. One was the State Prison, known as the largest walled prison in the United States. Every time an escaped convict showed up on the television cop show *San Francisco Beat*, it seemed he had busted out of Jackson's prison. The Sunday night *Ed Sullivan Show* also highlighted Jackson by featuring, several times, a precision drill team, the "American Legion Jackson Zouaves." Dressed like Algerian soldiers, with baggy pants, sash jackets, and fez hats—and carrying rifles—they quickstepped all over the stage, weaving in and out and creating numerous formations. At the end of seven and a half minutes of constant, rhythmic motion, they threw each other up and over a tall wall. There was no other act on television like the Jackson Zouaves.

The third jewel in Jackson's crown was the Cascades. It was a hill with cascading waterfalls. But more than that, it was a beautiful year-round recreation area. In the winter, it was the best sledding hill in town. The Schaffer Drive kids went there to ride Flexible Flyers or my wooden toboggan, a Christmas gift from Santa. The hill was a gentle slope in some spots, but much faster and bumpier in others. In one section, you seemed to be riding down steps—you flew off one, landed, and then flew off another. Sometimes, instead of sledding, we ice-skated at the frozen pond near the hill's base till our hands and feet froze and we retreated to the warming shelter.

There was more to do at the Cascades in the summer. I occasionally played Little League games on adjacent ball fields. I went golfing on the Cascades course with Rick, and sometimes we rode our bikes back in the early evening, took off our shoes and socks, and waded into water hazards to retrieve lost Dunlop or Spaulding Top-Flite golf balls. People went in droves to the Cascades on the Fourth of July to watch fireworks. The signature allure of the Cascades was the man-made waterfall that stepped down the hillside from top to bottom. Color postcards of the Cascades reached mailboxes in every state in the country.

First opened to the public in May 1932, the Cascades made concrete into something marvelous. Five hundred feet long and sixty feet wide, the Cascades had a vertical drop of sixty-four feet, which was divided into sixteen separate falls or steps. Eleven of these falls were lit from behind, so as the water fell four feet from one level to the next, it was backlit and became red, green, blue, pink, purple, or yellow. The colors could be changed and altered into different patterns, forming a crazy quilt of colors, or making the waterfall all red or blue or green from top to bottom. Three large pools captured the water as it flowed down, and six fountains sprayed water into the air. Each side of the Cascades carried 126 steps, so you could walk to the top on one side and come down on the other. When the colored lights were on in the summer, cars slowly drove by in a line to catch a glimpse, and many parked and then sat at the foot of the Cascades to watch the full progression of color changes. My buddies and I, on windy, hot evenings, liked to climb the steps and get wet from fountain spray blown off course by the breeze.

Some dirt lanes and one straight strip of pavement ran down the backside of the Cascades hill. On one weekend a year, American flags and hay bales lined this pavement, because it was time for the All-American Soap Box Derby—yet another institution or tradition, like the Pine Wood Derby and the Craftsman's Guild, that men initiated to teach boys skills and to pave the way for their future interactions with real automobiles.

Newspapers supported the birth of automobile racing in the United States in the late 1890s. They sponsored early races—and reported on them. The newspapers generated interest in the races, and the races created news that people wanted to read. Newspapers sold racing, and racing sold newspapers. And so it was with the All-American Soap Box Derby, launched and sponsored initially by two Ohio newspapers, the *Akron Beacon Journal* and the *Dayton Daily News*. In the mid-1930s, the Akron paper got other newspapers to participate, such as the *Detroit News* and the *Flint Journal*. They got Chevrolet to sign on as a national sponsor, and Chevy dealerships sponsored the Derby in their hometowns. In local competitions, boys drove gravity-powered racers they had designed and built down a long hill. They ran heat after heat, with winners advancing until only one unbeaten boy racer remained—the champion. That champion then traveled to Ohio to race against other champions. By 1935, the championship races took place in Akron, not on a city street but on a purpose-built Soap Box Derby track, three lanes of concrete about one thousand feet long, built by the Works Progress Administration (WPA).

Boys had always ridden wagons, scooters, bicycles, and all kinds of rudimentary vehicles down hills for the thrill of it. They raced other kids in their neighborhoods, but they never codified rules, organized their events, or played them out on a national scale. Adults, communities, and companies did all that. Nominally created to benefit the boys, which it did, the Soap Box Derby also fed the interests of many. The Soap Box Derby held its first local and national competitions in 1933, during the Great Depression. Many families, communities, and companies were suffering. They had seen rising unemployment and falling incomes, sales, and profits. The Derby was seen by its boosters as fun-filled philanthropy that made good business and civic sense. The newspapers wanted to sell more papers. Chevrolet and all its dealers wanted to sell more cars. If they sold more cars, Akron's tire-making companies would sell more tires—and there were several of them: Firestone, General, B. F. Goodrich, and Goodyear. Akron, with its depressed economy, wanted some positive excitement, something that would bring crowds and capital into the city.

With many influential supporters spread across the country—and with so many Depression-era boys looking for something new and exciting to do—the Soap Box Derby quickly became a success. In 1935, fifty-five cities ran a Soap Box Derby and sent the winner to Akron. The competition thrived until the war temporarily halted it. After the war, the Soap Box Derby flourished again, especially in the 1950s and 1960s. It became so popular it rivaled (and often surpassed) real automobile races in terms of public interest and press coverage.

When I went to the Cascades on Soap Box Derby Day in the 1950s, the track was lined with hay bales for safety, in case a driver lost control or a wheel fell off and the racer ran off the track. A long row of American flags on poles lined the track; this was now officially the *All-American* Soap Box Derby and something of a patriotic event. Nobody in Jackson, including me, seemed to question at the time the absence of Black boy participants, or girl participants. Those issues were still ten or fifteen years down the road. In the now, white boys came down the track driving a rainbow of colorful racers, all coasting as fast as they could, all cheered on by the large throng of watchers. In the end, one boy received a trophy for winning at Jackson and free passage to Akron, where he raced for $5,000, amid more hoopla and ceremony than he ever could have imagined.

In 1955, on Derby Day in Akron, 1,700 participants marched in a long parade that featured celebrities and several high school and college marching bands. All of the VIPs rode in new 1955 convertibles—provided, of course, by Chevrolet. Over the 1950s, an impressive list of celebrities showed up at the working-class city to watch boys whisper down the track under gravity power. They came to see the Derby and to be seen themselves by the public, which might number seventy thousand in attendance: Pat Boone, Jimmy Dean, Dinah Shore, Jimmy Stewart, Bob Cummings, Andy Devine, Abbott and Costello, Art Carney, the great Cleveland Browns quarterback Otto Graham, three-time Indy 500 winner Wilbur Shaw, and boxing champion Jack Dempsey. They all came to see the Derby. So did Ronald Reagan and Richard Nixon.

After the parade, the big Saturday crowd filed into Derby Downs. Bleachers flanked both sides of the track. At the start and finish lines, bridges built over the track were bedecked with signs and created space for photographers and important guests to watch the races from on high. Before the boys raced, three celebrities participated in an Oil Can Race, driving oversized Derby racers. Jack Dempsey won the first Oil Can Race in 1950. After all of the races concluded, the Soap Box Derby hosted a banquet, prizes were awarded, and pictures were snapped. The next day, newspapers across the nation posted news and photos of the Derby, often on the front page, and the winner from some small town might be whisked off to New York City to appear on NBC's *Today* show.

Not every boy wanted to race in the Soap Box Derby. They wanted the noise of an engine, even a small one, and the smell of gasoline and exhaust. They wanted an accelerator! They wanted to turn left and right on a twisty course. They wanted their fannies to be mere inches above the asphalt, which always accentuated the feeling of speed. In short, they wanted go-karts.

The go-kart was yet another creation with an engine and wheels to come out of California. Art Ingels worked for the Kurtis Kraft company that built hot cars for the street and track, including five cars that won the Indy 500. In 1956, Ingels and a neighbor friend put together the first go-kart. They would not have a monopoly for long, because many California companies and individuals started making go-karts. Compared to a full-grown race car, go-karts were incredibly small and simple. They had a welded tubular steel frame, a short wheelbase, and no bodywork. Many riders looked cramped as they sat in a rudimentary seat and had their knees bent up while their feet worked the brake and accelerator pedals. A small engine sat directly behind the driver's seat. The engine (like one you might find on a lawn mower or chainsaw) drove the rear wheels. The go-cart sat low to the ground on wheels that were small in diameter—but their tires had a broad tread for better traction.

The go-kart was a thrill to drive. Cheap to buy and own, it democratized racing. It could be bought as a kit or as a full kart with a McCulloch West Bend two-cycle engine, or something similar. Now, almost anybody could get into the racing game if they wanted—not just adults, but boys too young to drive real cars. Kart racing started in California in 1957 on tracks laid out with traffic cones on the Rose Bowl and in shopping center parking lots. In 1958, Azusa, California, claimed the first of many permanent go-kart tracks built across the country. By 1960, factory teams raced karts that could hit fifty-five miles per hour. Besides staging races, tracks rented out karts for people to ride just for fun. That's how I got a bit of experience in driving something so quick and nimble—buying laps at a go-kart track.

Some boy racers in the 1950s and '60s chose to drive quarter midgets instead of go-karts. The quarter midget—so named because it was about one-fourth the size of an adult's midget race car—had a full body, usually of aluminum or fiberglass, that resembled midgets, sprint cars, and Indy car roadsters. The little racers usually had a tubular frame, torsion-bar suspension, mechanical brakes, mag wheels, and, for power, something like a 7.5-cubic-inch Continental engine.

In February 1958, a lengthy article called "Cars for Kids" ran in *Hot Rod* magazine. An overhead shot of about twenty boys wearing helmets and sitting in quarter midgets adorned the cover. The main article's subtitle read, "Sleek, scaled-down race car bodies, modern chassis construction and a full complement of high-performance engine equipment are offered the Quarter Midget boys." Manufacturers sold them in kit form or ready to race, and speed equipment companies entered the fray too: "Already offered are high torque cams, high compression pistons and heads, roller bearing cranks, beefed gear boxes and hot ignition systems." Some famous race car builders got into the quarter midget business, most notably Frank Kurtis. His Kurtis Kraft company built 120 Indy cars. From the early 1950s to the mid-1960s, his company also built 1,500 quarter midgets that sold for $587, considerably more than most. Boys from six to sixteen raced them (in different classes) on one hundred paved or dirt oval tracks, one-twentieth of a mile around, spread across the country.

My movement toward driving a real car never included such a thing as a quarter midget. I had pumped my little legs to propel a pedal car. I had pestered Mom innumerable times to drop a dime into coin-operated kiddie rides found in front of stores. They moved me up and down and side to side in a pretend race car or Model T. I had ridden go-karts at go-kart tracks. They were great fun although a bit scary. Less scary, but still great fun, were the bumper cars I drove at the Jackson County Fair.

The fair came to Jackson every year, just before the start of school. It was a crowded, fun place, especially at night, when illuminated by the colorful lights that adorned the attractions. I got to see farm animals in the fairground's barns, but because I was allergic to hay, I couldn't stay there long. The fair had freak shows and a fun house. It had exhibition halls where judges awarded colorful ribbons for tasty pies and cakes and for handcrafted dresses, skirts, sweaters, napkins, and quilts. The fair featured fine foods for kids: snow cones, cotton candy, candy apples, and hot dogs. It featured live bands and other acts, and hucksters called to youngsters to come play the many contests designed to take their money, like ring toss. The fair had a merry-go-round, and other rides lifted you up high, spun you around fast, or just scared you to death. I always rode the Tilt-a-Whirl. My favorite was the Ferris wheel. I was excited when I first sat down in the Ferris wheel's seat, which swung a bit while they latched the safety bar down. The wheel rotated up and then stopped so the next car could be loaded, and so on and so on, until a friend and I were stopped at the very top of the wheel, laughing and swinging and looking out over the entire fairgrounds. Finally, the wheel went around and around without stopping. No matter how many times it went around, the trip always ended too soon.

But of all the rides, I liked the bumper cars best. They came in many colors. They had metal bodies, grills, and headlights, a seat that two could squeeze into, and a big steering wheel. A rubber bumper ran entirely around the bottom of each little roadster. Electricity drove the bumper cars. They rode on a metal, oval floor, and from the back of each car a pole reached up to a tented electrical grid. They were like trolley cars. Electrical contacts atop the pole contacted the grid, and, beneath the car, electric brushes contacted the metal floor. When an operator flipped the on switch, a motor in the front of each car was energized and all fifteen or so cars within the oval started to move. When he flipped the switch off, all the cars stopped. The former drivers headed out, while new drivers headed in to take their turn.

An early maker of these rides called the cars "Dodgem" cars. The maker told drivers to avoid running into other cars on purpose, and for sure don't hit them head-on. Instead, dodge 'em. Miss them. Such nonsense! Every boy driving a bumper car at the Jackson County Fair in the 1950s was a little demon, hell-bent on running into every car he possibly could, and hitting his friends' cars hardest. The faster my chosen car was, the better for chasing down a friend and ramming him. So, while the group in front of us was driving, I watched to see which car was fastest. Some cars had cleaner or better electrical contacts, picked up more power, and moved faster. At the entrance, I quickly gave my admission ticket to the operator and ran to the fastest car I'd seen. As soon as my car got up to speed, I rammed somebody, then turned the wheel to go ram somebody else. Sometimes three or four cars got wedged together and weren't going anyplace. That called for evasive action. If I turned the steering wheel all the way to the right or to the left, the car automatically and suddenly went into *reverse*! What a trick! I'd back out of the logjam, straighten the wheel, and head off to rattle somebody else's teeth. Although I didn't know it at the time, bumper cars presaged the type of driver I would be when I got my license at age sixteen.

On one especially good day at the fair, I rode the bumper cars a couple of times early in the evening, and then, while Mom and a friend headed off to exhibits of homemade goods to be worn or eaten, Dad and I took seats in the covered grandstand facing the dirt track at the fairgrounds. The 1950s and '60s were interesting, in terms of the range of things car fans got to watch. The grown-up version of bumper cars—the demolition derby—became very popular. Five to fifteen old cars ran around on a field, ramming one another, until only one was still running and all the others were smashed and stopped. There was also the exciting, hold-your-breath Figure 8 race. Instead of driving counterclockwise around an oval, drivers drove counterclockwise around half of the track shaped like an *8*, and then clockwise around the other half. In the middle of the *8*, all of the cars passed through an intersection where they crossed paths. Collisions were not only possible but likely. At this Jackson County Fair, father and son watched another kind of exhibition that flourished in the 1950s and '60s: the Joie Chitwood Auto Thrill Show, featuring the Hell Drivers.

Joie Chitwood was a successful race car driver, a sprint car champion

The over-and-under ramp-to-ramp jump was a crowd favorite at the Jackson County Fair. Before turning to Chevrolets, from 1948 to 1953 Joie Chitwood's Thrill Show used and abused Fords. (Courtesy of Joie Chitwood Jr./Joie Chitwood Collectibles)

inducted into the National Sprint Car Hall of Fame. Between 1940 and 1950, he ran in all seven Indianapolis 500 races that were not canceled due to World War II, and he finished fifth three times. Chitwood bought his thrill show from the widow of the previous owner, who died while trying to complete a ramp-to-ramp car jump. By 1950, the show was touring around the country, performing stunts in new Fords and, in some summers, four to six shows toured at the same time. The Jackson County Fair was a regular stop, and Chitwood drew big crowds year after year. In the mid-1950s, the show used Chevrolets and served as advertising for that make. Chevy provided new models for Chitwood to abuse, and the thrill show's stunts proved to the audience that Chevy cars were rugged and reliable.

Before the show, a caravan arrived at the fairgrounds: four to six new Chevrolets, including a convertible that Chevy wanted to show off; a jalopy that could be beat to death; a couple of motorcycles; and a truck carrying ramps for jumping. The crew consisted of four drivers, an announcer, and two clowns who could be used as drivers if needed. At the start of the show, four cars drove down the front straightaway, turned left a little bit, put on their brakes, and angle parked in perfect unison in front of the grandstands. Each driver was introduced as he opened his door and hopped out to give a jaunty wave to the crowd. They got back in their cars and spent an hour or so driving back and forth and doing tricks in front of the grandstands.

They drove forward at considerable speed and then did a quick 180-degree spin to continue on, but going backward. They went backward and did a quick spin to end up going forward. Four cars, only a foot or two apart, raced in a straight line down the straightaway, and then began alternately weaving left and right, coming back into line without colliding. Four cars nearly touched as they formed a moving square, with two nose-to-tail cars on the left and two on the right. The drivers aimed at some ramps. The cars on the left ran their right-side wheels up and over a ramp. Simultaneously, the cars on the right rode their left wheels up the ramp. All four cars came back to earth ever so close to one another, still in perfect formation as they reformed their square and headed off to jump three more ramps. For another trick, they ran the right side of the car up and then off a high ramp. The driver's left-side wheels stayed on the ground while the other wheels were way up in the air. The drivers played with the steering wheel—a little left, a little right—to keep the car balanced on only two wheels while it continued down the track.

For obvious reasons, the Hell Drivers didn't do stunts that would bang up or destroy their new Chevrolets. Their driving skills and the show's choreography were meant to keep the paint and bodywork pristine. If they wanted to add a sense of heightened danger, by purposely rolling a car over, maybe time after time, they chose to wreck some old jalopy, *not* a Chevy, but maybe a Ford. Drive it over a high ramp, roll it over, wheels to wheels, then have the driver get out, smile, and wave to the crowd. If they wanted to burst through a plank wall doused with gasoline and set on fire, the Chevrolets sat off to the side and riders hopped on motorcycles and powered them through the wall of flames. The last stunt was the biggest, and it required a tall up ramp, a big space, and then a tall down ramp. One new Chevy flew off the first ramp and launched itself into the air. At the same time, a second Chevy cut in to drive between the two ramps and *under* the flying car. The flying Chevy then landed hard on the down ramp. Its softly sprung suspension collapsed. The front bumper hit the ground, and the car bucked up and down while wallowing side to side. Chevrolet hoped that audiences didn't notice that and laugh. But Dad and I thought the landing was funny, and so did many others in the crowd.

In midsummer 1959, when I was twelve, Dad took me out for a ride. He often took me on errands and small trips here and there. This time Dad did something surprising. He turned into the large parking lot near the hardball diamond in Ella Sharp Park and brought the car to a stop. He shut off the engine, turned to me, and asked, "You want to drive?" He'd never asked that question before, and truth be told, I had not been itching yet to drive a real car. It seemed years down the road. Still, I said "Sure!" We switched places and pulled the car seat way, way up, as far as it would go. Dad sat in the middle of the bench seat, so he could have better control over the wheel if things went wrong. From there the instructions started: "Put your right foot on the brake pedal and push it down. Then, turn the ignition key to the right and let it go as soon as the engine fires. Keep your foot on the brake. With your left hand near the top of the wheel, take your right hand and put it on the end of the shifter. Got it? Now pull the shifter toward you and down until that arrow above the column stops at the 'D,' for Drive. Put your right hand back on the wheel. Okay, now take your foot off the brake, and the car will slowly move forward. Give it some gas—hey, not so much!—just enough to pick up some speed. That's it! Now turn the wheel left and go in a big circle."

We made many stops and starts. I put the shifter in "R" and we went backward. At a stop, Dad told me to push the turn signal lever down and then to turn left; then to push it up and turn right. Just for the heck of it, we honked the horn and came to a sudden stop. "Good, good," he said. "Are you having fun?" Any time I hit twenty miles per hour, my dad told me to slow down a bit. We didn't hit anything, but there wasn't really anything to hit, the lot was so big and empty. This went on for maybe fifteen minutes before we switched places. "Thanks, Dad!" I said as I got back in the passenger seat. "Good job," he said, reaching over to give my knee a little pat.

It was the first and only time I drove my father anywhere. Lawrence Alfred Lankton died on September 4 the next year, 1960. When a thirteen-year-old boy loses a good father, the loss makes extra special the times they had spent together. After a death there are no new times to be shared in the future, only old times in the past, and they slip farther away each day. Feelings and memories dim and some utterly vanish. But other memories, even if they seem buried deep beneath the surface of subsequent life, occasionally rise to the surface and take a person back dozens and dozens of years. Suddenly you remember the fun of being in a rowboat, fishing for bluegill and sunfish early on weekend mornings in the summer. You remember how scared you were when being taught how to ride a red Schwinn American bike that was way too big for you. You remember how you learned to swim after Dad carried you out to deep waters in Vandercook Lake; he offered encouraging words and then let you go. You remember playing catch in the front yard at Uncle Elmer's farm, when a hard ball thrown by your dad with some velocity popped you right in the eye.

Most relatives called my dad "Big Larry," so naturally I grew up being called "Little Larry." Big Larry's death changed Little Larry's life in myriad ways, some small, some very large and transformative. No more help with perplexing math problems. No more trips to see Tiger night games, followed by a couple of coney dogs. No more watching Dad crumble saltine crackers in his hands, drop the crumbles into a bowl, cover them with milk, and eat them like cereal. Never in my life did I ever see anybody else do that. They say don't sweat the small stuff, but life is made up of small stuff, and when that small stuff is gone, it is gone forever.

When Dad died, neighbors sent condolences. I always remembered the sympathy card that was handmade by the Horn family's little girls from down the street. It simply said, "We are sorry Mr. Lankton died," written in crayon. Friends and family came to the house after the funeral, including Rev. Kendall Cowing. Seven years earlier he had conducted my sister's wedding ceremony in the Methodist church in Vandercook Lake. Now, he had buried my dad. We all talked, reminisced, and ate food brought in by friends. After the guests left, my mother and I got in the Packard and drove back to Hillcrest Cemetery at dusk to stand by the grave buried under flowers. This was our private goodbye, and it was sad as hell. We felt so alone in the world, even though just hours before we had been surrounded by other mourners. It started to rain gently, so we walked downhill toward the car. I put my arm around Mom's tiny waist and said, "Don't worry, Mom. We'll make it."

From that moment until I went to college, Mom and I lived in a single-parent household. That seemed so strange, so different. I had no friends with only one parent. Rick had Roy and Wilma. Phil had Earl and Ginny. Bruce had Arnold and Patricia, Danny had Roy and Alice, brothers Bill and Terry had Art and Shirley, Jim had Bob and Joanne, Cheryl and Mark had Uncle Darrell and Aunt Millie, and my little nephew and niece, Rhys and Dana, had Ben and my sister, Lynn. I would learn that having only one parent had consequences.

In the summer of 1961, my mother splurged on a guided tour that took us on the Santa Fe Railroad's El Capitan Vista Dome train from Chicago to Los Angeles and back. The train was posh. All of our lodgings and food were posh. I thought Mom did it for me, a grand trip after hard times to bring some joy to life. Later, I figured maybe she had done it for herself, too. As a young woman from Kingman, Indiana, with a tenth-grade education, she had moved out to Los Angeles. She never talked to me about her time in California, but I found a stack of postcards she had written to Aunt Ruby back in Danville. According to the cards, my mother had a man friend in Los Angeles, and they were both doing well. That romance apparently died, and Dorothy Mary Atkinson returned to the Midwest in the late 1930s and lived with some friends in Detroit. She met Lawrence Lankton, got married in 1945, had her first and only child in 1947, and became a widow in 1960. As a fifty-year-old woman, she was returning to Los Angeles after an absence of twenty or twenty-five years. Maybe she was going back to revisit some good times herself. At any rate, Mom and her boy certainly enjoyed the train trip across America, especially when sitting up in the Vista Dome car.

I enjoyed Las Vegas. I played some slot machines at the station right after getting off our train—until a guy stopped me because I was too young. We stayed at the Riviera Hotel, where at age fourteen I watched the stage show *Gypsy* about the famous stripper Gypsy Rose Lee. That was quite an eye-opener. I was taken by the beautiful scenery at Yosemite and impressed by the fact that we got to stay in the Ahwahnee Hotel, the same grand hotel that I had read about in Herman Wouk's *The Caine Mutiny*. One hotel guest was a bat. I caught it in a towel and released it outside. In San Francisco we stayed at the Fairmont Hotel. Buddy Hackett was performing there, but he had such a potty mouth that Mom wouldn't let me see him. I did get to ride the cable cars, which was much fun. At Disneyland, I experienced Tomorrowland's Autopia. The sporty looking car I jumped into could seat two, but Mom let me ride it alone. The course, modeled after a freeway, ran for about a mile. It incorporated overpasses, underpasses, turns, and hills. I steered my own car and operated the accelerator. The car had a gas engine of 7.5 horsepower, made putt-putt exhaust noises, and could hit eleven miles per hour. It had a big aluminum bumper wrapped around front, back, and sides, just in case two cars tried to occupy the same space at the same time. After Disneyland, we stayed at the Inn at the Mission in San Juan Capistrano and took a tour down to Tijuana, Mexico. I spent most of my time in gift shops with Mom, looking for a souvenir. I settled on a high-quality, all-metal, windup toy model of the Volkswagen Bug. I remained more interested in cars than in miniature Mexican sombreros.

Not long after we returned home from this trip, Mom set into motion her plan to move us from Jackson to Danville. If the death of my dad was the single most important event in my life, this move was the second most important. I went along with it. What else could I do? But it was something she wanted to do, not something that I wanted. Like going to California, she was going home again, but on a permanent basis. Her roots and most of her family were in central Indiana around

Kingman and in the border city of Danville. The move was prompted by her understanding that she couldn't make enough money to keep the house on Schaffer Drive, so if we had to move anyway, we might as well move to Danville. Once there, after getting a job as dining room hostess at the Danville Country Club, she still had trouble with housing costs. We started in a worn-out second-floor apartment on Chandler Avenue near Lincoln Park. Then, wanting a house for us again, she bought a small bungalow on Chester Avenue, on the northern end of town. But after a short stay there, she moved us to another worn-out second-floor apartment on Oak Street, close to downtown. To help make ends meet, she sold Avon cosmetics and, for a short time, Mutual of Omaha insurance.

At the time, I never gave my mother full credit for what she could or did do. I just always *expected* her to be competent and able to get anything and everything done. She never graduated from high school, but she was smart and sharp. In short order, she sold the Packard and the house on Schaffer Drive. She arranged for the move, sorted out all the stuff to get rid of or to keep, and moved us into an apartment three hundred miles away, then into a bungalow, and then back into an apartment. She worked both outside the home and inside it. She never remarried, or even had a date. She spent almost no money on herself. Sure, she would have liked to have lived in a better place, but above all else she did not want to become house poor. She protected her money so she could take good care of her son.

I was familiar with Danville. I had visited it many times on family vacations. I knew all my relatives in Indiana and Illinois, and for those who died after I got to know them, like my grandmother, a couple of uncles, and an aunt, I knew where their graves were and visited them. But the move took me away from some favorite family members, sister Lynn and her husband, Ben, in Jackson and Aunt Millie and Uncle Darrell in Grosse Pointe Woods. Those folks had been important parts of my life since day one. They had always been fun and always treated me well.

The move also cost me my childhood friends. From the time the big move happened in January 1962, I felt I had only half friends in this world, and I was often jealous of folks who had whole friends they fully grew up with. In Jackson, my best half friends were Rick, Bill, Terry, Bruce, and Phil. I knew them as young boys. I attended the Boy Scout Camp Teetonkah with them in 1958. I played in their houses and knew their parents well. I knew what kind of car their parents drove and what job they had. We kids went to school together, played pickup baseball and football together, and learned to bowl and play golf together. We bicycled everywhere, explored woods, and trudged through swamps with hip boots on. But then I moved away, and although I saw some of my friends briefly on short trips back, I never got to see their second halves develop. I never got to see them grow up and go into high school and beyond. I heard about it later, but I never saw Bruce do well, become a doctor, and head off to Alaska. My best buddy, Rick, attended Michigan State, ultimately got a PhD, bought seventeen Corvettes, and became the dean of Purdue University's Krannert School of Management. I didn't anguish over the Vietnam War with any of these boys, or see Phil go into the Navy and then come home to build Goodyear tires for thirty-eight years. Terry took over his grandpa's plumbing business, and Bill, so I was later told, sold used cars for a living. I never knew who or when they married, or if they ever had kids who did some of the same stuff we had done.

In Danville, I ended up with a totally different set of half friends—friends I never met until age fourteen or fifteen. I went through high school with them. I knew how smart they were in math class. I sat with them at basketball and football games. I knew their girlfriends and who they went to the prom with. I knew their favorite hangouts. I knew when they were choosing colleges, and what they wanted to be. But I never played Little League or went sledding or skating with any of them. I never played with Lincoln logs or an Erector set on their den floor. Indeed, I had never been in their houses. I didn't know their parents, didn't even know their parents' first names.

After moving to Danville, I was lonely and fell back on putting models together to pass the time. I created, in my head, a model car club called "The Dragoons," and I designed a membership card for the club, using a graphic style I stole from Ed "Big Daddy" Roth. Roth was all over the car culture in the late 1950s and early 1960s. He was a key figure in the Kustom Kar movement out of Southern California. They changed the spelling because their Kulture was building customs so radical and different that new words (or old words with new spellings) were needed. They were artistic, colorful, shape-bending, and, in many cases, impractical creations. Roth built Kustom Kars featured in *Car Craft* and *Rod and Custom* magazines and others, and he also published artwork in magazines and on T-shirts. He was famous for illustrating colorful, outrageous creatures (such as Rat Fink and "Mr. Gasser") joined by equally outrageous vehicles. When I finished my Big Daddy-esque membership card for the Dragoons, I thought it was perfect. I had artfully captured Big Daddy's style. I only had to make one card, because I was the club's only member. Then I started on my last models.

First I tackled an AMT plastic model of a 1961 Ford Falcon Ranchero pickup truck. This was a "Styline" kit that cost a bit more because it came with some special parts to encourage customization. The supplementary parts created optional front and rear ends, and the kit included upholstery stickers, body putty, and sandpaper. I had been influenced by the Kustom Kars created by Roth and George Barris, so I decided to make the Ranchero into my own Kustom. I used some extra parts provided by AMT, but made the Ranchero my own by radically changing the rear end. I used a coping saw to cut away the rear fenders on the truck bed, so the rear wheels stood totally outside the bodywork. I created minimal wheel wells, shortened the bed, and changed the taillights. Body putty, then small files and sandpaper, smoothed over the new shapes. I flocked a custom interior and sprayed the model with candy burgundy paint. I entered my creation in a model contest at the hobby shop off Main Street and won second place and a little trophy.

The model car industry enjoyed a large boom in the late 1950s and early 1960s. Their kits first allowed you to build a stock Ford or Chevy, just like you would see at a dealership. Then they offered 3-in-1 kits—using different parts and decals within one kit, you could build a stock model, a custom, or a hot rod. Then came Kustom Kar Kulture, and you could build a model car that did not come from Detroit at all but from creative Californians like George Barris and Ed "Big Daddy" Roth. In 1961, AMT released the first model of a pure show rod, "Ala-Kart," a heavily customized 1929 Ford Model A roadster pickup built by George Barris. Similar model kits followed that replicated Roth's wild creations, such as the "Outlaw," the "Beatnik Bandit," and the "Mysterion." The model industry continued to evolve by offering model kits of engines. In 1958, Renwal, a small company that had produced plastic models for a few years, released its "Visible V-8." This was a generic V-8 of no specific make. A battery-powered small motor turned the model engine's crank, and because the cylinder block, heads, and valve covers were made of clear plastic, you could see its internal parts move.

In 1961, Revell introduced its model of a Chrysler Slant Six engine. (Chrysler had introduced this six-cylinder engine in 1959; its engine block was slanted thirty degrees from vertical to lower its height under the hood.) Revell had planned to make a model of a popular Chevy V-8, but $100,000 from Chrysler changed the model maker's mind. The Slant Six model, one-quarter the size of the real engine, was exceptionally precise, accurate, and true to the engines running in Plymouths and Dodges.

Assembling the model was almost like putting a real engine together. As I worked on it, I thought it was time well spent for a boy planning to go to the General Motors Institute to get a degree in mechanical engineering. The model had about three hundred parts molded of red, black, silver, and gray plastic. It came with a long instruction manual and a pamphlet on the workings of internal combustion engines. The Slant Six was the most complicated, difficult, and educational model I ever put together, and it took me a couple of weeks to finish it. Some parts snapped together, some were glued, and some were held in place with screws. When completed, the model sat on its engine stand, which held the batteries and the switch for sending the Slant Six into motion. The fan turned, the rocker arms rocked, and the pistons went up and down. This model had no clear plastic parts, so to see internal parts do their thing, and to see small lights flashing to mimic spark plugs firing in proper sequence, I had to take off a removable piece of the block. I could watch the valve gear work by taking off the rocker cover. It was a great model, and when I finished the Slant Six, I felt like I'd really accomplished something.

Next came a Monogram model of a Model T that seemed huge, because it was. Done in one-eighth scale, it was nearly seventeen inches long. Monogram released its Big T model in 1962 at a price of $11—over five times the price of an ordinary model. It had 203 molded parts in five colors, including 97 pieces of simulated chrome that really made the model stand out. The engine was fashioned after Chevy's popular 283-cubic-inch engine. The body was patterned after a '24 Ford roadster body, with a short pickup bed behind it. The front wheels turned. The tires were soft rubber whitewalls. The kit came with some extra parts, so a builder could customize the interior and radiator shell. It also came with a twenty-four-page-long instruction manual to guide assembly.

The Big T was much easier to put together than the Slant Six. It was a fun project from start to finish, and handsome when completed. Monogram followed the Big T with a Big '32 Ford, a Corvette Stingray, a Jaguar XKE, and a Firebird Trans Am, but I didn't build any of those. When I finished the Big T, my driver's license was only months away. My vroom vroom days were over. My production line of model cars came to a halt, and I, as they say, put away my childish things. It had been two and a half years since I told Mom, "Don't worry. We'll make it." Well, we were making it, and I was beginning to thrive in my new town and school.

# 12

## CAR TUNES

Top 40 radio originated in the early 1950s. Todd Storz, at radio station KOWH in Omaha, began compiling a list each week of the most frequently played songs on jukeboxes across the country. Storz used the data to create a playlist for his radio station, and other stations quickly followed suit. Stations believed they were playing the tunes that listeners really wanted to hear. Borrowing from that idea, what if you were interested in car songs from their "golden age" of the postwar era through the mid-1960s? What would you want to hear, if (like Chuck Berry) you were "cruisin' and playin' the radio with no particular place to go"?

### One Man's Top 40 Car Songs

40. The Rip Chords, "Hot Rod USA," 1964
39. Dinah Shore, "See the USA in Your Chevrolet," commercial jingle, 1949
38. Ferlin Husky, "The Drunken Driver," 1954
37. Robert Mitchum, "Ballad of Thunder Road," 1956
36. Nervous Norvus, "Transfusion," 1956
35. Paul Evans, "Seven Little Girls Sitting in the Back Seat," 1959
34. The Beach Boys, "Drive-In," 1964
33. The Beach Boys, "In the Parking Lot," 1963
32. Marilyn Michaels, "Tell Tommy I Miss Him," 1960
31. Paul Revere and the Raiders, "SS 396," 1966

30. The Rip Chords, “Three Window Coupe,” 1964
29. Jimmy Liggins, “Cadillac Boogie,” 1947
28. Roy Brown, “Cadillac Baby,” 1950
27. Ike Turner, “Rocket 88,” 1951
26. The Beatles, “Drive My Car,” 1965
25. Ray Peterson, “Tell Laura I Love Her,” 1960
24. The Beach Boys, “A Young Man Is Gone,” 1963
23. J. Frank Wilson and the Cavaliers, “Last Kiss,” 1964
22. Everly Brothers, “Wake Up Little Susie,” 1957
21. Mark Dinning, “Teen Angel,” 1960
20. The Playmates, “Beep Beep,” 1958
19. Jan and Dean, “Bucket ‘T,’” 1964
18. Chuck Berry, “No Particular Place to Go,” 1964
17. Arkie Shibley, “Hot Rod Race,” 1950
16. Charlie Ryan, “Hot Rod Lincoln,” 1955, 1959
15. Simon and Garfunkel, “America,” 1968
14. Beach Boys, “Shut Down,” 1963
13. Beach Boys, “409,” 1962
12. Wilson Pickett, “Mustang Sally,” 1966
11. The Rip Chords, “Hey Little Cobra,” 1964
10. Nat King Cole, “Route 66,” 1946
9. Beach Boys, “Fun, Fun, Fun,” 1964
8. Jan and Dean, “Drag City,” 1963
7. Beach Boys, “Don’t Worry Baby,” 1964
6. Ronny and the Daytonas, “GTO,” 1964
5. Chuck Berry, “Maybellene,” 1955
4. Jan and Dean, “Dead Man’s Curve,” 1963
3. Jan and Dean, “Little Old Lady from Pasadena,” 1964
2. Beach Boys, “Little Deuce Coupe,” 1963
1. Beach Boys, “I Get Around,” 1964

* * *

In the decades after World War II, Americans put more music into their cars and more cars into their music. Car radios and car songs loomed large in the lives of teenagers. Between 1955 and 1965, the car radio secured its place in the center of dashboards. It often came equipped with AM/FM, tuning dials, push buttons, and an automatic station search function. Teens cruised down their Main Streets listening to tunes like "Wake Up Little Susie" and "Mustang Sally."

Motorola marketed the first successful car radio in 1930. Some feared this innovation, thinking a radio would distract drivers and lead to accidents. Several states proposed car radio bans and fines, but to no avail. Philco and other companies joined Motorola in producing car radios in the 1930s. The industry grew until slowed by World War II. Still, by 1946, an estimated 9 million cars in the United States had radios. That number climbed to 26.5 million by 1953. By 1965, 80 percent of America's cars offered passengers the opportunity to listen to news, sports, opinions, music, and commercial jingles. As I tooled around town as a high school senior, listening to "Wooly Bully" and "I Got You Babe," one minute my radio told me to drink Coke, and the next minute it said that Pepsi was for the young generation.

The radio industry and its audience changed dramatically after World War II. The radio once provided family entertainment. Everyone gathered around it in the living room, listening to network programming: news, live music played by bands or orchestras, dramas, comedies, quiz shows, and travel adventures. Then television arrived, and ABC, CBS, and NBC largely neglected their radio partners and concentrated on developing content for television. As radio listeners became television watchers, many stations disappeared from the dial, and at surviving stations, managers generated more local content to fill airtime. They hired disc jockeys who could attract advertisers and hold an audience. They played more recorded music, and the rise of rock and roll and the Top 40 playlist brought them a major new market: teenagers. Many teens listened to their car radios or new pocket-sized transistor radios they could take anywhere. The decline of radio reversed, and the number of stations rose from about 2,000 in 1950 to 3,500 in 1960 and to 4,000 in 1965.

I did not buy 45s or albums, because for a long time I had nothing to play them on. I listened to music on three radios: the red-and-silver transistor radio I got in 1959; the family's big Zenith radio in the living room; and the car radio in the big Packard. I also listened to music on television. Ed Sullivan brought many young artists to his stage: Elvis, Bill Haley and the Comets, Buddy Holly, Roy Orbison, the Everly Brothers, the Beach Boys, and the Beatles. Dick Clark's *American Bandstand* brought in new singers all the time: Freddy Cannon, Bobby Darin, Bobby Rydell, Chubby Checker, Frankie Valli, Jan and Dean, and Gene Pitney.

Songs reflected the desire of many American families to enjoy the freedom of automobility and the scenery that America had to offer. In 1946, Bobby Troupe wrote "Route 66," one of the best road songs. Car travel had been curtailed by the war, but now the war was over, and Americans could hit the road again. First popularized by Nat King Cole, "Route 66" played throughout the 1950s and '60s. The song was covered by Bing Crosby, Patti Page, Perry Como, Chuck Berry, and the Rolling Stones. "Route 66" lyrically followed the route of the legendary highway from Chicago to Los Angeles: When you take your trip to California, "get your kicks" on Route 66. Motor west through Saint Looey and Joplin, Missouri; Oklahoma City; Amarillo, Texas; Gallup, New Mexico; Flagstaff, Winona, and Kingman, Arizona; and Barstow and San Bernardino, California. The song didn't carry listeners from sea to shining sea, but it did take them from Lake Michigan to the Pacific.

Another song heard repeatedly on television from 1956 to 1963 encouraged Americans to see the great USA On her popular television show, Dinah Shore, a pretty and personable entertainer from Tennessee, sang "See the USA in your Chevrolet. America is asking you to call. Drive your Chevrolet through the USA—America's the greatest land of all." This commercial jingle rattled around in the heads of millions of people. The song told them you can travel great distances in a Chevy without worry. Disneyland had just opened, and millions of Americans wanted to go visit the Magic Kingdom. The Rockies way out West tempted Americans to travel too. Whether you were traveling east or west, north or south, Dinah Shore let you know that Chevy offered the best car service, and service was important to Americans taking long road trips. They feared being stranded in the middle of nowhere. Not to worry, they could always find a Chevrolet dealer to service their car. Buy a Chevy, pack it up, and go.

One of my favorite car songs reached number 4 in 1958. Sung by the Playmates, "Beep Beep" tells the story of a lowly Nash Rambler that keeps beeping its horn at the Cadillac in front of it. The Caddy driver speeds up, trying to shake the impertinent Rambler, because it would be a disgrace to get passed by such a little, cheap car. The music speeds up as the cars speed up. The Caddy finally tops out at 120 miles per hour. The Rambler driver pulls alongside the Caddy and asks how he can get his little car out of second gear. The song was funny, because everybody knew that a Nash Rambler could never go 120 miles per hour.

Other car songs were not so humorous. The open road symbolized romance, opportunity, and freedom. Roads led to the future, but only if you lived to get there. When I was young, it seemed like America—through the medium of car songs—was trying to scare me and other baby boomers to death. Like the writer of adolescent fiction Henry Gregor Felson, lyricists killed off teenagers left and right. Thank God it was all make-believe.

In 1960, "Teen Angel" reached number 1 on the charts. A young guy and his gal find themselves in a car stalled on railroad tracks. He leads her to safety, but she runs back to the car to retrieve his high school ring. She is killed by the oncoming train, and her boyfriend will never get to kiss her again. "Tell Laura I Love Her" reached number 7 in 1960. Tommy and Laura are lovers. He wants to give her a wedding ring, so he signs up to run in a stock car race. Instead of winning the $1,000 purse, he dies as his car overturns and bursts into flames. With his last breath he says to tell Laura his love for her will never die. Within months, the pathos of "Tell Laura I Love Her" was doubled up by an "answer song." Laura asks a little star in heaven to "Tell Tommy I Miss Him," and that her love for him will never die. Another song in the same vein, "Last Kiss," reached number 2 on the Top 40 charts in 1964. A young man and his date are out driving in his daddy's car. Suddenly he sees a stalled car in his lane. He swerves to the right, loses control, and crashes. In the wreckage the driver finds his dying girlfriend. He holds her close and gives her a last kiss.

I heard these teen tragedy songs dozens of times on the radio. To me they were never sad, because they were never real—they were just musical entertainment. Popular music thrived on the breakup of young couples in love. The car crash was just a new way to do it. Instead of her running off with another guy, kill her on the highway.

Not all car death songs were intended to pluck at listeners' heartstrings. Novelty songs like "Transfusion" encouraged teens to laugh at death. Written and sung in 1956 by Nervous Norvus (Jimmy Drake), "Transfusion" reached number 8 on the charts that year. Every verse in the song leads to the same driver's apparent death in another accident, but a blood transfusion always pulls him through. He speeds, runs a stop sign, crosses the center line, passes a truck on a hill, passes on the right, races down a mountain in the rain, passes without honking his horn—and crashes. But give him a gallon of blood and he's out on the road again.

A macabre novelty song appeared in 1965. "I Want My Baby Back," sung by Jimmy Cross, played for laughs from start to finish. The song pokes fun at a car death song ("Last Kiss") *and* a motorcycle death song ("Leader of the Pack"), both released in 1964. A young couple is returning home from a Beatles concert, and it starts to rain. The driver can hardly see, and then he suddenly spots a stalled car right in front of him. He swerves left to miss it—and a pack of motorcyclists is coming right at him. The driver and his baby meet the leader of the pack head-on. Body parts of the motorcyclists and the girlfriend are scattered all over the horrific scene. Months later, the young driver finds he can't make it without his baby. He still digs her so much that he digs her up at the cemetery. The creaking coffin top opens, and he gets into the coffin with her. The creaking coffin top then closes. His last line, "I've got my baby back," is muffled. Mercifully, "I Want My Baby Back" pretty much closed the lid on the era of car death songs.

In the 1950s and '60s, popular songs played for two to three minutes. The Beach Boys' classic "Little Deuce Coupe" ran only 1:48. The songs were short and well suited for radio play. No one song painted a panoramic picture of car or youth culture in America. But if you listened to a Top 40 of car songs, taken collectively, their lyrics created a montage that captured how young Americans felt about cars and the teenagers who drove and rode in them. The songs weren't written by cultural anthropologists who carefully observed behavior at drag strips, drive-ins, or high school parking lots. Young songwriters wrote their songs for young performers to sing, and the word pictures they painted were sometimes realistic, but often fanciful. Just because a singer sang some words didn't mean they were true. A stock GTO could not beat a rail job at the drags, and it would have been highly unlikely for a little old lady in Pasadena to race a super stock Dodge with a legendary 426-cubic-inch Hemi engine under the hood and a four-speed tranny. But wasn't it fun to picture her at the wheel on Colorado Boulevard, spotting young men a length and then shutting them down?

The songs got one thing right: there was a pecking order of cars, and in the late 1940s through the 1950s, Cadillacs reigned supreme. They were big, fast, stylish, comfortable, and expensive, a premier status symbol that attracted young ladies. White Americans and Black Americans sang songs lauding Caddies. In 1947, Jimmy Liggins, a twenty-nine-year-old Black guitarist and bandleader from North Carolina, recorded "Cadillac Boogie." Liggins sang about a travelin' man, a hep cat daddy, who drives a long Fleetwood Cadillac with a V-8 motor. He goes sportin' around town, pickin' up all the fine chicks who are enamored with his car. In 1950, Roy Brown, a Black member of the Blues Hall of Fame, recorded "Cadillac Baby," a sexually charged song about a woman who wants to ride (have sex) all night long. In 1955, Chuck Berry's frustrating girlfriend drives a Cadillac Coupe de Ville at over 100 miles per hour, while he has a V-8 Ford. The Caddy in "Beep Beep" hit 120 miles per hour. In "Hot Rod Lincoln," it's a fast passing Caddy that sets off a race, and the Rip Chords sing about the owner of a Shelby Cobra who takes his sports car to the track, hitched to the back of his Cadillac.

Other Detroit-built automobiles made it into song if they sported prestige, powerful engines, and high performance. In 1951, a Black musician from Mississippi, Ike Turner, wrote "Rocket 88." His band recorded the song in a Memphis studio. The Rocket 88 was both an engine and a car produced by Oldsmobile. Introduced in 1949 and continued for many years, the Rocket was an overhead valve, 303-cubic-inch engine that developed 135 horsepower. Olds put this engine in its Olds 98 model and in the smaller, lighter—and therefore faster—Olds 88. The Rocket 88 Olds became a big winner on the NASCAR circuit and in the new car marketplace. One of its sales slogans was, "Make a Date with a Rocket 88." That's what Ike Turner's song was all about—let's have young women make a date with the man driving a Rocket 88.

"Rocket 88" was a song of consequence. It was inducted into the Blues Hall of Fame, the Grammy Hall of Fame, and the Rock and Roll Hall of Fame. Many music historians credit "Rocket 88" as the first rock and roll song. It has the beat, instrumentation, and lyrics to support that claim, plus all the youthfulness and energy of rock and roll. The lead singer, Jackie Brenston, was the oldest in the band at age twenty-three. All the other musicians were between seventeen and twenty, including Ike Turner. The song sounded like rhythm and blues, but it was not about hard or difficult times. To the contrary, it was a celebration of the good life, thanks to the stylish and fast new convertible that attracted young women. The men and women in the Rocket 88 enjoyed riding all around town for joy, cruising and boozing.

The muscle-car era of the mid-1960s ushered in songs dedicated to the hot cars produced by Detroit's Big Three. To reach younger buyers and to invigorate the Pontiac Division at GM, in 1964 John DeLorean put a larger engine in the Tempest, which had first been introduced as a midsize car. Pontiac swapped out the Tempest's 326-cubic-inch engine for a bigger 389-cubic-inch engine of 325 horsepower that could be ordered with three two-barrel carburetors and a four-speed. Pontiac gave this variant a name that conjured up an image of speed. "GTO" stood for Gran Turismo Omologato, the name of a Ferrari race car. The March 1964 cover of *Car and Driver* magazine helped push the comparison. It depicted a GTO chasing down a red Ferrari on a twisty road course.

Pontiac did not expect to sell many GTOs in 1964. It placed few ads in the mainstream media. But things changed when the new Pontiac started being hailed as America's first muscle car, thanks in part to popular music. In Nashville, John Wilkin was a teenager bitten by the GTO bug. He wrote the lyrics to "GTO," reportedly while sitting in a high school physics class. Wilkin was the son of a successful country song writer, and he patched together a band of session musicians called Ronny and the Daytonas. The group put out a single and an album dedicated to Pontiac's 1964 muscle car. This group was Nashville's main contribution to the car culture. Their greatest hit by far, "GTO" reached number 4 on the charts. The song highlighted the allure of a small, sleek hardtop or convertible with a big motor that was engineered to do one thing particularly well: go fast. A young man saves his money, buys a GTO, equips it with a roll bar, and takes it to the drag strip, where it beats the gassers and the rail jobs. Like the song, the real GTO was a big hit. Pontiac originally estimated sales of five thousand units. Dealers delivered thirty-one thousand GTOs to enthusiastic buyers in 1964.

The Beach Boys also recorded "GTO," and Jan and Dean and John Lee Hooker sang their own songs about the muscle car. Meanwhile, Jan and Dean called attention to super stock Dodges in "Little Old Lady from Pasadena," and the Beach Boys told the world that a Chevy with a 409-cubic-inch engine always turned in the fastest times. Paul Revere and the Raiders costumed themselves as old-time colonials, but in 1966 they performed "SS 396," about the modern Chevelle Super Sport. Chuck Berry bragged about his 1965 cherry-red Ford Mustang. With 385 horsepower, Berry believed it was a shame to ask it to comply with the seventy-mile-per-hour speed limit on Interstates.

Some sports cars made it into song, but not all of them. MG, Triumph and Mercedes sports cars were left out, while Jaguar was featured in many songs, especially after introducing its XKE in 1961. Jaguars won some and lost some when it came to musical drag races; it was an unlucky driver of an XKE who died in Jan and Dean's "Dead Man's Curve." In 1963, a new California group, the Rip Chords, helped introduce America to another sports car, the Shelby Cobra. The Cobra was derived from a British sports car, the Ace, hand built by AC Cars. American sports car driver and auto designer Carroll Shelby took interest in the Ace, known for its excellent handling, and he replaced its six-cylinder engine with a Ford V-8. The reengineering started in Britain and was completed in California in 1963. With Ford's 289-cubic-inch engine, the rebadged Shelby Cobra became a very lightweight and fast sports car. It became a car of renown, thanks to a song.

Annette Kleinbard, a California-born singer and songwriter, once suffered life-threatening injuries when her sports car tumbled down a mountainside. At the age of twenty-two, she wrote "Hey Little Cobra," reportedly with help from her little brother, Marshall, who was only thirteen. The Rip Chords recorded Kleinbard's song as their third single, and it was a big hit. It told the story of a sports car race, where the new Cobra raced against plenty of Jaguar XKEs and Corvette Stingrays. From the drop of the flag, the Cobra flies by the other cars and the driver waves bye-bye to the vanquished. The idea is not just to beat them but to "Shut 'em down." At the end, the Cobra driver is so far ahead that he takes his car out of gear and coasts across the finish line.

The Corvette—especially the Corvette Stingray of the 1960s—was the one American sports car worthy of racing Cobras and XKE's. Corvettes successfully competed in American sports car races since the mid-1950s. They were successful in song too. In 1963, Stingrays lost out to the Rip Chords' new Cobra, but that was not the only race run on vinyl that year. In "Shut Down," the Beach Boys ran a drag race between a Stingray and a super stock Dodge. The Dodge Dart has a 413-cubic-inch engine, and the Corvette Stingray has a fuel-injected 327. They rev up their engines and accelerate off the line. The Stingray's rear slicks lose traction, while the Dodge digs in and goes ahead. The Stingray driver power shifts and starts to catch up. His clutch's pressure plate is burnin', but with the Stingray's accelerator to the floor, the 413's lead starts to shrink. Finally, the Stingray goes in front, shutting down the Dodge.

From 1955 to 1957, the two-seater Ford Thunderbird was a half-hearted sports car. The high-water mark of the Thunderbird in song was the Beach Boys' 1964 release, "Fun, Fun, Fun." Before her daddy took her car keys away, a sexy girl cruised alone in daddy's T-Bird, leading potential suitors on a wild goose chase. The Beach Boys didn't specify the year of the car, but as far as I was concerned, the desirable girl just had to be driving a two-seater from the 1950s. The film *American*

In 1963, a Shelby Cobra leads a Corvette Stingray into the corner at a race in Los Angeles. (Dave Friedman Collection of The Henry Ford)

*Graffiti*, set in 1962, saw it the same way. Susanne Somers teased young men by tooling around town in a '56 T-Bird.

Lyricists and groups paid considerable attention to hot rods, customs, and what might be called jalopies. The hot rods often turned up in songs like Jan and Dean's "Drag City," a mythical place where drivers and their cars burned up the quarter mile and ran the fastest drag races in the nation. The whole point of a hot rod was to go fast. Often the hot rod started as a Model T or Model B Ford, a coupe or a roadster. Owners and mechanics gutted the machine and rebuilt it with a tricked-out engine, a custom exhaust, a strong transmission, and a stout differential at the rear end geared to maximize acceleration. A hot rod was built to *go*. A custom car, on the other hand, was made for *show*. Owners built customs for car people to admire while the cars were standing still. Look at all that chrome! Check out the metal-flake paint, the pin striping, the tuck and roll upholstery!

The Rip Chords and Jan and Dean both recorded the hot rod song "Three Window Coupe." This car shuts down all the competition. It's the

The '32 Ford, coupe or roadster, has always been a favorite of hot-rodders. Dick Smith built this exquisite customized '32 roadster, powered by a Chrysler V-8, in the early 1950s. (Collections of The Henry Ford)

toughest and fastest. It doesn't look like much, but when the driver pops the clutch and gives it the gas, the coupe wins the Trophy Run at the drags. The Beach Boys had a great hot rod song too. The cover of their "Little Deuce Coupe" album depicts a custom 1932 Model B Ford coupe. It is all prettied up with paint and chrome. But the lyrics paint a different picture, a picture of a different car—a real hot rod. The owner brags that he has the fastest car in town, and other guys won't even challenge him. Its flathead Ford engine has been bored and stroked to produce more horsepower, and the coupe will run 140 miles per hour. A competition clutch and a limited slip differential at the rear end allows the coupe to lay rubber in all four gears. The song is entirely about performance, not looks.

In the late 1940s, Charlie Ryan, a singer and songwriter from Spokane, Washington, acquired a 1940 Lincoln Zephyr four-door sedan. He turned it into a hot rod. He shortened the frame by two feet, did away with the Lincoln's body, and replaced it with a 1930 Model A Ford coupe body. He dropped a 1948 twelve-cylinder Lincoln engine onto the frame, along with a '48 three-speed transmission with overdrive. While completing his transformation, he wrote "Hot Rod Lincoln," a song he first recorded in 1955 and again in 1959. In it, the youthful driver is clearly proud of his Lincoln/Ford with its souped-up motor. While out driving with friends one night, a Cadillac passes him by. His friends rib him for being behind the Caddy, so he puts his car into overdrive and winds it up to 110 miles per hour. At that speed the telephone poles alongside the highway looked like a picket fence, and the lines on the road looked like dots. He passes the Cadillac. When he does, a flashing red light shows up in his rearview mirror. The cops arrest him and put him in jail, and he calls his pop. The father makes his bail and laments that his son is going to drive him to drinking if he keeps on hot rodding that Lincoln.

The Beach Boys poked fun at cars that looked good but lacked performance. The "No-Go Showboat" is a show-winning custom car that is not suited for drag racing. She has plenty of chrome and metal-flake paint. She wins over chicks but wins no races. In the best of worlds, a California car would look good *and* run fast. The hot rod in "Cherry, Cherry Coupe" is sharp looking, with custom bodywork, tuck and roll upholstery, chrome reversed wheels, and whitewall slicks. At the same time, it wins drag races. Another car with similar attributes is the Beach Boys' "Custom Machine." It has metal-flake paint and Naugahyde bucket seats front and back, and everything is chromed, including the jack. It has been lowered to within an inch of the ground, and when the driver steps on the gas, its Corvette engine roars to life.

As Henry Gregor Felson warned in his hot rod books for adolescents, a kid working on an old car had all his money and free time tied up in it. In song, like in life, not every car-crazy kid had enough money or skill to build a top-notch hot rod. Just purchasing a car and getting it to run was a challenge. In the Beach Boys' "Ballad of Ole' Betsy," a young man loves his unrestored jalopy. Betsy was born in '32 in Detroit and shipped west by rail. Over decades she traveled many miles before her adoring last owner found her. He knows she is rusted iron, but to him she is solid gold. He sheds tears, knowing that Betsy's growing old, and he'll run her till she can run no more. Another Beach Boys' song,

"This Car of Mine," starts out with the same story as "Ballad of Ole' Betsy," but ends on a happier note. A young man buys a car that's old and broken down. He takes it home and has enough resources to fix her up. He makes his car so fine that no amount of gold could convince him to sell her. Jan and Dean sang about another auto salvage project in their 1964 song "Bucket T." A Bucket T was a popular type of small hot rod that used the body of a Model T roadster that had room for two people at best, and sometimes only one. It had an exposed engine and chromed exhaust pipes, a vertical windshield, a polished, original radiator surround, and sometimes a small pickup box. In "Bucket T," a boy finds his Model T roadster in a barn in Tennessee, buys it for five bucks, and spends three years turning it into a hot rod. Only then does the fun start. He gets his kicks by popping the clutch and laying down some rubber. The young driver is proud of what he built: she's first class and can outrun anything. She attracts girls, too, but to no avail, because his Bucket T's seat has room for only one.

Young men wrote and sang almost all the car songs. In many, a young driver tours his town. He cruises the strip, drives by his high school, visits the beach, and pulls into drive-in restaurants. He finds a cute girl who hops into his car, and they cruise around together for a while. By the time the short song ends in two minutes, not much has happened, really, including any intimacy or sex. Car songs in the 1950s through the mid-1960s presented teenagers in a favorable light. Teenagers were looking for fun, not trouble. They seemingly had only a few flaws: they drag raced over public roads and sometimes had deadly crashes. Otherwise, they lived innocent lives. Lyricists put a positive spin on teens, ignoring social problems such as juvenile delinquency.

Many older Americans in the 1950s feared that teenagers were growing too wild, too free. Teens rejected parental supervision, social authority, and social norms. They spent little time at home. They lived out on the streets and made their own rules. Too many dropped out of school. Teen pregnancy became a problem. Teen crime became a problem. Drinking, drugs, and mental illness became issues. It seemed to many that teens were going to hell in their hot rods.

Car songs written and sung by the younger generation, especially whites, ignored all of this. Songs sanitized the new youth culture in America, especially when compared to the movies. Delinquency starred in many films, such as Marlon Brando's *The Wild One*, about a violent outlaw motorcycle gang, and James Dean's *Rebel Without a Cause*, about suburban, middle-class high schoolers who have lost their way. Those two movie classics were joined by many B-grade movies awash in juvenile delinquency: *Hot Rod Girl. Hot Rod Rumble. Hot Rod Gang. Drag Strip Riot.* In the 1955 film *Teen Age Crime Wave*, two delinquent teens break out of reform school and go on a shooting spree across their state. 1957's *Teen-Age Thunder* was about "Young Love and Teen Age Kisses . . . Hot Rods and Hot Tempers." Two young men wanting the same girl play "chicken"—they drive straight at each other to see who chickens out and turns aside first. That same year, in the film *Eighteen and Anxious*, an eighteen-year-old girl elopes to Mexico and gets pregnant. The baby's father dies, and she is abused by other young men. The movie's poster read, "Parents may be shocked . . . [but] youth will understand." *High School Confidential*, released in 1958, builds drama around high school narcotics use. *T-Bird Gang*, a 1961 film, is about a group of young men: "The one year out of high school crowd—fast cars, girls . . . no place to go." They kill a night watchman and go on to commit a series of crimes.

The antisocial, illegal, and dangerous behavior so rife in movies was absent in car songs played over the radio. In song, no teenager dropped out of school to become a violent criminal. No teenagers joined a gang; instead, they joined respectable car clubs. The hot-rodders of song did not take narcotics or smoke pot—they didn't even drink alcohol. And they didn't have sex and knock up their girlfriends. They were remarkably clean cut.

In the teenage car death songs of the 1950s, the cause of the accident was never drunk driving. Only older performers recorded songs about drunk driving and its tragic consequences. In 1942, bluegrass singer Roy Acuff put out "Wreck on the Highway," later covered by George Jones and Gene Pitney in 1965. "Wreck on the Highway" was unusual in a few regards. First, its bluegrass sound, with fiddles and banjos, made it very different from pop music. Secondly, it was about adults, not teenagers. A man hears a crash on the highway and stops. He sees whiskey, blood, and broken glass on the road. He hears the groans of the dying, but sadly he doesn't hear anybody praying over this scene.

The "don't drink and drive" message was repeated in a country song recorded by Ferlin Husky in 1954. "The Drunken Driver" is a didactic, spoken-word song that warns not to drink a drop while at the steering wheel. Two little kids walk side by side along the state highway. A speeding car comes around a curve with an intoxicated driver at the wheel. His car strikes and kills the youngsters. The driver staggers out of his car and discovers he has run over his own children.

The lyrics sung by Black musicians working in the rhythm and blues and boogie genres sometimes included people sharing a bottle and strongly hinted at people sharing each other. Young white singers did not go there. They sang of romances marked by innocent flirtations. In the mid-1960s, readily available birth control pills were a bit into the future, as were feminism and the sexual revolution. Society strongly encouraged girls to say no, not yes, to the predatory desires of young men. In 1959, a novelty song, "Seven Little Girls Sitting in the Back Seat," reached number 9 in popularity. In this song story, an unfortunate young male driver is alone in the front seat, while Fred sits in back, accompanied by seven little girls busily huggin' and kissin' him. The driver asks if one of the girls could come up front and sit with him. They tell him to keep his mind on the drivin', his hands on the wheel, and his snoopy eyes on the road ahead. The girls are having fun with Fred. Nobody joins the driver. He is feeling unneeded and unwanted. He keeps drivin' and Fred keeps getting hugs and kisses—but nothing more.

Songs were full of playfulness. Young couples just cruised around, playing the radio, sometimes stopping in a secluded spot to share some kisses. Teen "sex" concluded with a little cuddling, and that was it. Nobody got naked and sweaty. Nobody got a young girl drunk just to take advantage of her. Nobody became a front seat contortionist, curling around a Hurst shifter to have sex. Nobody got pregnant. Even the hint of sex could make trouble for a young couple. In the Everly Brothers' number 1 song in 1957, "Wake Up Little Susie," little Susie has gone on a date with her beau to the drive-in. They fall asleep in the car and the boy doesn't wake up until four o'clock. He had told Susie's momma he'd have her home by ten. Now they are in a pickle. Whatta they gonna tell her momma? Whatta they gonna tell her pa? They fell asleep, their goose is cooked, their reputation is shot. Since society in the 1950s believed that a girl's sexual innocence was more important than a boy's, Susie has more at stake in this song and will have to answer to her parents.

A few songs put the female's hands on the wheel and gave her control of trolling the streets, looking for boys and amusement. The girl driving her daddy's T-Bird enticed and frustrated boys as she cruised the streets, but she was nothing compared to Maybellene and Mustang Sally, two of the strongest young women of car song renown. Maybellene tormented her man in the mid-1950s and Mustang Sally did the same in the mid-1960s. Making the girl or woman the driver was an important role reversal that had consequences. It put her in charge.

In 1955, a twenty-nine-year-old Black musician from St. Louis walked into Chess Records to record his very first song, one he had written, called "Maybellene." The song was meant to appeal to a young audience, Black and white, that was taken with cars, speed, and a suggestion or hint of sexuality. The song proved a great hit for Chuck Berry, and it helped define rock and roll. It sold a million copies, rose to number 1 on the rhythm and blues charts, and to number 5 on Billboard's pop chart. The moral of the story: if a woman has her own car, she has the freedom to go off on her own and cheat on you and break your heart. "Maybellene" is a car chase song where the woman drives the best, a Cadillac, while her man—or the fellow who *wants* to be her man—drives a V-8 Ford. The Ford races the Caddy; they go bumper to bumper and roll side by side, language suggestive of the intimacy he misses. The Ford driver catches up to Maybellene at the top of a hill, but to no avail. She's still back doin' the things she used to do, getting on without him.

In April 1964, Ford introduced the Ford Mustang, also known as a pony car. The top model had a 289-cubic-inch engine, and its fresh, trim design led to great success in the automotive marketplace. One Black artist, Mack Rice, quickly wrote and recorded a song about the pony car in 1965. His recording of "Mustang Sally" did not find a big audience, but in 1966, Wilson Pickett released a more popular version that went to number 6 on the rhythm and blues charts and number 23 on the pop charts. The song, like "Maybellene," showed that it was risky to desire a woman who enjoys the freedom of having her own car. In this case, the man causes his own problem by giving Sally a 1965 Mustang. When he does that, Mustang Sally acts like a mustang herself, an untamed wild horse. She drives fast; she runs all over town. All she wants to do is ride around. It is reasonable to interpret the word "ride" as meaning that Sally wants to have sex all the time. Mustang Sally is the opposite of true. The poor fellow who gave her the car laments that she doesn't wanna let *him* ride, just other guys.

Chuck Berry and Wilson Picket sang about sex using metaphors. The same was true for the Beatles in their 1965 song "Drive My Car." A young man meets a girl who wants to be famous, who wants to be a star of the silver screen. Before that happens, she says he can do something for her, he can chauffeur her around, he can drive her car, and maybe she'll love him. He's willing, but then she admits she has no car, only a willing driver. In this song, "drive my car" is another euphemism for having sex, one that Paul McCartney claimed went back to rhythm and blues songs.

In 1964, Brian Wilson and Mike Love of the Beach Boys wrote "Drive-In," a song that addressed youthful sex more directly than their earlier recordings. At the drive-in, enjoy chili dogs, buttered popcorn, and a Coke. But enjoy your date too. Watch enough of the movie to know the plot (just in case a parent might ask about it), but you know you'd be lying if you said you really watched the movie. Go ahead and make love. The young man and the young woman both enjoy sex. But remember the saying "only you can prevent forest fires." In a song about drive-in sex, the word "prevent" implies that if the boy used a condom, a pregnancy might be averted.

In the automotive world, "TDC" means top dead center. The piston has gone up as far as it can go in an engine's cylinder, and its next movement will be down. The TDC for car songs in American youth

This white convertible was the first Mustang to come off a Ford assembly line in 1964. Designated as 1965 models, early Mustangs were not muscle cars, but those with a 289-cubic-inch V-8 engine moved along pretty well. (Collections of The Henry Ford)

culture was 1963–64. At that time, groups from Los Angeles produced the most popular car songs (and surfing songs), and, listening to them, it seemed that all the sunshine from heaven fell upon California. That magic land had the best beaches, prettiest blondes, handsomest boys, and highest waves—plus the best drag strips. hot rods, and custom cars. Message after message reaffirmed California's exalted state. Three musical groups in particular—the Rip Chords, Jan and Dean, and the Beach Boys—sent California vibes over the airwaves, reaching me in oceanless Illinois, a state where we suffered the triple indignities of cold, snow, and brunettes.

These groups had a great deal in common. They sang both surfer songs and car songs, and their careers took off in late 1962 or 1963. They often covered each others' songs, and sometimes helped write them. All members of these groups attended high schools near or in Los Angeles. The members were of a like age. In 1963, Phil Stewart of the Rip Chords was twenty-five and Ernie Bringas, twenty-four. Jan Berry and Dean Torrence were twenty-two and twenty-three years old. The Beach Boys—brothers Brian, Dennis, and Carl Wilson, plus cousin Mike Love and friend Al Jardine—were all between seventeen and twenty-two.

Except for Ernie Bringas, who was born to a Mexican mother and immigrated to the United States as a child, the Californians in these groups were about as white as possible and remarkably clean-cut when their careers soared. No beards or mustaches. No long hair. They presented themselves as super-wholesome and handsome all-Americans enjoying the good life. They were unabashed, happy heterosexuals at a time when heterosexuality was the unquestioned norm. In song, they depicted other young men (and their cars) as rivals or challengers on the track, strip, or street, and they saw young women as enticing ornaments to be pursued and acquired as they cruised the beaches and streets of Los Angeles. They drove hot rods, nostalgic woodies, sports cars, or the latest high-powered products of Detroit.

In 1963, the Rip Chords produced the highly successful single "Hey Little Cobra." Backed by some of the best session players available, the Rip Chords put out a fifteen-track album, *Hey Little Cobra and Other Hot Rod Hits*, early in 1964. The album included covers of great California car songs previously recorded by Jan and Dean and the Beach Boys: "409," "Little Deuce Coupe," "Shut Down," and "Drag City." The Rip Chords put out their second and final album later in 1964, a fifteen-track mix of instrumentals and car and surfer songs. One track, "Hot Rod U.S.A.," sings of the spread of hot rod culture from California to the entire country. Cincinnati hot-rodders build Deuce coupes; drag racers burn up the quarter mile in New Orleans; and in every town, hot rods shut down other hot rods. The song immodestly adds that all this hot rod culture started in 1963 with the release of songs by Jan and Dean, the Beach Boys, and—of course—the Rip Chords.

The Rip Chords were up on the news and had a sense of humor. One track on their second album was "One Piece Topless Bathing Suit."

Not long before the album debuted, fashion designer Rudi Gernreich titillated the world by introducing his monokini, which did not cover a woman's breasts. The Rip Chords sang a song about it. Who would wear such a thing? That Rip Chords song begins with a few words familiar to every teen fan of car songs, "Go granny go," and another part of the lyric says that the little old lady doing the Watusi in a topless bathing suit is about ninety-four. For the Rip Chords, Jan and Dean's "Little Old Lady" from Pasadena did more than drive a super stock dodge. She also hung out, bare breasted, on a California beach.

Jan Berry arranged and produced Jan and Dean's original songs, often with significant contributions from Brian Wilson and others. Berry and Wilson were collaborators who influenced each other and came up with the California sound, often called surfin' music. In May 1963, Jan and Dean released a single, "Surf City." This city was an imaginary yet ideal place of play where young men and women mingled freely on the Pacific coast with no responsibilities and no inhibitions. The guys especially had it good at Surf City, because there were two girls for every boy.

"Surf City" hit number one on the Billboard charts in July 1963. Five months later, the duo released a *Drag City* album. The two titles said it all; they switched from surfin' music to car songs. The *Drag City* album featured a Beach Boys' hit from 1963, "Little Deuce Coupe," and two Jan and Dean songs that became big hits: the title track, "Drag City," and "Dead Man's Curve." "Drag City" rose to number 10 on the Billboard chart, and "Dead Man's Curve" rose to number 8. Written by Berry and Wilson, "Drag City" is about hard-core drag racing from its very first line about burning up the quarter mile. A radio DJ says that the races at Drag City are the nation's fastest. The excitement, the smells, the sounds of revving engines, the anticipation of drag racing—it is all there on this record.

The exhilaration of speed turns into a fatality in "Dead Man's Curve," another song written by Barry, Wilson, and others. "Dead Man's Curve" tells the tale of a race between two young men and their cars, a Corvette Stingray and a Jaguar XKE. It's late on a Friday night and the streets are deserted at Sunset and Vine. The driver of the XKE rolls down his window and calls over to the Stingray driver, challenging him to a drag race. The Stingray driver responds that they should race all the way to Dead Man's Curve. They wait for the traffic light to turn green and then pop their clutches and take off. The race extends toward a dangerous stretch of road. One car is ahead, then the other. The Stingray swerves, but its driver pulls out of it as he goes into Dead Man's Curve. The singing stops, and in a spoken voice we hear the Stingray driver telling a doctor that he started to swerve, and then he saw the Jag sliding into the curve. The crash was a horrible sight he would never forget. He found out that people were right—you might not return from Dead Man's Curve. Screeching tires can be heard in the background, and the young Jag driver is dead.

The title track from a 1964 album, *Little Old Lady from Pasadena*, was a huge success for Jan and Dean. It reached number 3 on the charts. It was also the last Jan and Dean song to chart in the top ten. On April 12, 1966, two years after recording "Dead Man's Curve," Jan Berry was driving his new Corvette Stingray at high speed down Whittier Drive in Beverly Hills when he crashed into the back of a parked truck. Only twenty-five years old, Berry suffered debilitating injuries, including severe brain damage. He had to learn to walk and speak again. He had partial paralysis of his right arm. He eventually got back on stage to perform, but if Jan Berry survived the accident, for all intents and purposes Jan and Dean did not. They had produced sixteen Top 40 hits, and five had cracked the top ten. One was a silly song, "Baby Talk." One was a surfer song, "Surf City," their only number 1 hit. Three of their car songs made the top ten, "Drag City," "Dead Man's Curve," and that fun song about the granny with a shiny red super stock Dodge.

In the mid-1960s, the Beach Boys were golden. Their first album, released in October 1962, included two hit songs. The title track, "Surfin' Safari," captured the excitement of taking up surfing when everybody was just learning how to do it. Load your woody wagon with boards, meet up with young honeys, and have a good time. Another prominent track on the album was "409," which extolled the virtues of Chevrolet's 409-cubic-inch big block engine.

The Beach Boys' second album, *Surfin' USA*, released in March 1963, included another hit car song, "Shut Down." Their third album, "Surfer

Girl," released in September 1963, included the songs "Little Deuce Coupe" and "Our Car Club." "Little Deuce Coupe," later covered by the Rip Chords and Jan and Dean, helped cement California as the epicenter of car songs. In "Our Car Club," a group of young men have been cruising with one another and they want to organize themselves into a real club. They'll get the finest cars—a Deuce coupe hot rod, a Stingray, a rail job, and an XKE (quite an ambitious inventory). They'll be the fastest at the drags, and they will wear matching jackets when out cruising.

Album number 4, released just one month after album number 3, included four car songs already found on other albums. New recordings included two tribute songs. "Spirit of America" sang praises to Craig Breedlove, who had just set the world land speed record on the Bonneville Salt Flats. "A Young Man Is Gone" tells of the tragic death at age twenty-four of actor James Dean. This charismatic young movie star seemingly had a boundless future in films, but he was killed in a horrific accident on a California highway on September 30, 1955. Dean participated in sports car racing and was driving his small Porsche 550 Spyder at high speed when he struck another vehicle that turned in front of him When they recorded this song, the Beach Boys were nearly the same age as Dean when he died. The song is heartfelt with great harmonies. Far less solemn was the song "Car Crazy Cutie," about a beautiful girl who is a hot-rodder's perfect girlfriend, because she has mechanical skills and can help in the pits at drag strips.

In March 1964, the Beach Boys released their fifth album, *Shut Down Volume 2*, which included four car songs. "In the Parking Lot" sings the slice-of-life history of a high school couple who spend time each morning in the high school parking lot. They don't go right into the building but sit in the car. She turns on the radio and they sit and listen for a while. While other kids are at their lockers, these two kids are making out. Time for one long kiss, and when the news comes on, it is time to hustle inside.

*Shut Down Volume 2* also included the hit single "Fun, Fun, Fun," written by Brian Wilson and Mike Love, which reached number 5 on the Billboard chart. A young woman drives around in her daddy's

T-bird, going fast and blasting the radio. She's cruising. She's not at the library, like she told her old man. She continues to have fun till her daddy gets wise to her and takes the T-bird's keys away. The song had a ring of truth to it for every kid, including me, who cruised in a parent's car.

Another song on the album, written by Brian Williams and Roger Christian and sung by Wilson, is not buoyant and light like "Fun, Fun, Fun." A young woman keeps telling her man "Don't Worry Baby," things will turn out all right. But he is not reassured. He has bragged too much about his car, and now he can't back down from a race, even though he thinks that something bad is going to happen. She keeps telling him not to worry. If he takes along her love for him, nothing could go wrong. This song struck a whole new chord for the Beach Boys. The young man is not confident and carefree; he has doubts and is afraid. The song was a success, hitting number 24 on the Billboard charts as a single. Later, *Spin* music magazine rated "Don't Worry Baby" as number 11 on the list of the 100 greatest singles of all time, and *Rolling Stone* put it at number 178 of the 500 greatest songs of all time. Wilson thought this "heart and soul" song was one of the Beach Boy's finest records.

The Beach Boys' sixth album, *All Summer Long*, debuted in July 1964, when Beatlemania was sweeping the country. America's band changed its California sound and songs to compete with the British invasion. Most tracks were less tied to cars or surfing, and more reflective of the overall lives being lived by California teenagers. Still, this album had two car culture songs on it. "Drive-In," a song that addressed youthful sex, and "I Get Around," written by Brian Wilson and Mike Love. "I Get Around" is important in the history of the Beach Boys. It was one of the last car culture songs they recorded in the mid-1960s, so it represented the end of a music era. At the same time, it was the very first Beach Boys' song to ever reach number 1 on the Billboard charts, and in 2017 it was inducted into the Grammy Hall of Fame.

The Beach Boys performed "I Get Around" on the *Ed Sullivan Show* on September 27, 1964. The Californians shared the New York stage with three hot rod roadsters loaded with chrome. The song is about cruising from town to town, but with a twist. "I Get Around" is a

Surrounded by hot rods, in 1964 the Beach Boys performed their new hit song, "I Get Around," on the *Ed Sullivan Show*. (Courtesy of Bettmann)

semi-autobiographical tale of the Beach Boys, and the guys in the car have a past. The driver has done this before, over and over again. He isn't just a kid anymore. He and his buddies have made some good money and are getting to be well known. Now it bugs them to be cruising up and down the same old streets. They have to find a new place to go. It sounds like the driver and his buddies are ready to leave the cruising scene, but the end of the song puts them right back into it. They still cruise in a cool car and pick up girls, but in a new place. Cruising remains seductive. Cruisers go down the strip, turn around and go back again. Round, round, round, they get around.

The Beach Boys put out six albums of new material between October 1962 and July 1964. Their biggest car song hits on the Billboard charts were "Little Deuce Coupe" at number 15; "Fun, Fun, Fun" at number 5; and "I Get Around," which finally reached number 1. Despite the success of "I Get Around," the Beach Boys stopped producing car songs. Popular culture changed, as it always does, and the Beach Boys, led by Brian Wilson, pivoted to remain important and popular in a multifaceted music industry now populated by British groups, protest music, folk and folk rock, and early psychedelic rock. The group released a new album, *The Beach Boys Today!* in March 1965. The album used many more musicians, new orchestral arrangements and instruments, and adult themes. Indicative of the change was the song "When I Grow Up to Be a Man." The voice is still self-possessed and expresses a very limited worldview, but at least it asks new, more mature questions. Will he love his wife for the rest of his life? What will his kids think of him?

Other rock groups abandoned car songs at about the same time. In my adolescence, I often turned up the radio when a favorite car song came on, especially "GTO." The songs fanned my adolescent enthusiasm for cars, cruising, and speed. I sang along and slapped the steering wheel to keep time to the Beach Boys' latest. Many car songs played out in my own life. Like the girl who drove her daddy's T-Bird, I didn't own my own car; I drove my mother's. I cruised with my male buddies and drove through all the drive-ins. I had my own Maybellene, but she was named Marilyn, and one night I futilely chased her over a good part of Vermilion County, Illinois, trying to catch her and win her back. As with Jan and Dean, there was a dangerous curve, and I didn't make it all the way around. I rolled the car wheels to wheels. I went to the Dixie Drive-In with Linda and other attractive young women. I sat snuggling in the front seat with pretty Sue while parked in the dark on her street. I sat in the high school parking lot and listened to "GTO" on the radio before going inside. I drag raced 327s, 396s, and 409s on US 1 and Interstate 74. Once, like in "Hot Rod Lincoln," a red light came on behind me and a police officer kindly escorted me to the county jail.

I was often stupid, but mercifully I lived through it, and eventually other things besides cars, cruising, cute girls, and car songs occupied my time and thoughts. I found provocative ideas, but no revving engines or car-crash sounds, in my new favorite music, the protest and peace songs of the 1960s. My brain filled with the poetry, pain, and protests of Bob Dylan and others: "Where Have all the Flowers Gone?" "Turn, Turn, Turn." "If I Had a Hammer." "The Times They Are A'Changin'." "A

Hard Rain's a-Gonna Fall." "Masters of War." "The Lonesome Death of Hattie Carroll." "The Ballad of Hollis Brown." Suddenly, Little Susie and the Everly Brothers seemed a thousand miles and a thousand years away.

One afternoon, just before I headed off to college in September 1965, I sat in my car in the K-Mart parking lot, straining to hear the words to Barry McGuire's "Eve of Destruction," a song about how the world was going to hell in a handbasket in innumerable ways: violence flarin', bullets loadin', the threat of thermonuclear war, racism and segregation, hate in Red China and in Selma, Alabama, and a lack of respect and concern for people, even neighbors. This growling song was overwrought, to be sure, but I found much of it to ring true. How could I not? Six months before I got my driver's license, the nation lived through the Cuban Missile Crisis. For thirteen days, from October 16 through October 28, 1962, we teetered on the brink of war with the Soviet Union over the issue of Russian nuclear missiles being placed ninety miles south of Florida. Six months after I got my license, on November 22, 1963, a Lincoln, a car named in honor of an assassinated president, carried President John F. Kennedy to his own assassination in Dallas. In turbulent times folk music and protest songs filled me with a greater awareness of a dangerous and complex world, and their lyrics affected me more than any car songs ever did—or could.

# 13

## DANVILLE GRAFFITI

When I first saw the George Lucas film *American Graffiti*, I absolutely loved it. I was in my mid-twenties, young enough to remember well the end of my high school years. I had gone through the rite of passage from adolescence to adulthood not that long before, and I sympathized with the film's four main characters—all male—who faced some basic questions in life: What am I supposed to do now? What should I aspire to be? Can I shape my own future, or will the future shape me? *American Graffiti* carried heavy messages about growing up in America and about social mobility, but the film on the surface was all fun and games. I loved the characters and the young, new actors who played them, the rock and roll soundtrack, the cars, the dream girl in the Thunderbird, and the crazy shenanigans that happened at Mel's Drive-In and along streets and highways.

*American Graffiti*, arguably the best American car movie of all time, is set in Modesto, California, in 1962. All the characters belong to the subculture of "cruisers." They pile into their cars and go up and down the main street, and then they go up and down again. *American Graffiti* showed that cruising was not inconsequential in the lives of participants. It was not just an activity that let you kill some time, enjoy your car, and see some friends. It was much more than that. When guys and gals left home and their parents behind to take up residence at Mel's Drive-In and nearby streets, they discovered new friends and new things to do, for sure, but they also collided head-on with personal doubts and insecurities, threatening strangers, exciting but frightening freedoms, and important life choices to be made.

Four likeable boys-to-men head up the cruisers of *American Graffiti*, and we ride shotgun with them over the course of a long and eventful night, just as summer is ending and schools are ready to start. We watch to see just where Curt Henderson, Steve Bolander, Terry Fields, and John Milner are going to go, or if they are going anywhere at all, except endlessly up and down the strip. Curt (played by Richard Dreyfuss) and Steve (Ron Howard) are promising, freshly minted high school grads, and both are set to fly off to a distant college the following morning. But will they leave for a world of challenge and opportunity or will they settle for staying home? Will Curt fly off to college with dreams of being a White House intern someday? Or will he stay home to pursue a seductive, gorgeous blonde who cruises in a '56 Thunderbird? Will Steve leave home to find a new home? Will he leave friends to find new friends? Or will he stay put and marry his high school sweetheart?

Terry (Charlie Martin Smith) and John (Paul LeMat) are good guys, too, but they lack potential. Unlike Curt and Steve, they seem to have no chance of seizing any positive, life-changing opportunities. Terry's greatest aspiration is to move up from his current Vespa scooter to car ownership. If he could become a bigger player in the world of cruising, maybe he could shuck off his pejorative nickname, "Toad." John is what Toad would love to be. John is the king of the local cruisers. He owns the sharpest and fastest hot rod, a bright yellow '32 Ford, a Deuce coupe. John takes on all challengers to his crown and shuts them down. But John is uneasy, thinking maybe he has overstayed his welcome in the street world of cruising and drag races. He senses he should move on to something else but has no idea of what that would be.

The teenagers in *American Graffiti* act out many kinds of ritualistic behavior. Friends pile into cars and roam up and down streets. They listen to their own music, the tunes of Fats Domino, Chuck Berry, Buddy Holly, Del Shannon, and a host of other rock and rollers. While doing their male bonding thing, the guys also cruise for chicks. Banter passes from car to car, in hopes of seducing some pretty young things into hopping out of one car and into another. Periodically, each car swings into the hub of the cruisers' world, Mel's Drive-In. Folks put down a burger, chili dog, or Coke, but food is secondary to socializing. They stop to find out who's doing what and who's riding with whom. Back out on the street, it's a competitive, sometimes hostile environment. All the kids in one car might be friends, but the kids in the next car might be challengers. The guys judge each other by the cars they drive and the girls who ride with them. They hurl insults and play pranks on one another. Sometimes, pranks become minor crimes, and they bait the police. They race from stoplight to stoplight or drag race on the highway just out of town. Simply put, they act up. They moon people on the strip; pull down a guy's pants; and give others the finger. They test their newfound freedom and experiment with adult things, especially alcohol and sex. They park in the woods and puke in parking lots.

*American Graffiti* winks at cruising and presents it as an okay thing to do. It is a way American kids learn to grow up, so it's okay to be foolish, play pranks, joust with cops, disobey traffic laws, drive aimlessly, and ignore or challenge adults. It's okay to score some illegal booze and to fumble at sex and artlessly grope your partner. But it's okay only to a point. It's only okay if this rite of passage is a temporary, transitional period. It is okay to go into it, but you also must come out of it. And you must be of the right age, both when you enter this passage and when you leave it. If you are a girl too young to know what "cop a feel" means, then you should still be at home and not out on the street, where predatory males might, in fact, cop a feel. But you can't stay too long, either: "You just can't stay seventeen forever." When John Milner hops the fence into the local auto junkyard, he changes from hot-rodder to archaeologist. He knows all these wrecks. He knows who drove them, who was fast. He knows who was killed. He knows all this because he's stayed too long on the strip. *American Graffiti* takes about 110 minutes to follow its characters around for one night and morning, and then it takes an additional minute to show what happened to them over the next several years. One way or another, they all left the subculture of cruising.

John Milner never left the cruising scene until he was killed by a drunk driver in 1964.

Hapless Toad, who never had any real plans for himself, became part of the Army's plan. No doubt drafted, he went missing in action in Vietnam in 1965.

Steve played it safe and stayed home with his high school sweetheart. Appropriately enough, for someone who didn't take big risks in life, he ended up as an insurance salesman.

Curt had gotten on the morning plane and left home with ambitious plans for college and for a White House internship. Events beyond his control destroyed these plans. Kennedy was assassinated early in his sophomore year, and later Curt protested against an escalating Vietnam War. He ended up as a writer living in exile in Canada. There are no guarantees. Sometimes life can turn sour, even if you are the one who does all the right things.

When I saw *American Graffiti* in 1973, my mind flashed back to my own cruising days in Danville, Illinois. *Graffiti* was, indeed, an *American* story, one that belonged not only to culture-bending California but to towns across the nation, including those in the heartland. Curt, Steve, Milner, Toad, and the girls of *American Graffiti* seemed just like the kids who cruised up and down Danville's Vermilion Street in the mid-1960s.

Danville, a city of about forty thousand and the seat of Vermilion County, had one foot in agriculture and another in industry. Danville sat surrounded by farm fields, long-abandoned saltworks, and worked-out strip mines. Near the heart of town, served by rail lines, stood the Lauhoff Grain Company, with its tall, concrete elevators full of corn. Lauhoff's made the whole town smell like milled grain in the summer. While Danville helped feed Americans, it also helped move them along highways, thanks to its mammoth General Motors Central Foundry, which made gray iron castings for GM. Danville also boasted a Hyster plant that made lift trucks, a General Electric ballast plant, a Windbreaker jacket plant, and a new boat-building company. Adding a touch of levity to its production capacity, thanks to the Fred W. Amend Company, Danville also gave the world Chuckles jelly candies, five pieces per package: licorice, lemon, cherry, lime, and orange.

Danville had two principal streets, Main and Vermilion. Main, on the south end of town, ran east and west near the Vermilion River.

Vermilion Street intersected Main at the county courthouse and town square and ran due north from there. Much of Main Street seemed to represent old Danville, while Vermilion Street represented newer, more modern Danville. The heart of downtown occupied the first three blocks of Vermilion and the first block or two of the cross streets intersecting Vermilion. Most of the merchandising, servicing, and governing done in Danville was done right here. Besides the main department store of Meis Brothers, several specialty clothing stores catered to men, women, and children: Bill Vogt's, Deutsch's, The Fashion, Snider's Cotton Shop, Jules Straus, Overstreet's, and others. There were banks, insurance companies, and doctor's, dentist's, and lawyer's offices. The Hotel Wolford, just a few blocks from the town square, still offered lodging to travelers, because it had not yet been done in by new motels on the fringe of town. The downtown offices of the *Danville Commercial-News* newspaper stood near furniture stores, two large drugstores, Danville Paint and Wallpaper, and Woodbury's stationery shop. Several restaurants occupied downtown buildings; they ran the gamut from the second-floor Chinese restaurant; to the Deluxe, a meat-and-potatoes place that offered belly-filling meatloaf and hot beef and hot turkey sandwiches, smothered in gravy, accompanied by real mashed potatoes and canned corn or green beans. The Nook was a real curiosity, a very narrow hamburger joint that looked like it had been built to fill in an old pedestrian alleyway.

After a downtown lunch, Danvillians could easily stroll their downtown in a half hour, walking along Vermilion, plus a few blocks of Main, Walnut, Harrison, and North Streets. In this compact world of storefronts, if they wanted they could stop to get their shoes resoled; buy a trombone, a wedding ring, or a watch; purchase a thirty-two-inch Louisville Slugger or a Danville High letter jacket; check out the newest toys and AMT model car kits; or attend a movie at the Fischer or Palace Theaters. They could also attend to business at the local and federal courthouse, city hall, the post office, and the library.

Anybody who needed anything ended up regularly in downtown Danville. In the mid-1960s, at least, it remained intact and offered a wide range of things to buy and things to do. Still, it was a modest place.

Most of its businesses were small. Danville was a low town that didn't jut up much above the prairie around it. The First National Bank Building, at the corner of Main and Vermilion, twelve stories tall, towered over the rest of the downtown, which was filled mostly with two- or three-story storefronts.

At one time, electric streetcars running down both Main and Vermilion had delivered shoppers and businesspeople to downtown Danville. But a half century into the age of the automobile, the streetcars and their tracks were long since gone. Vermilion Street downtown was a busy two-way, two-lane street with a stoplight on every corner and parallel parking on each side. If a driver couldn't find a place to park on Vermilion, there were a couple of handy parking lots nearby, one behind Woodbury's and another just a block away at Walnut and North Streets, near the Pioneer Buick-Pontiac dealership, which was right downtown. Seven other new car dealers were scattered around Danville, some close to downtown, some further out. They sold Chevrolets, Ramblers, Chryslers, Plymouths, Dodges, Fords, Lincolns, and Mercurys. In Danville—and indeed in all of mid-America—the American car was still king. The only odd man out was Danville Import Motors, which sold Volkswagens.

My buddies and I—in our American cars—sometimes cruised through downtown. We headed south on Vermilion, through downtown, and turned left on Main to check out the girls who might be standing on the sidewalk outside the Knights of Columbus, which held weekend teen dances. Or we went to the Steak 'n Shake on Main. Sometimes, if some high-speed travel seemed in order, we turned off Main onto Bowman Avenue, which had an entrance onto Interstate 74, where you could really give it the gas. Mostly, though, we cruised north of downtown on Vermilion Street, which, if we kept on going, became Route 1, the Dixie Highway that ran up to Chicago.

High schoolers drove to many places along this route. Danville had a second Steak 'n Shake on Vermilion, only a few blocks north of downtown. This popular drive-in restaurant served the best burgers and fries in town. Inside, the Steak 'n Shake had only ten chromed stools at the counter and a few tables and chairs, so almost everybody ate in their cars and got curb service. A lot of kids just cruised through the lot, hollered at friends, and kept on going. Marty K's, a new joint that advertised "Hamburgers, Shakes, Fries, 15 Cents Each," stood right next to Steak 'n Shake. Marty K's was especially popular in late fall and throughout the winter, after football or basketball games, because the food was cheap, nobody hassled you, and you ate inside where it was warm. Right across Vermilion from these two places, a Clark gas station offered the cheapest fuel in town. Gas ran twenty-nine to thirty cents per gallon for regular, and maybe up to thirty-three to thirty-five cents per gallon for premium.

A bit further north, Ben Carson's Pharmacy, just a few blocks from the high school, offered an old-fashioned soda fountain. Kids walked there after school or drove and went inside. The 1960s were on their way to becoming the era of sex, drugs, and suggestive rock and roll, but not at Carson's. Even in a decade of tumultuous social upheaval, not all parts of a culture change simultaneously. At Carson's, you got a Coke, a chocolate soda, maybe an egg salad sandwich. You talked to a gaggle of girls or guys. You laughed with the soda jerk, Steve, a handsome, athletic high schooler (a diver on the swim team) who always had a joke to tell. Maybe you picked a magazine off the rack to read or talked about the most recent assignment in English Lit.

Carson's was a safe environment, a throwback to the days of poodle skirts, a haven, really, left over from the 1950s, or maybe even earlier. So was the family-owned Custard Cup a couple miles to the north, on what was then the outskirts of Danville. You might stand in line with moms, dads, and kids to get a soft vanilla or chocolate cone or a sundae. Luana, one of the prettiest gals in town, who became Danville High's 1965 homecoming queen, worked the window at the Custard Cup, so you might stop for a cone just to get a chance to say "hi" to her. Some other pretty gals worked just up the road from the Cup at the A&W drive-in. They carried trays loaded with root beers, floats, and chili dogs out to kids in cars. I found one of those gals to be very attractive one summer, and I finally got the chance to take her home one night, only to discover that she smelled totally of onions, which brought an end to a very short romance.

Out by the Custard Cup and A&W, surrounded by a vast parking lot, a new retailer, K-Mart, had just opened its doors. K-Mart seemed like a giant, like an entire downtown under one roof. It had so much stuff and such low prices. Many Danville residents raised issues with the place. It didn't carry quality stuff like the downtown stores; it didn't give shoppers personalized attention and good service; and instead of taking a rest from commerce on the Sabbath, it was open on Sunday. But other Danville residents flocked to the place, filling its parking lot with cars, day after day. K-Mart was more than a store; it was the opening salvo of a consumer revolution in Danville. It sucked people out of downtown, and in a few years started putting serious hurt on stores there. Also, K-Mart's existence seemed to accelerate development north of town, along Vermilion Street (Route 1). That's where new shops and stores would go, as well as much residential development. This strip of road was the town's future, which was reached by car. As for me, one thing I liked about K-Mart was its big parking lot, especially after a snow. When the store wasn't open and the lot wasn't plowed, that was a great place to throw your car into a skid and then try to steer yourself out of it before the rear end came all the way around.

If the K-Mart parking lot offered some entertainment in the winter, just to its north the Dixie Drive-In Theater offered entertainment in the summer. Families with kids went there. If everybody went it was a cheap night out because the parents avoided the cost of a babysitter. The little tykes could just fall asleep in the back seat. Cars full of guys went to the Dixie, maybe sneaking one or two into the drive-in in the trunk to save a few bucks. Cars full of gals went there too. And many cars with just one guy and one gal turned into the Dixie Drive-In. Maybe they watched the movie, or maybe they just "made out." Since the Dixie was known as a "passion pit," some high school girls, like Carol, received strict orders from Mom *not* to go there. If she did and got caught, like Carol said, "I'd have been dead meat!" So instead of heading to the drive-in, some couples played it safe, passed it by, and went to "Swing 'n Spring," so named because it offered mini golf and trampolines. Swing 'n Spring was pretty much the northern end of the road for kids in their cars. For a couple of summers, in 1964 and

1965, my friends and I headed out to Swing 'n Spring several times a week. We played mini golf for money, betting three dollars on each nine and another three on the total score. This, for us, was serious competition. We knew how to bank the ball off the boards on every hole to have the best shot at an ace. Earl missed an important putt once, and in anger he spun around and let go of his putter, sending it not just out of bounds but clear over the Dixie Highway.

I arrived in Danville in January 1962, in the middle of ninth grade. I was a short, chubby boy of fifteen who just wanted to fit in and find some new friends. A growth spurt finally came, and overnight I was five feet eleven. I was quite unremarkable, except in a few ways. I had been taking second-year algebra in Jackson, a level that Danville didn't offer. So, I went back into first-year algebra in my new school, Northridge Junior High. I could do problems in my head that others struggled with on paper, so I became a math whiz who offered help to others. Then there was a student talent show in the spring. Having no recognizable talent, I wasn't in it, at least not officially. I was just watching it. A couple of girls performed a Tom Sawyer skit, and one of them took a bite out of an apple and casually tossed it over her shoulder, into the audience. I leaned over the seat in front of me and caught it. I sat back down, and some boys in my homeroom urged me to throw it back. I stood up, pumped once, thought the girls onstage saw me, and let the apple fly. But they hadn't seen me, and the apple struck unsuspecting Martha Bailey right in the head. When I sat back down, I was far better known in school than I had been just moments before.

The boys in my junior high homeroom became my first friends in Danville, and as we moved up to high school and passed from fifteen to sixteen, they became the first kids I cruised with in cars. John drove a two-tone, '56 Ford convertible with a V-8. If you dared take the top down, it was a devil to get back up. Starting this car was not a sure bet, but when it did start its Glass-Pack mufflers sounded a deep, throaty rumble that was music to any car-crazy kid's ears. Brad had a '49 Ford, which when manufactured was one of the freshest postwar designs. But by the '60s, Brad's root-beer-colored Ford looked as old as dirt. It was a rolling antique. It rode so high; it had such a large steering wheel, but such a tiny windshield; and when you sat in Brad's Ford, it felt like you were on your grandmother's stuffed sofa, rather than on a car seat. Ronnie drove an early '50s Studebaker pickup truck, painted red. Studebakers were rare enough; Studebaker pickups were rarer still. Ronnie, always sporting a flat-top haircut and a smile, really liked driving that thing on the edge. Surprisingly, he survived, and so did his passengers, despite all the fishtailing and power sliding the Studebaker did on gravel roads. None of these vehicles were any great shakes, but while I was driving my mother's 1958 Hillman Minx, John, Brad, and Ronnie had their own wheels.

But my day was coming. I was soon to move up a thousand big steps in the teenage world of automobiles. In May 1963, I received my driver's license. In the fall of that year, I accompanied Mom to the Pioneer Buick-Pontiac showroom. Mom wanted to replace the Hillman with a smallish American car, and she had the idea that a Pontiac Tempest might fill the bill. Inside the showroom sat a Tempest of sorts, but underneath its hood lurked a 389-cubic-inch, 325-horsepower V-8. This hot-looking machine—a white two-door hardtop with a black interior—had two chromed, fake air scoops on top of its hood, and instead of white sidewalls, a thin red stripe ran around its "Tiger Paw" tires. This was the first iteration of a Detroit muscle car, the legendary Pontiac GTO. *Car and Driver* wrote that "hairy chested," bold product men had designed this car, "the best American car we have ever driven and probably one of the five or six best cars in the world for enthusiast drivers." What can I say? My mother bought it. In the annals of automotive lore, was there ever anything more surprising, or more out of character than tiny little Dorothy Mary Atkinson Lankton, all 105 pounds of her, at fifty-three years of age, plunking down more than three grand to buy the hottest new car in America?

I later figured Mom bought the car partly out of guilt. Back in 1958, Dad and I drove one Saturday from Jackson to a foreign-car dealership some forty miles away in Lansing. My fifty-five-year-old dad signed to purchase an Austin-Healey Sprite, a tiny, entry-level two-seater sports car. My Dad, Big Larry, had to work to just get in and out of it. Still, its sportiness appealed to him. Maybe it was the manifestation of a belated

This '64 GTO looks just like the one my mom bought in the fall of 1963, except it has alloy wheels and different tires. She paid a little over $3,000. Six decades later, this one sold for fifteen times that much. (Courtesy of Coyote Classics)

midlife crisis. Regardless, he was to pick up the car and take it home the next weekend. In the meantime, we took some promotional literature about it back home. When Mom saw the pictures, she immediately announced that the Sprite was so small you couldn't carry the family in it—or even a week's worth of groceries! What good was a car like that? So, Dad tucked his tail between his legs, canceled the deal on the Sprite, and bought our four-door Hillman Minx instead. Two years later, Big Larry died, never owning a sports car. I figured my mom felt guilty about that, and to appease her guilt, she bought a GTO for the other "man" in her family, her son.

Thanks to Pontiac and an overindulgent mother, in my junior year I started cruising Danville, not in Hillman but in a GTO. True, it was not the fastest iteration of the car. There was a 348-horsepower version, with three two-barrel carburetors and a four-speed Hurst shifter. Our GTO was a two-speed automatic, and its 325-horsepower engine had a single four-barrel carburetor. But the car was hardly slow. If you put your foot into it, it stayed in low gear and accelerated rapidly to nearly eighty miles per hour before shifting into high. Automatic transmission or not, life didn't get much better than this: sitting in the high school parking lot in a GTO while listening to Ronny and the Daytonas sing "GTO" on the radio. That car truly transformed my life. I was no longer just an average-looking, glasses-wearing kid who had gone from too chubby at age fifteen to seven inches taller and too skinny at age seventeen. I wasn't a stud. I wasn't an athlete. But as Marilyn wrote in my 1965 yearbook, I *was* "Mr. GTO," and that counted for a lot. "Come see me at the Cup when you're bombing around in your GTO," Luana wrote in the same yearbook. "Even if you didn't have a GTO," wrote Lish, "I'd still love, honor and respect you!! (Let's have an affair sometime, ok?)" Alison penned, "Now that you've got that GTO you'll have to take me for a ride sometime." Bonnie simply encouraged me to "Have fun this summer in your GTO!" I felt like a rock star.

By the time the GTO came to bless my life, I was growing a new group of best friends, while my junior high buddies, John, Brad, and Ronnie, moved to the background. At the two-thousand-student Danville High School, I had no classes with them. From my sophomore year I spent at least a few hours a day with new kids who were in the same advanced classes in English and math. From September till the beginning of June, during the school day we thought serious thoughts and did serious work: algebra, geometry, trig, analytical geometry, chemistry, and physics. We acted in and directed school plays. (Turns out I did have some talent after all.) We deciphered "Beowulf" and "Paradise Lost" and read Emerson, Thoreau, Melville, and Stephen Crane with John Sanders. We read John Ciardi poetry and the *Saturday Review of Literature* with Martha Kay. Sanders and Kay were simply the best English teachers you could ever hope to find in a public high school. They opened new literary worlds to students who had only recently put away their baseball cards and bicycles. They challenged me to think, and they encouraged me to work hard on my writing. They expected a lot from me, and I tried to deliver because I respected them and wanted their approval. They changed me from a wanna-be mechanical engineer into an English major. John Sanders picked up the phone and made one call that got me acceptance and a scholarship into a private college, DePauw University.

After classes were done for the week at Danville High, on Friday and Saturday nights during the school year, and throughout the summer, I spent my nights in cars, learning life lessons with Dan, Dave, and Doug. Dan was a bit of a contrarian, a kid who seemingly always kept a bit of distance between himself and even his friends, one who was always poised to challenge you about something. He drove a blue-and-white 1964 Chevy Impala convertible with the 327-cubic-inch engine. Dan signed my yearbook on the advertising page sponsored by Danville's New Car Dealers Association. He underlined the word "Chevrolet" in the ad and wrote that Chevrolets were "better known as GTO eaters." Where a line in the ad originally read "Buick and Pontiac," Dan altered it to read "Buick and Dogs."

Dave, a handsome blonde kid who played a good rock and roll saxophone, was the most reckless of the group; he'd launch himself into some potentially dangerous activity first and think about it later. Moderation was a stranger to Dave, especially when there was a six-pack around. Once, after trying to go beer for beer with Moose, a six-foot-six, 230-pound mountain of a kid, Dave wasn't feeling so good. When a cop pulled them over, to try to hide his underage drinking, Dave (as quietly as possible) barfed down the sleeve of his shirt. Dave drove a green-and-white 1955 Chevy with unpainted body filler over the rust spots. His ride was not a hot rod but a ten-year-old, six-cylinder beater car.

Doug was the best-looking of the guys. In his first two years of high school he claimed Barb, a cute, petite varsity cheerleader, as his girlfriend. Then, as a senior, he switched over to Cheri, a member of the Pompette squad. Doug was a gregarious, confident kid whom everybody liked. He had a dual capability unusual in young men; he could be both very foolish and yet very sincere. Doug had a depth to him that most lacked. When entertained, his face wore a bright, infectious grin from ear to ear—but he could also flash a countenance of earnest interest and concern if you were talking to him about some serious subject.

Doug drove his parents' dark-blue-and-white Ford Fairlane 500 with a 289-cubic-inch engine.

Since we were separating from our families and going through our rite of passage, Dan, Dave, Doug, and I almost never met at each other's houses. In fact, I knew next to nothing about their families, their parents, or their siblings. But we knew each other away from home, at school and out on the street. In the fall and winter, we often met after the high school football or basketball game on Friday or Saturday night and then jumped into cars and drove to a popular hangout, like Marty K's. In the summer we always seemed to run into one another each evening, any night of the week, without any conscious planning. We'd get into one car to cruise Vermilion, or take two or three cars all the way from downtown to out past the Dixie Drive-In to play mini golf. On most of these nights, nothing of any consequence happened. We joked around, smoked Marlboros, and bantered with other guys who were pretty much doing the same things we were. We listened to a rock station that played "Hey Little Cobra," "409," and "Little Deuce Coupe," mixed in with "I Want to Hold Your Hand," "Oh, Pretty Woman," and "California Girls," mixed in with "Wild Thing" and "Wooly Bully."

In Danville in the mid-1960s, the drug of choice was alcohol, more specifically beer, and the cheaper the better. If some kids scored a six-pack or two, they sometimes headed out to the country to party out of view, or maybe to the Dixie Drive-In. Their drinking, still in the experimental stage, not infrequently led to drunkenness. It was not exceptionally rare to see a car door open, and then someone who'd imbibed too much Pabst Blue Ribbon lean out to spill his guts by the side of the road. But kids had remarkable recovery rates. They could make themselves miserable one night, then laugh about it the next and go out and do it again.

There were many laughs to be had on the street. One night we drove thirty miles from Danville over to Urbana-Champaign and drank a pitcher or two at Cam's, a student hangout near the University of Illinois campus. Upon returning to Danville, we stopped at the Clark gas station on Vermilion and we all got out of Dave's '55 Chevy to stretch our legs while filling up. Dave—who'd taken in considerable beer, so he hadn't been driving—slid out of the back seat. While we stood by the pumps, a furry little mutt of about twenty-five pounds came over to greet us and get pats. When we started piling back in the car, the dog jumped in, too, getting in back with me and Dave. Then suddenly, with no warning or provocation, just as the car started to move, the little animal jumped all over Dave, snarling and biting at him.

Dave started crying out for help: "Get this dog off me! Get this dog off me!" The '55 Chevy shot across Vermilion Street, went straight into the Marty K parking lot, and came to a screeching halt, parked askew. In full sight of all the folks at Marty K's, as well as those eating in their cars next door at Steak 'n Shake, the Chevy's doors flew open and four kids and a dog jumped out. Three of us, for whom the dog held no malice, laughed hilariously, bent over, slapping our legs. We had never seen anything so funny, and if anything, we cheered for the dog. Poor Dave, on the other hand, raced around the car like a broken-field runner, but the quicker dog kept up and leaped repeatedly at Dave's backside. In desperation, Dave, now shouting foul epithets at his four-legged tormenter, finally hopped up on the trunk and then crawled up on the roof of his car. The dog still ignored the rest of us and leaped and leaped and leaped up at the car, trying to get at Dave. I finally held the dog so Dave could get down and back in the car. The others got in, carefully banning the dog. We pulled out of the lot, and the dog chased us for a block before giving up. Dave was now safe.

Looking back, we boys were lucky to survive all our foolishness. We survived not only dog attacks and beer but all manner of fast and reckless driving. Twenty-five years after actor James Dean died on a California highway, a *Washington Post* journalist wrote a commemorative piece about the legendary actor. In it, she theorized that Midwestern boys, like the Hoosier actor Dean, learned to love speed because there was nothing of interest to look at in their local landscapes. They drove fast just to pass through boring country in a hurry. Maybe there was some truth to that. The boys I rode with lived in a town surrounded by cornfields, and we all had a love of speed, which put us at much risk. My risk increased when Mom traded in the Hillman for the GTO. That car was not meant to go slow, nor was I.

Cruisers in Danville often raced away from stoplights, doing a quick half block before slowing for the next light. They peeled out or smoked their tires, piercing the night with tire squeal and leaving two black patches on the road. There was one residential street in Danville that had slippery asphalt. Unfortunately, for those poor residents trying to sleep in their ranch houses along this street, it was a great place to put down some fantastic rubber. Rear wheels instantly broke traction, and while they continued to spin and smoke, the car seemed only to inch ahead. In the GTO, or in Dan's 327 Chevy, we laid rubber for way more than a block. On stickier pavement, in less settled country, Dan and I often dragged each other. Dan's 327 was a remarkably strong runner, and it often kept up with the GTO until about eighty miles an hour, when the GTO left the Impala in the dust.

Once I was away from my residence and Mom, I sometimes took the air cleaner off the GTO and stuck it in the trunk. When I floored it, the big four-barrel carburetor positively honked as it sucked in air. The third or fourth time I did this, the honk abruptly stopped and the engine shut down. I thought I'd blown it. Turns out, the carburetor had sucked down the sound insulation mounted on the underside of the hood, smothering the engine. I remedied this problem by criss-crossing wires under the hood to hold the insulation up. A few times, I headed out to the Shell station next to the Custard Cup, where a young guy let me use the lift and tools. I pulled off the mufflers, ran with a powerful, V-8 roar for several hours, and then put the mufflers back on before returning home.

Right after the Pontiac GTO came out, Detroit put out other muscle cars with large displacement engines that appealed to baby boomers just coming of age. The car companies competed with one another for bragging rights, and so did the drivers of their products. Whenever a new muscle car cruised Vermilion Street—such as a Chevelle Super Sport 396 or the Olds 442, with its four-hundred-cubic-inch engine—drag races inevitably followed. I was playing mini golf at Swing 'n Spring one night when a new Chevelle SS pulled in. A bit later, just beyond the mini golf course on Route 1, the GTO and the Chevelle raced side by side until a red light flashed behind us. A bit later still, I was at the county jail, waiting for Mom to bail me out. The very next week, another challenger to the GTO arrived at Marty K's parking lot, and soon two cars drag raced along I-74. This time, however, rendered cautious by my recent arrest, I merely went along for the ride. Doug did the driving.

The gang of four spent one pleasant night in October 1964 in cars on an oval circuit—not a racetrack, but the quarter-mile cinder track that ran around Danville High's football field. As vice president of the student council, I had the enviable task of lining up four convertibles to parade the queen and her attendants past the grandstands during the homecoming game against Bloomington. This one lap showed off four of the school's prettiest and most popular girls—Luana, the senior queen; plus Sandy R., her senior attendant; Sandy B., the junior attendant; and Su, the sophomore. My buddies and I expected that slowly motoring past a waving, cheering throng would be a lot more fun than the game itself, because the Danville Vikings were having a poor season. They had lost five of their first six games, while being outscored 119 to 26. Besides, we knew that afterward we could drive around in the convertibles before turning them back in to the dealerships by noon on Saturday. Predictably, the Vikings lost again, 33 to 7. I hardly remember anything about the game itself. But I do remember that as I drove the convertible by the grandstand, I looked in the rearview mirror to see pretty Sandy R., sitting atop the back of the rear seat, waving and crying. "This is the best thing," she said, "that will ever happen to me."

Romance was in the air that night, with pretty girls in their best formal dresses, riding around in pretty automobiles. But it didn't take homecoming to link, in my mind, girls and cars. Guys and cars got together to do guy things, like drag race, swear, smoke, listen to loud music, give obnoxious strangers the finger, and drink. Guys and gals got together in cars for other purposes, to discover love or sex, or both. It had always been this way, it seemed. The 1904 song "In My Merry Oldsmobile" linked romance and sex to the new-fangled horseless carriage almost as soon as it hit the streets. Six decades later, kids cruising Danville still paired off in cars, boys and girls.

Invariably, the boy drove, and the girl—in a time free of seat belt restraints and laws—slid over to sit as close as she could to his side, maybe with her arm draped over his shoulders or with her fingers playing with the nape of his neck. As they drove the strip, or as they headed out to park along some dark and quiet lane in the country, a key question remained the same old one: just how far was somebody willing to go in an automobile? The answer to this question was up for grabs in the mid-1960s. A few years before, everybody was expected to be a Goody Two-shoes, and the girls were expected to say "no." A few years later, along came the sexual revolution and birth control pills, and girls were expected to say "yes," sooner rather than later. But in between, in the mid-1960s, about the best a young guy could hope for was a "maybe." My friend Lish later recalled that, "We wanted to be bad, but didn't know how." She played at sex, without really doing it. Once she went with Dave to the A&W in a 1959 Simca, which had reclining seats. With their frosty mugs sitting on the window tray, Dave and Lish lowered the seat backs so the two of them disappeared from sight. Occasionally, they let their bare arms reach up high enough to be seen. That was all: just bare arms, waving around. They encouraged nearby folks to guess what they were doing. Pretend sex was funny and amusing, which was good, if that was all you were getting.

Not all that many guys hit sexual home runs in their cars in those days. As they used to say, they got stopped at first, second, or third base. In lieu of that tired old baseball metaphor, Dan invented his own drag-racing metaphor. In describing a recent date to Doug, Dave, and me, Dan said the girl was "quick off the line, but not too much top end." We knew exactly what he meant. As for me, I never even got off the line with most of the girls I coveted. In my sophomore and for much of my junior year, I had all the desire a teenager could muster but lacked the confidence to go after tall Lish, who seemed too bold and strong to take on as a first love; or Luana, who was simply too beautiful and seemed way above my class; or Nan, who sat right next to me in trigonometry for a full year. We flirted and passed notes back and forth all the time. I admired her legs from the top of her knees to the hem of her skirt, a glorious and tantalizing six inches. We even went out on one date. But Nan was already leaning toward Ben, a couple of years older. Still, I gave her serious thought and didn't give up easily. Nan lived on Denvale Drive in a new subdivision by the country club and Lake Vermilion. Time after time I cruised by her house in the GTO, hoping to spot her outside so I could pull over to chat and win her heart. But all I kept finding was her dentist father, cutting the grass.

Slowly, but faster after getting the GTO, I gained more confidence, and at the end of my junior year I dated Sue, a thin, pretty gal. She sat next to me for a full year of chemistry, and as she admitted, I helped her get through the class. Sue was a senior, an enticing "older woman" with a good sense of humor. We were an item only briefly, because early in the summer I left town to go to a National Science Foundation pre-engineering program at the University of Illinois. While there, I learned that I didn't want to be an engineer, which was a valuable lesson, but one that cost me my girlfriend, Sue, who started dating my "friend" Dan while I was gone. Still, it was a pleasant experience that ended without rancor. Sue was always fun to be around, and in dating her I became a little more familiar with female anatomy, and how wonderfully smooth and soft parts of it could be. While it lasted, I regularly tooted my horn when passing by her house, just to let her know I was thinking of her, and we made out in the dark, parked right on her street.

And then there was Marilyn, the sophomore with straw-colored hair, big brown eyes, and a constant smile. She had a good body to go along with her pretty face, and she had nice athletic legs. I first spotted her playing tennis with her best friend, Linda, at Cannon Park, and she rapidly became the first love of my life. I began stopping at the outdoor Sun 'n Swim pool on the north side of town just to see her. Chatting with Marilyn, as she stood dripping wet in her two-piece, was a pleasant way to spend part of an afternoon. Marilyn wore her sexiness very casually. She seemed unaware of it, but I surely noticed.

We walked high school halls together, went to football and basketball games, and went to Marty K's and Steak 'n Shake. We cruised north up Vermilion Street until it became the Dixie Highway, and then turned left on Newell, a winding dirt road. Out near the metal truss bridge over the North Fork of the Vermilion River, we parked. That was our place, which we occasionally shared with fishermen. Sometimes we walked along the riverbank, which was often mucky, so we jumped from log to log. Sometimes we went out in the adjacent field with a blanket. Marilyn liked moonlight, liked "stars on the ceiling," as she called them, meaning stars in the night sky. Sometimes we just stayed in the car, especially if the mosquitoes were bad or rain was falling. On one very soggy evening, I started to back the GTO out of its secluded patch of ground so I could take Marilyn home. The rear tires bogged down. To assess the situation, I opened my door, stuck my head out, and gave the GTO some gas. In reverse, the spinning wheels promptly threw mud all over my face and the inside of the door.

On the blanket or in the car, we never did go all the way. I never pressed the issue. We were too young and just getting started in the romance of life. Silently, in the dark, without ever discussing it, we both recognized boundaries, which did become more liberal over time. After several months we necked in intimate ways that released emotions and sensations never felt before. Stopping short was frustrating, but it kept us out of trouble.

A few months after this love affair began, it hit a bump in the road. Marilyn's mom laid down the law, and for whatever reason (and I was never sure what it was) she said that Marilyn could not date me anymore. This dictum didn't end the romance but did drive it underground. Marilyn's mom was happy as long as no white GTO stopped by to pick up or drop off her daughter. This meant that some of my friends got to drive the GTO, because I swapped cars with them. While cousin Jim tooled around in the "Goat," I took Marilyn home in Jim's Rambler. For a sweet gal like her, nothing was too great a sacrifice. Marilyn and I conspired weekend after weekend to get together. Our biggest covert operation came on prom night in the spring of my senior year. My buddy, John Johnson, drove up Marilyn's driveway in his car. He went into the house, said hello to Marilyn's parents with a smile, and presented Marilyn with a corsage. He then drove off with her, only to deliver her to me a little ways away. After the all-night prom party, John took Marilyn back to her mom, safe and sound. John called this deception "operation mirage."

What I found most attractive about Marilyn was her spirit. She was born happy. I was prone to thinking too much, worrying too much. I was ready to bolt high school and get on to college. Marilyn was smart, to be sure. But as a sixteen-year-old sophomore, living was more important to her than thinking. She had a lot of high school left to enjoy, and she was going to do what she wanted to do and have a good time. The romance didn't last. I proved to be a drag on Marilyn's free spirit, and I was leaving town soon to go to college. What Marilyn's mom couldn't kill, handsome Denny did. Denny, a year older than I, was a car guy. He had a '31 Ford roadster hot rod and a '63 Pontiac Tempest with a strong 326-cubic-inch engine. But more importantly, he knew how to have a good time, and he spent Friday and Saturday nights looking a whole lot like a member of Paul Revere and the Raiders, wearing a tricorne hat, a red colonial coat with big white cuffs, white pants, and tall black boots.

Marilyn loved music (she played first-chair viola in the high school orchestra). She loved to dance and helped organize youth dances. While I, being a stick-in-the-mud, didn't go to any weekend dances, Denny headed the most popular rock and roll band in town, "The Villagers." It was no contest. On May 30, 1965, just as I was graduating high school, Danville's paper, the *Commercial-News*, ran a picture of Marilyn meeting with the leaders of three local bands. Denny stood closest to Marilyn and held a bass guitar. The look in his eyes said it all. He was interested in this girl. Denny soon won Marilyn over. She moved into his 1963 Tempest and left the GTO behind. I spent a terribly lonely summer pining over my loss. On my last night in Danville before leaving for college, Susann—a smart, pretty gal who was just a good friend, never a girlfriend—showed what true friends were for. She charitably volunteered to go out to the Newell Road field with me and a blanket and give me some goodbye kisses. But it wasn't the same.

The following summer, all the guys, with one year of college under their belts, returned home to tell stories about life and love at the University of Illinois, Southern Illinois, or DePauw. Truth be told, I didn't have as many entertaining stories as the other guys, and the summer of 1966 was without many highlights, either, until the very end, when Dave and I decided to take a long road trip together. We piled some camping gear into the trunk of the GTO and headed off on an adventure, better defined, perhaps, as a pursuit of young women in the Midwest. We first stopped at Lake Shafer, Indiana, which had drawn a throng of teenagers to hear Sonny and Cher perform. Dave and I went to the concert, listened to "I Got You Babe," "Baby Don't Go," and "All I Really Want to Do," and then hustled up two playful gals for a bit of harmless necking in the car. Next stop: Jackson, Michigan, my old stomping grounds. We looked up Mary. I had had a crush on her in junior high school before I moved away. In some ways, she was like Marilyn. Mary, too, loved music, played music, and was full of energy and always smiling. At Mary's urging, we drove down to a dance bar in Toledo. While I did my poor imitation of dancing, Mary attracted the attention of every guy in the joint when she positively shook it to tunes like "Working in a Coal Mine." The next night, we drove Mary back to school at Western Michigan University. I went in to snuggle all night with her, while Dave—another example of what friends are for—graciously volunteered to sleep in the car.

Next stop: further north, at the Traverse City State Park on Lake Michigan. We pitched our tent, went for a swim, and then toured the campground on foot, looking for friendly faces. Each of us found one, but while my date left early to rejoin her folks, Dave's date settled into our tent for the night. Try as I might, I could not fall asleep while Dave and the girl made out just a few feet away. When I heard her softly say "please, please, please," I had no idea if she meant please stop, or please do it. Either way, I couldn't take it anymore, so I left the tent and took a prolonged walk under the stars.

The next day we drove over the mighty Mackinac Bridge to St. Ignace, in Michigan's Upper Peninsula. We didn't know it at the time, but we had seen our last young women of the trip. In the sleepy U.P., we had also seen our last Sunoco gas station selling top-grade 260 premium, my gas of choice—and we'd seen about the last of any gas stations that stayed open after nine at night. After eating a late dinner in St. Ignace, we passed up buying some inferior Clark gas and headed out on US 2 toward Marquette, 160 miles away. We started with only a little over a quarter tank of gas and soon learned an important geography lesson about Upper Peninsula gas stations: they were few and far between, and all of them closed early. It became apparent that we'd have to get all the way to Marquette to have any hope of finding an open station. The drive became a game: could we make it that far? We treated it like one of those old Mobil Gas Economy Runs. Trying to maximize mileage, we held the accelerator gently and steadily and drove at thirty-five miles per hour in the dark. Never had the Pontiac gone so far, so slowly. We switched drivers on the fly, and to avoid all stopping, peed in a container and then dumped the contents out the window. We cursed a construction zone that made us take a slight detour and finally ran out of gas about five miles shy of Marquette. Nobody was going to come by to help us; we had hardly seen a car on the road for the last two hours. Dave and I looked at one another. Well, what about the gallon of white gas, for fueling the camp lantern, that was in the trunk? We poured its contents into the GTO, and the engine fired. Amazingly, at idle or cruising at a steady, low speed, the engine sounded normal. But if you gave it the gas—the white gas—you never heard such pinging in your life. So, we limped into Marquette, where the only twenty-four-hour station carried the same cheap Clark gas we had passed up in St. Ignace. We were happy to get it. We drove a bit farther and pulled into a roadside rest area to sleep away what little was left of the night.

In the last days of our trip, we pitched a tent at the Porcupine Mountains Wilderness State Park in the western Upper Peninsula on Lake Superior, where the weather can change in an instant. As soon as the tent went up, fog and heavy rain rolled in. Spending the night chilly, wet, and hungry seemed like a bad bargain, so we broke camp right after making it and headed south through Wisconsin on a two-lane road that had a small bar with a lighted beer sign about every five miles, but little else. Little else, that is, except for frogs. In the GTO's headlights, thousands (maybe tens of thousands) of little frogs with white bellies jumped all over the road in the wet night. I couldn't dodge a herd of frogs. After the GTO's Tiger Paws had squished a huge number of them, Dave and I stopped the car and captured a frog to examine. When we took it inside the car, it escaped Dave's hands and disappeared under a seat, never to be seen again.

After the foggy, froggy night, we visited Wisconsin Dells and then hightailed it back to Danville. Within days we headed back to college, as did Dan and Doug. As it turned out, the eventful trip that Dave and I took from Danville to Lake Shafer, to Lake Michigan, to Lake Superior, and back to Danville in 1966 was just about the end of it, the end of our cruising, the end of our hanging out so much together. We did not stay seventeen forever. Jobs and career plans separated us. Big romances separated us. Plus, we all spent nine months away at college and only three months a year at home. To repeat the language used in *American Graffiti*, we left a home to find a home; left a life to find a life; left friends to find new friends. Even as the bonds between us weakened, we knew we had spent very important time together, a short span of years unlike all those that came before, and certainly unlike all those adult years that came after. From age sixteen to eighteen or nineteen, while cruising up and down Vermilion Street, we had acted up together in ways that later would bring laughter, embarrassment, even tears. We had grown up together and it was time to move down new roads and take new trips. In 1967, my big trip was not to chase skirts in the Midwest in a muscle car but over a weekend to ride a bus from Indiana to Washington, DC, and back to join the March on the Pentagon, the first big protest of the Vietnam War.

In 1968, I spent the summer half a world away from Vermilion Street. I did a semester abroad with Rachel, my college sweetheart and future wife, and then we toured Europe from Denmark down to Yugoslavia in a car that was about as far removed from a GTO as a car could be: a tiny Fiat with an 850-cubic-centimeter engine that had trouble making 105 kilometers (65 miles) an hour. Driving across Austria, Rachel and I discovered a mini golf course sitting twenty feet below the outside deck of a restaurant and bar. Patrons sipped drinks while casually looking out over the green-carpeted miniature golf course. Given all the nights in 1964 and 1965 that I spent gambling on mini golf at Swing 'n Spring in Danville, I just had to play. Rachel and I got to one particularly difficult hole, where there was no straight shot to be had because the cup was tucked away on a dogleg. I assessed the terrain and figured an ace was possible, if I played a three banker. The ball had to carom off three boards to get to the hole. It took me three tries to get my ace. The bar crowd sitting above had been watching me figure the angles, and when I sank my third putt they broke out in applause. I looked up at them, grinning. I wished Dan, Doug, and Dave had been there for that shot; it would have made them proud.

* * *

I received conscientious objector status during the Vietnam War. I married Rachel and got a PhD in American civilization from Penn. Never outgrowing my adolescent need for speed, over the years I raced along on six-cylinder Honda CBX motorcycles, and then in a Ford Taurus SHO and a Subaru WRX STi. For thirty years, I taught a course called "The Automobile in America" at Michigan Technological University.

Source: Danville High 1965 yearbook

Dan got an engineering degree from the University of Illinois. He moved to California and dropped out of sight for almost forty years. Finally, he sent word that he had married three times and worked in the space and computer industries before retiring early. As an amateur, he raced a BMW on road courses for a decade. He owned a Corvette ZR1 and a Dodge Viper, and then a Shelby Mustang.

Source: Danville High 1965 yearbook

Doug graduated from the University of Illinois and married Cheri, his senior-year love from Danville High. He worked for several large corporations, had a family, and became a devout Christian. Doug then retired from profit-making enterprises to become a vice president and major fundraiser for Habitat for Humanity. He was very proud of the work he did alongside Jimmy Carter on several projects.

Source: Danville High 1965 yearbook

Dave graduated from Southern Illinois University. He married his high school sweetheart, Karla, who was the perfect blonde for him. Her conservative influence calmed the boy down, kept Dave out of trouble, and probably saved his life. Dave became a vice president of the Pekin Insurance Company near Peoria. He and Karla retired to The Villages in Florida.

Source: Danville High 1965 yearbook

Marilyn married my rival and successor, rock and roller Denny, in 1967. They soon had one daughter, Michele. Marilyn taught French and English at a small-town high school near Danville and commuted thirty-five miles to the University of Illinois to work on her master's degree. While driving home from a class, she died on November 22, 1972, in a car accident on I-74, just west of Danville. I served as one of her pallbearers.

Courtesy of Michele Hecht

# 14

## CARS AND MEMORIES

In the summer of 1993, things were busy as usual in small-town Houghton, on the western end of Michigan's Upper Peninsula. I taught two summer school classes at Michigan Tech and coached Little League. My eight-year-old daughter, Laura, played softball, swam on a team, took figure skating lessons on Tech's rink, and went to a hockey camp there. My twelve-year-old son, David, played Little League and made the All-Star team that I coached. David went to hockey camps, too, and started playing soccer. Mom kept a family calendar on the wall in the kitchen, the kind where every date sat in a big square of open space. She filled those squares with notations, allowing the family to keep track of who went where and when. Whenever there was a break in the schedule, you had to take advantage of it. After Little League ended, I decided to take David on a 550-mile trip down to Detroit. I wanted to see some exhibits at the Henry Ford Museum, drop in on my sister and brother-in-law in Jackson, and take in a Tiger game. Mom and Laura were happy just to stay home and spend time together without the guys.

David and I headed east across the Upper Peninsula. Thirty-five years earlier, my dad and I stopped at the ball diamond in Williamsport, Pennsylvania, where they played the Little League World Series. In Munising, Michigan, David and I stopped at the Little League diamond near the shore of Lake Superior. We stretched our legs and played some catch. At St. Ignace we ate a lunch at Big Boy before crossing over the Mighty Mac Bridge to Lower Michigan. In a mere nine or ten hours, we arrived in Jackson. After spending the night at Lynn and Ben's, I drove David over to Schaffer Drive, where I lived when I was twelve. I parked the car, and we walked up and down the short street, looking at the houses while I told stories.

From Schaffer Drive we headed downtown to Jackson Coney Island to have coney dogs with everything: a layer of finely chopped spiced beef (made of beef heart, the secret ingredient!), a thick blanket of sweet onions (chopped into the tiniest pieces possible), and mustard. I thought they tasted the same as they had in the 1950s. Full and content, we got back in the car. En route, David was amazed by the eighty-foot-tall tire standing next to Interstate 94 near Detroit's airport. Once a Ferris wheel at the New York World's Fair in 1964, since 1966 it had served as a roadside statue advertising Uniroyal Tires. We easily made it into Detroit in time to watch all of batting practice before the Tigers' night game against the Texas Rangers. It was memorable, thanks to Cecil Fielder. With a man on in the eighth inning, Cecil hit a mammoth home run that landed on the upper deck roof of Tiger Stadium. The Tigers tied the game in the eighth and won it in the tenth, 6–4.

After sleeping a bit late and having a nice breakfast, we drove to the Ford Museum in Dearborn. I took David to the "Made in America" exhibit, which was about how Americans had made all kinds of stuff, including the assembly line and the Model T. Thankfully, they had some interactive modules and exhibit signs written especially for kids. David was happy for a while—but his interest was not unlimited. After a few hours, we left the museum, planning to return the next day for more.

When we came back, David voted to go to the Play-Doh Fun Factory and then over to the "Imagination Station," a participatory exhibit that thirty-five people could enjoy at a time. It had a gazillion small colored balls mixed together, and the participants operated pulleys, levers, and Archimedean screws to separate them by colors. I left David to go look at the "Automobile in American Life" exhibit at the other end of the museum. "When you are done here," I said, "come find me. I'll be somewhere around that big 'Holiday Inn' sign." Yes, one of those iconic "The Nation's Innkeeper" signs fit easily into the huge Ford Museum.

I had been coming to the Ford Museum since I was a boy on grade school field trips. For a few years in the early '70s, I worked there as a curator. Back then, the auto exhibit was a dark, colorless collection of maybe two hundred cars sitting on a teakwood floor, looking for all the world like an archaeological parking lot. No flash, no glitter, no real interpretation. But this exhibit, opened in 1987, was something wholly different. I smiled at the prospect of finally seeing it.

I admired how the exhibit brought the outside world of car culture into the museum. It showed how the car altered the look of America in so many familiar ways. Besides the Holiday Inn sign, the museum had recreated, in fine detail, a mid-1950s Holiday Inn room. I thought it looked sparse and sterile, especially with its cinder block walls, but it was clean and comfortable enough. Nearby I spotted what the motel room replaced, a circa 1935 tourist cabin with a potbellied stove for heat and a chamber pot—a chamber pot!—for a bathroom. The cabin came from the Irish Hills of Michigan, not far from Jackson. The cabin once stood with other roadside kitsch along US 12, one of those highways largely put out of business by Interstate 94.

Car travelers get hungry and seek out places to eat. How about the museum's 1946 "Lamy's Diner"? You've never seen that place before. If you drove by it in its original location, Marlborough, Massachusetts, would you stop? What's on its menu? Is it any good? Are you willing to chance its meatloaf? Maybe you'd rather choose McDonald's instead, represented here by its signature Golden Arches up-and-over sign, all lit up, touting fifteen-cent hamburgers and 160 million sold. Maybe you crave a White Castle slider or an A&W chili dog with a root beer float? What'll you have, a one-of-a-kind diner, or standardized architecture and food that you know is the same from sea to shining sea?

Cars always need gas, and you need a potty break. Start looking for a gas station. It won't take long; they're easy to find, even in the middle of the museum. There's a tall, freestanding Texaco sign right there, white with a big red star in the middle of it. A complete Texaco station stands beneath it, clad in white porcelain enameled panels. TEXACO is spelled out in big red letters along the top, and thin green bands ring the building. Big windows trimmed in green set off the office/sales area on the left. Inside, tires and cans of oil stand ready to be bought. On the right, a service bay has a green door of jointed panels that can roll up or down. Over the door in green letters it reads, "MARFAK LUBRICATION." Gas pumps stand at attention in front of the station, ready to dispense Texaco's Fireflyte gasoline. This station is an exceptionally good example of corporate identity expressed in three dimensions. In its architecture, colors, and familiar forms, it yells out to drivers: Pull in and stop for Texaco gas!

I loved seeing this station but had three issues with it. What the hell was Marfak Lubrication? Texaco never did a good job of branding that. Secondly, why doesn't the service bay have a hydraulic lift in it, the kind a mechanic would use to raise a car up to change oil or tires or mufflers? And lastly, where is Texaco's "Clean Restroom" sign? All stations had one. In its advertising in the 1950s and early 1960s, Texaco *bragged* about its restrooms. They were *registered* (whatever that meant) and clean. Look at the glistening porcelain enamel panels on the station's walls. They scream out, "This place is clean!" So, where's the clean restroom sign? (Turns out the museum had it in storage.)

If there's a bit of romance in your heart, then take your sweetheart to the exhibit's mock-up of the Douglas Auto Theatre, a drive-in whose big neon sign tries to lure you in. All around me I saw the architecture of American car culture: restaurants, motels, gas stations, and drive-in theaters, along with their signs. Mix in a hundred cars and I could cruise, on foot, the America I grew up in.

I have always liked to watch people touring museums. How do they react to historical stuff? Do they study every label? Do they quickly rush past some artifacts, but linger at others? Why do people care enough to stop and take a real look? The Ford Museum, at great expense, built a flashy new exhibit. When the museum puts an object on the floor, it is tacitly saying that this thing is important. Some label may tell you exactly why it is important, but maybe not. Does the visitor really care about historical, economic, social, or design significance? Does the visitor give a damn whether this was the very first or the very last, the biggest or the smallest, the most expensive or the cheapest, the most typical or the most revolutionary, or the best or the worst gizmo on the planet? Are visitors keen on learning something, or are they, in July, just killing a day of vacation amidst a treasure trove of stuff?

I watched people looking at cars and learned something. Visitors walked right past most cars but lingered at others. They walked right by buggy-like horseless carriages, but they stopped to look at—no, to admire—a pink-and-gray '56 Chevy Bel Air convertible. I leaned in to hear what they said about it. They said things like "I had one just like it, honey." Or, "I always wanted a convertible!" Or, "My neighbor had one like it, except it was a two-door hardtop." Visitors responded in very *personal* ways. They responded because a particular car meant something *to them*. A certain car reminded them of Mom and Dad and summer vacations, of riding backward in the rear seat of that station wagon, or of high school dates, fondling in the back seat, speeding tickets, going to the drive-in theater, playing mini-golf at Swing 'n Spring, or drag racing a Chevelle Super Sport on the Dixie Highway.

Many cars from the 1950s and '60s sat clustered near the Holiday Inn, McDonald's, and Texaco signs, making me feel right at home. I lingered to take a close look at the '55 Corvette, '56 T-Bird, and '65 Mustang convertible. I saw a '57 DeSoto Fire Flight hardtop with push button drive and mammoth fins (from the Chrysler Corporation's god-awful styling period), a '58 Edsel with push-button drive (Ford's god-awful mistake), and a '59 Caddy (from GM's god-awfully huge period). On the bottom end of the food chain, I ran across a '49 Volkswagen sedan and a '60 Corvair, which was in perfect condition and, despite Ralph Nader's warning, had never rolled over. But it might well could have, according to Nader's book exhibited near the Corvair, *Unsafe at Any Speed: The Designed-In Dangers of the American Automobile*. Speaking of safety, look at that! They had the 1957 Cornell-Liberty Insurance safety car on exhibit! I never, ever expected to see that.

I had a good time touring through the cars, until one stopped me in my tracks. It was much longer than most. It was very dark blue or black. The Ford Motor company made it at its Wixom plant in January 1961 and then sent it to the Hess & Eisenhardt Company of Cincinnati. They cut the car in half and put a new section in the middle, lengthening it by three and a half feet. Altogether, the car cost about $200,000. Ford kept ownership of the vehicle, code-named X-100, and rented it to the Secret Service for only $500.

After landing at Love Field on November 22, 1963, President John F. Kennedy and his wife, Jacqueline, climbed into this car and drove into Dallas. The president did not come out alive. He was assassinated in this custom Lincoln Continental. I had never seen it in person before, had never wanted to see it, but there it was. This car was personal to me. I was sixteen when Lee Harvey Oswald assassinated President Kennedy. I was growing up and starting to think in a more political way. Standing in the museum, my mind replayed Kennedy's assassination and the devastating days that followed.

On November 23, Kennedy's body lay in repose in the East Room of the White House. On November 24, they carried his body to the US Capitol Building, where long lines of mourners came to pay their respects. Jacqueline Kennedy stepped out of the White House dressed all in black, her face barely visible behind a black veil. She walked holding hands with her two young children, Carolyn and John-John, one on each side. My mother and I sat in the living room of our little bungalow in Danville, watching on television. As soon as I saw Jackie and the two children, I started to cry. It seemed impossible not to, and it would happen again, several times.

On November 25, a funeral cortege moved the casket from the Capitol to the White House to pick up assembled mourners, and then to St. Matthew's Cathedral. At the conclusion of the funeral service, Jackie, Caroline, and John-John stood outside the cathedral. It was John-John's third birthday. At the sight of his dad's casket, he offered a child's salute. Tears flowed again at our house and across the nation. The funeral cortege passed on to Arlington National Cemetery, where they buried John Kennedy and lit an eternal flame.

All three television networks carried the ceremonies of November 24 and 25. They provided unprecedented coverage of live events, and Mom and I watched it all. That's why the Kennedy presidential limousine in the museum was so personal to me. I felt like I had lived it all, from shooting to burial. One thing particularly touched me whenever they moved Kennedy's casket. A Lincoln or Cadillac would not

The two most significant cars in my life in the 1960s were juxtaposed at the Ford Museum: a GTO and Kennedy's limousine. They represented, for me, the best of times and the worst of times. (Collections of The Henry Ford)

do. Only horses would do. I felt the solemnity and near majesty of the six clip-clopping gray horses that pulled the black caisson with its high wheels, followed by the single black horse, named Black Jack, whose saddle was empty and whose stirrups held boots that symbolically faced backward.

In the museum, Kennedy's presidential limousine looked a bit different than it had in Dallas. Because presidents after Kennedy used it, they made it safer. It now had a permanent top of armor plate and bulletproof glass. In 1963, the limousine had a top, but it was removable. Kennedy didn't like the top, so he rode into Dallas without it.

I looked over the new bulletproof top and spotted a car just twenty or thirty feet beyond the limo. My god, what a contrast! The car was not black but gleaming white. I saw it in full profile, so there was no mistaking what it was. It was a Pontiac GTO, the same color as the one I drove in high school. I went over to the GTO and stood as close as I could get to the little Pontiac with the big engine. I could tell by the headlights that this was a '65, while mine was a '64, but they were essentially the same. Viewed from the side they were damn near identical. I hadn't seen such a pristine GTO in years. "You're really lookin' fine," I muttered, echoing a long-ago song lyric. Standing beside the old muscle car, I fell in love with it all over again.

I had always believed there was considerable truth to the idea that you are what you own, that things, the stuff of life, go a long way in determining and defining your life. Our culture is materialistic. Your stuff presents you to others and influences how they see you. And your stuff influences how you see yourself. I stood there, happy that this car had been part of my life. Surely, it changed me.

Looking back on my rite of passage, my growth from boy to man, I divided my young life into two parts: the time spent in Jackson, Michigan, and the time spent in Danville, Illinois. In Jackson, the one thing that mattered most in my life was 1861 Schaffer Drive, the just-built single-story ranch house with a two-car garage and a big yard where, for a time, Mom, Dad, and I all lived. It sat in a neighborhood occupied by my best buddies, near empty fields, streams, wetlands, and woods to play in and explore. It was a mile from a great park with ball diamonds and a golf course. Day after day I left this house to go places, most often by car. The car took me all over town, and to some distant places too. It took me to relatives in Indiana and Illinois, and in 1958 it took Dad and me all the way to Niagara Falls, Gettysburg, Washington, DC, Uncle Charlie's, and back. That was the important point: I left in a car and always came back home in a car. The house Mom and Dad bought was like a magnet. It was the center of everything, and life was good and stable and fun, until it wasn't. My dad's company, Mechanical Products, brought a drafting table to the house in 1960 so he could do some work while he was sick. But after a half year he couldn't push a mechanical pencil along a T square to draw a straight line.

Dad was in and out of the hospital several times. A few visits to see him were memorable. Sister Lynn and I played a game of Scrabble with Dad, and we all finished within one point of one another. That seemed like a happy victory for everyone. Mom and I left the hospital with Dad one weekend morning. On the way home Dad pulled the car to the curb in front of a Francis Street bakery. Dad stayed in the Packard while Mom and I went inside to select some pastries. Suddenly there was a commotion. We went back outside to find that a car had collided with the front of our car. The driver, an elderly man, had died at the wheel while heading downtown. He slumped forward and his car kept on going. It went over a railroad crossing, crossed the centerline, and hit the curb, which steered his car right into ours. Somebody asked my dad why he didn't pull our car out of the way. "Somebody had to stop him," was all he said. A dying man stopped a dead man. Later, Mom had to fight his insurance company. They argued they weren't liable for collision damages because they insured a living driver, not a dead one. The collision was an act of God. It took time, but Mom finally won the dispute.

Dad got weaker over time. In September he left for the hospital and did not come back home. Sixteen months later, I left 1861 Schaffer in a car, and for the first time ever I did not come back home. Mom drove us three hundred miles to Danville, where I completed ninth grade and then high school. By any objective measure, Mom and I moved several rungs down the socioeconomic ladder. Without Dad, we had a much lower income, even though I received Social Security survivor's benefits. The quality of our housing declined, from the new house with a big yard in Jackson to an old second-floor flat without a yard, close to downtown Danville.

In Danville, the thing that mattered most in my life was not a dwelling but a car, a 1964 Pontiac GTO. My mother and I moved to Danville in a 1958 Hillman Minx, which, to put it mildly, was nothing special. The GTO, on the other hand, was very special. Ronny and the Daytonas recorded a song about it, and so did Jan and Dean and others. It arrived at a difficult time in my life, and it gave me a big boost that I needed to feel better about myself and my place in the world, and especially my place in Danville, where I had cousin Jim but no lifelong friends, and for a while, too few new ones. After the GTO came into my life, Patricia wrote in my yearbook, "You know, last year you seemed sort of shy to me, or maybe quiet. I can really see a change in you this year! (Of course, it's for the better.) You've made so many friends and have been so busy!"

In 1964, Jan and Dean hit number 3 on the charts with "Little Old Lady from Pasadena." The year before, my mom, the little old lady from Danville, splurged beyond belief to buy a GTO, and you had to know it was for her son. She gave me the gift of love, confidence, and optimism. Life had been tough and disappointing of late, but it would get better again, I would be happy again, I just had to go for it. Thanks in no small part to a car, life did get better, and Danville turned out to be more than okay. It turned out to be a great place for me.

When I was in college at DePauw University in Greencastle, Indiana, sometimes I got to take the GTO over to campus for a week or so. In 1966, early in my sophomore year at DePauw, I met Rachel, a pretty blonde whose dad was president of a savings and loan in Peoria. She asked me out on our first date, and I felt like I was pretty special. On some of our dates we took the GTO out to secluded spots. As juniors, after we finished our semester abroad studies in Germany and England in 1968, Rachel bought a tiny new Fiat 850 and we toured much of Europe. We had wonderful pastries for breakfast. We slept out in the open on a hillside above the Adriatic and woke up surrounded by the biggest bees we had ever seen. We laughed at my inability to find the road out of Trieste that led to Yugoslavia. How could I not find an entire country? On a rainy night, we put our sleeping bags down inside a huge concrete sewer pipe laying on its side at a construction site; it kept us dry. In Le Havre, we went to the cinema to see "Nevada Smith." It was dubbed. We had a fun time listening to Steve McQueen speaking French as he sought revenge in the American West.

Not all times were fun times, of course. Some times were solemn, like when we toured Verdun and Normandy. We enjoyed Europe, but we knew that 1968 was a terrible year in many ways. Nearly seventeen thousand Americans died in Vietnam. Martin Luther King Jr. fell dead to a gunshot in Memphis. Bobby Kennedy fell dead to a gunshot in Los Angeles. Everywhere we went, Europeans kept asking us, what the hell is wrong with America? We had no good answer for them.

At the age of twenty-one, after seven months abroad, I returned home to Illinois. After a few days in Danville, I stopped by the local draft board office to pick up the papers needed to claim conscientious objector status. The secretary who handed them to me had the ironic name of Hazel Slaughter. Back in the kitchen of our flat, I told Mom what I was up to. She quickly burst into tears and told me that it was a good thing my dad wasn't alive to see this. Dad had been dead for eight years, and this was the first and only time Mom ever told me I was a disappointment to him. Throughout the Vietnam War we heard stories of how this divisive conflict drove a wedge between fathers and sons, how it split families apart. This was my time to feel a bit of that.

My folks were not overtly political. I never heard them engage in a political discussion or argument. I guess they were Republicans, because I voted for Richard Nixon in my junior high school's mock presidential election in 1960. Why else would I have done that? Later, that never would have happened. In the 1960s, events—first the civil rights movement and then the Vietnam War—pushed me to the left. I never supported that war, and as the 1968 Democratic National Convention drew close, I supported the peace candidate, Eugene McCarthy. I bought red and blue poster paint, and, in August 1968, our white GTO drove around Danville with "McCARTHY" painted on both sides in large letters. My mother, bless her, never complained about this.

Just before returning to DePauw for my senior year, I learned that my draft board had approved my CO status, based not on my religious beliefs but on my ethical, moral, and humanistic opposition to war. Nine months passed at DePauw, and Rachel and I graduated together in mid-1969, and then we temporarily went in separate directions. In grad school in Philly, I discovered that when we were apart, I missed Rachel too much. So, I wrote her a letter that beat around the bush for a few paragraphs but ultimately asked, "Do you wanna get married?" She said "Yes." Our wedding took place on a hot, hot day in mid-August in Peoria in 1970.

After the wedding, more graduate school at Penn beckoned. With Rachel's folks in Peoria and my mom still in Danville, Rachel and I drove back to Illinois at Christmas and maybe once a summer in a new Fiat, a 124 Sport Coupe. We had enlarged our family; we had a springer spaniel in the back seat who wanted to attack every toll taker on the Pennsylvania Turnpike. On a trip to Danville in 1971, Rachel and I got together with Marilyn and Denny and met their little girl, Michele. The two married couples went out for dinner on New Year's Eve and everybody had a good time. We'd be friends for life, I thought.

I never lived in Danville again after the summer of 1969, when I first left for the University of Pennsylvania. About the time I left, Mom drove the GTO to a dealership and traded it in for a 1969 Plymouth Satellite, light bronze with a black vinyl top. She didn't consult me about this. She just did it. After all, it was her car. A decade later, when she died of a stroke in 1979, I inherited the Plymouth. I had no emotional attachment to that car and promptly sold it.

Standing in the Ford Museum by the GTO, my thoughts went back to my mom, who skimped and saved so she could get me the best. A brown suede winter coat, Hart Schaffner & Marx sport coats, a Swiss Tissot watch for graduation, a gold tigereye ring for Christmas—and a GTO. I remembered all the days I took Mom to work at the country club about four o'clock and picked her up about nine o'clock. In between those hours, I often made dinner for myself and then went out to cruise around. Steak 'n Shake. Marty K's. The Custard Cup. A&W. The Dixie Drive-In. Swing 'n Spring Mini-Golf. Sun 'n Swim pool. And those secluded spots along Newell Road. They all seemed so trivial and yet so important to me at the same time. I thought of my best friends. We grew up together. I will never forget cruising in the GTO with Doug, Dave, Dan, and, of course, Marilyn.

After my son David was done playing at the Imagination Station, he wandered through the auto exhibit until he found me.

"Hey, Sport. Did you have fun?" I asked.

"Yep," David said. The boy looked at the shiny white car in front of him.

"What's that?" he asked.

"That's a Pontiac GTO," I said. "I had one of those once. I had one of those."

# BIBLIOGRAPHY


Alexander, Brian B. *Atomic Kitchen: Gadgets and Inventions for Yesterday's Cook*. Portland, OR, 2004.

Auto Editors of Consumer Guide with Jeffrey Godshall. *Designing America's Cars: The 50s*. Lincolnwood, IL, 2005.

Automobile Club of Southern California. [Map] *Southern California Car Culture Landmarks*. Los Angeles, CA, 2000.

*Automotive Industries*. Annual "Statistics Issues," 1950–60.

Baird, Dwight G. "Bright Car Colors Gain Favor." *American Business*, July 1953, 12–13, 39.

Belasco, Warren James. *Americans on the Road: From Autocamp to Motel, 1910–1945*. Cambridge, MA, 1979.

Blair, John, and Stephen McFarland, comp. *The Illustrated Discography of Hot Rod Music, 1961–1966*. Ann Arbor, MI, 1990.

Breedlove, Craig. *The Spirit of America: Winning the World's Land Speed Record*. Chicago, 1971.

Brockmole, Jessica A. *Pink Cars and Pocketbooks: How Women Bought Their Way into the Driver's Seat*. Baltimore, 2025.

Brody, Leon, and Herbert J. Stack, eds. *Highway Safety and Driver Education*. New Jersey, 1954.

"Cars of the Fabulous Fifties," VHS tape released by Video Cassette Sales. Hauppauge, NY, 1987.

Cohen, Lizabeth. *A Consumers' Republic: The Politics of Mass Consumption in Postwar America*. New York, 2003.

Cross, Gary C. *Machines of Youth: America's Car Obsession*. Chicago, 2018.

Davidson, Justin. "The Kitchen Debate's Actual Kitchen." *New York Magazine*, May 5, 2011, n.p.

"Design Features of 1953 Cars." *Product Engineering*, February 1953, 135–67.

DeWitt, John. *Cool Cars, High Art: The Rise of Kustom Kulture.* Jackson, MS, 2001.

Duffett, Mark, and Beate Peter, eds. *Popular Music and Automobiles.* New York, 2020.

"Dream Cars of the 50s and 60s: Vintage TV Commercials," VHS tape released by Goodtimes Home Video Corp., New York, 1986.

Editors of *Hot Rod* Magazine. *The Best of "Hot Rod" Magazine, 1949–1959.* St. Paul, 2003.

Eyerman, R., and D. Lofgren. "Romancing the Road: Road Movies and Images of Mobility." *Theory, Culture & Society* 12, no. 1 (1995): 53–79.

Federal Highway Administration. *Benefits of Interstate Highways.* Washington, DC, 1970.

Felson, Henry Gregor. *Boy Gets Car.* New York, 1960.

Felson, Henry Gregor. *Crash Club.* New York, 1958.

Felson, Henry Gregor. *The Cup of Fury.* New York, 1954.

Felson, Henry Gregor. *Hot Rod.* New York, 1950.

Felson, Henry Gregor. *Street Rod.* New York, 1953.

Felson, Henry Gregor. *To My Son, the Teen-Age Driver.* New York, 1964.

Felson, Henry Gregor. *Two and the Town.* New York, 1952.

Finch, Christopher. *Highways to Heaven: The Auto Biography of America.* New York, 1992.

Fitch, Steve. *American Motel Signs.* Berlin, 2008.

Flink, James J. *The Automobile Age.* Cambridge, MA, 1990.

Flink, James J. *The Car Culture.* Cambridge, MA, 1975.

Foster, Mark S. *A Nation on Wheels: The Automobile Culture in America Since 1945.* Belmont, CA, 2003.

Frumkin, M. J. *Classic Muscle Car Advertising.* Iola, WI, 2002.

Garner, Art. *A. J. Foyt: Survivor, Champion, Legend.* Vol. 1. Portsmouth, VA, 2025.

Garton, Jane Dwyre. *Pedal Cars: Chasing the Kidillac.* Atglen, PA, 1999.

Genat, Robert. *The Birth of Hot Rodding: The Story of the Dry Lakes Era.* St. Paul, 2003.

Gerl, Ellen J., and Craig C. Davis. "Selling Detroit on Women: Woman's Day and Auto Advertising, 1964–82." *Journalism History*, 38, no. 4 (2013): 209–20.

"The Good Wife's Guide." *Housekeeping Monthly*, May 13, 1955.
Green, Bob. "Cars for Kids." *Hot Rod Magazine*, February 1958, 26 ff.
Grushkin, Paul. *Rockin' down the Highway: The Cars and People That Made Rock and Roll.* St. Paul, 2006.
Gunnell, John, ed. *Standard Catalog of American Cars, 1946–1975.* 3rd edition. Iola, WI, 1995.
Gutfreund, Owen D. *Twentieth Century Sprawl: Highways and the Reshaping of the American Landscape.* New York, 2005.
Halberstam, David. *The Fifties.* New York, 1993.
Hawley, Samuel. *Ultimate Speed: The Fast Life and Extreme Cars of Racing Legend Craig Breedlove.* Chicago, 2018.
Heimann, Jim. *50s All-American Ads.* Koln, 2002.
Heining, Duncan. "Cars and Girls: The Car, Masculinity, and Pop Music." In *The Motorcar and Popular Culture in the Twentieth Century.* Farnham, England, 1998.
Heitmann, John. *The Automobile and American Life.* Jefferson, NC, 2009.
Highway Safety Foundation. *Mechanized Death.* Directed by Richard Wayman, 1961.
Highway Safety Foundation. *Signal 30.* Directed by Richard Wayman, 1959.
Highway Safety Foundation. *Wheels of Tragedy.* Directed by Richard Wayman, 1963.
*Highway to Hell: The True Story of Highway Safety Films.* Written and directed by Bret Wood, 2003.
Hine, Thomas. *Populuxe: The Look and Life of Americans in the '50s and '60s.* New York, 1987.
Horowitz, David. *American Social Classes in the 1950s: Selections from Vance Packard's "The Status Seekers."* Boston, 1995.
Horowitz, David A., Peter N. Carroll, and David Lee. *On the Edge: A History of America Since World War II.* St. Paul, 1989.
Howell, Mark D. *From Moonshine to Madison Avenue: A Cultural History of the NASCAR Winston Cup Series.* Bowling Green, KY, 1997.
Hyde, Charles K. *Arsenal of Democracy: The American Automobile Industry in World War II.* Detroit, 2013.

Hyde, Charles K. *Storied Independents: Nash, Hudson, and American Motors.* Detroit, 2009.

Ikuta, Yasutosh. *Cruise O Matic: Automobile Advertising of the 1950s.* Hong Kong, 2000.

Ingrassia, Brian M. *Special Capital: Indianapolis, Auto Racing, and the Making of Modern America.* Champaign, IL, 2024.

Ingrassia, Paul. *Crash Course: The American Automobile Industry's Road from Glory to Disaster.* New York, 2010.

Ingrassia, Paul. *Engines of Change: A History of the American Dream in Fifteen Cars.* New York, 2012.

Jackle, John A., and Keith A. Sculle. *The Gas Station in America.* Baltimore, 1994.

Jackle, John A., Keith A. Sculle, and Jefferson S. Rogers. *The Motel in America.* Baltimore, 1996.

Jackson, Kenneth T. *Crabgrass Frontier: The Suburbanization of the United States.* New York, 1985.

Kay, Jane Holtz. *Asphalt Nation: How the Automobile Took Over America and How We Can Take It Back.* Berkeley, 1997.

Keats, John. *The Insolent Chariots.* Philadelphia, 1958.

Keefe, Melinda, and Peter Schletty, eds. *The Hot Rod Reader.* Minneapolis, 2011.

Key, Mike, and Tony Thacker. *Dream Cars of the Fifties.* Secaucus, NJ, 1990.

Kinstler, James. Howard. *The Geography of Nowhere: The Rise and Decline of America's Man-Made Landscape.* New York, 1994.

Lawrence, Floyd G. "Power Devices on Way to Becoming Standard Equipment on Even Lower-Priced Cars." *Steel*, April 27, 1953, 69–70.

Lewis, David L., and Laurence Goldstein, eds. *The Automobile and American Culture.* Ann Arbor, MI, 1983.

Lewis, Tom. *Divided Highways: Building the Interstate Highways, Transforming American Life.* New York, 1997.

Lezotte, Chris. "Born to Take the Highway: Woman, the Automobile, and Rock 'n' Roll." *Journal of American Culture* 36, no. 3 (September 2013): 161–76.

Lezotte, Chris. "What Would Miss Daisy Drive? The Road Trip and the Woman Behind the Wheel." *Journal of Popular Culture*, 36, no. 3 (September 2013): 987–1011.

Liebs, Chester H. *Main Street to Miracle Mile: American Roadside Architecture*. Baltimore, 1985.

*Life* magazine. Automobile advertisements, October through December, 1950–69.

Lucsko, David N. *The Business of Speed: The Hot Rod Industry in America, 1915–1990*. Baltimore, 2008.

Marling, Karal Ann. "America's Love Affair with the Automobile in the Television Age." *Design Quarterly* 146 (1989): 5–20.

Marling, Karal Ann. *As Seen on TV: The Visual Culture of Everyday Life in the 1950s*. Cambridge, MA, 1996.

Matheson, Whitney. *Atomic Home: A Guided Tour of the American Dream*. Portland, OR, 2004.

May, Elaine Tyler. *Homeward Bound: American Families in the Cold War Era*. New York, 1988.

McCarthy, Tom. *Auto Mania: Cars, Consumers, and the Environment*. New Haven, CT, 2007.

McLoud, Ken. *Driving Identities: At the Intersection of Popular Music and Automotive Culture*. New York, 2021.

Montgomery, Charlotte. Column, "The Woman and Her Car." *Good Housekeeping*, 1950–1956.

Morgan, James. *The Distance to the Moon: A Road Trip into the American Dream*. New York, 1999.

Mueller, Mike. *Motor City Muscle: The High-Powered History of the Muscle Car*. Osceola, WI, 1997.

Mumford, Lewis. *The City in History*. New York, 1961.

Mumford, Lewis. *Technics and Civilization*. New York, 1934.

Nabokov, Vladimir. *Lolita*. Paris, 1955.

Nader, Ralph. *Unsafe at Any Speed: The Designed-In Dangers of the American Automobile*. New York, 1965.

National Film Board of Canada. *The Cars in Your Life*. Directed by Terence Macartney-Filgate, 1959.

Newman, Joshua. "Old Times Are Not Forgotten: Sport, Identity, and the Confederate Flag in the Dixie South." *Sociology of Sport Journal* 24, no. 3 (2007): 261–83.

Peterson, Richard A. "Why 1955? Explaining the Advent of Rock Music." *Popular Music* 9, no. 1 (1990): 97–116.

Oldenziel, Ruth. "The Fisher Body Craftsman's Guild, 1930–1968, and the Making of a Male Technical Domain." In *Boys and Their Toys*, edited by Roger Horowitz. New York, 2001.

Rae, John B. *The American Automobile Industry*. Boston, 1984.

Railton, Arthur B. "Push-Button Manor, Jackson, Michigan." *Popular Mechanics*, December 1950, 84–87, 252.

Redbook Magazine. *In the Suburbs*. Directed by Tracy Ward, 1957.

Ritzer, George. *The McDonaldization of Society*. Thousand Oaks, CA, 2004.

Rodriguez, Robert. *The Fifties Chronicle*. Lindenwood, IL, 2006.

Rothschild, Emma. *Paradise Lost: The Decline of the Auto-Industrial Age*. New York, 1973.

"Safety Features of 1957 Cars." *Public Safety*, January 10–12 and February 8–11, 1957.

Scalzo, Joe. *Indianapolis Roadsters, 1952–1964*. Osceola, WI, 1999.

Scharff, Virginia, *Taking the Wheel: Women and the Coming of the Motor Age*. Albuquerque, 1991.

Shackleford, Ben A. "Going National While Staying Southern: Stock Car Racing in America, 1949–1979." PhD diss., Georgia Institute of Technology, 2004.

Shackleford, Ben A. "NASCAR Stock Car Racing: Establishment and Southern Retrenchment." *International Journal of the History of Sport* 28, no. 2 (2011): 300–318.

Shelden, C. Hunter. "Prevention: The Only Cure for Head Injuries Resulting from Automobile Accidents." *Journal of the American Medical Association* 159, no. 10 (January 1955): 281–85.

Steinbeck, John. *The Grapes of Wrath*. New York, 1939.

Steinbeck, John. *Travels with Charley: In Search of America*. New York, 1962.

Szatmary, David P. *Rockin' in Time: A Social History of Rock-and-Roll*. Upper Saddle River, NJ, 2000.

Tillotson, Kristin. *Retro Housewife: A Salute to the Suburban Superwoman*. Portland, OR, 2004.

*Time* magazine. Automobile advertisements, October through December, 1950–69.

Turner, Victor. *The Ritual Process: Structure and Anti-Structure*. Chicago, 1969.

Volti, Rudi. *Cars & Culture: The Life Story of a Technology*. Baltimore, 2004.

Walsh, Margaret. "Gender and Automobility: Selling Cars to American Women After the Second World War." *Journal of Macromarketing* 31, no. 1 (March 2011): 57–72.

Widmer, E. L. "Crossroads: The Automobile, Rock and Roll, and Democracy." In *Autopia: Cars and Culture*, edited by Peter Wollen and Joe Kerr. London, 2002.

Wolfe, Thomas. *The Kandy-Kolored Tangerine-Flake Streamline Baby*. New York, 1977.

"Women Buy a Lot—But Not Everything." *Business Week*, January 7, 1950, 30, 33.

"Women Customers—They're in Every Market Now." *Business Week*, December 25, 1954, 35–36.

Yates, Brock. *The Decline and Fall of the American Automobile Industry*. New York, 1983.

Yenne, Bill. *Going Home to the Fifties*. San Francisco, 2002.

## ABOUT THE AUTHOR

LARRY LANKTON is professor emeritus of history at Michigan Technological University. His scholarly career focused on the history of mining, technological development, and labor in Michigan's Upper Peninsula. His book *Cradle to Grave: Life, Work, and Death at the Lake Superior Copper Mines* won a Great Lakes History Prize. Lankton is also the author of *Hollowed Ground: Copper Mining and Community Building on Lake Superior, 1840s–1990s* (Wayne State University Press).

Photo credit: David Lawrence

## DISCOVER THESE RELATED TITLES
## FROM WAYNE STATE UNIVERSITY PRESS

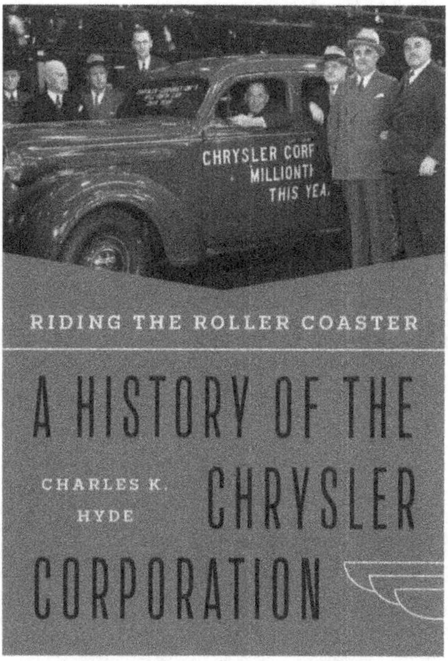


**Riding the Roller Coaster**
**A History of the Chrysler Corporation**

*Charles K. Hyde*

A comprehensive history of the highs and lows of the Chrysler Corporation and its lasting impact on the automotive industry.

ISBN 9780814352205, $34.99 paperback

**The Dodge Brothers**
**The Men, the Motor Cars, and the Legacy**

*Charles K. Hyde*

The enduring legacy of John and Horace Dodge and the history of their company.

ISBN 9780814332474, $24.99 paperback